MATHEMATICS CURRICULUM TOPIC STUDY

This material was supported with funding from the National Science Foundation under the Teacher Professional Continuum (TPC) program—ESI-0353315 "Curriculum Topic Study—A Systematic Approach to Utilizing National Standards and Cognitive Research," awarded to the Maine Mathematics and Science Alliance, principal investigator: Page Keeley. Any opinions, findings, conclusions, or recommendations expressed in this material are those of the authors and do not necessarily reflect the views of the National Science Foundation

MATHEMATICS CURRICULUM TOPIC STUDY

PAGE KEELEY
CHERYL M. ROSE

Foreword by Joan Ferrini-Mundy

Bridging the Gap Between Standards and Practice

CORWIN PRESS
A SAGE Publications Company
Thousand Oaks, California

For information:

Corwin Press
A Sage Publications Company
2455 Teller Road
Thousand Oaks, California 91320
www.corwinpress.com

Sage Publications Ltd.
1 Oliver's Yard
55 City Road
London EC1Y 1SP
United Kingdom

Sage Publications India Pvt. Ltd.
B-42, Panchsheel Enclave
Post Box 4109
New Delhi 110 017 India

Printed in the United States of America.

Library of Congress Cataloging-in-Publication Data

Keeley, Page.
Mathematics curriculum topic study: Bridging the gap between standards and practice / Page Keeley, Cheryl M. Rose.
    p. cm.
Includes bibliographical references and index.
    ISBN 1-4129-2643-2 (cloth) — ISBN 1-4129-2644-0 (pbk.)   1. Mathematics—Study and teaching—Curricula—United States.   2. Mathematics teachers—Training of—United States.
3. Teacher participation in curriculum planning—United States. I. Rose, Cheryl M. II. Title.
QA13.K44 2006
510.71'073—dc22   2005032721

This book is printed on acid-free paper.

06   07   08   09   10   9   8   7   6   5   4   3   2

Acquisitions Editor:	Rachel Livsey
Editorial Assistant:	Phyllis Cappello
Production Editor:	Diane S. Foster
Copy Editor:	Jacqueline Tasch
Typesetter:	C&M Digitals (P) Ltd.
Proofreader:	Dennis Webb
Indexer:	Molly Hall
Cover Designer:	Michael Dubowe
Graphic Designer:	Scott Van Atta

Contents

List of Curriculum Topic Study Guides

NUMBERS AND OPERATIONS

ALGEBRA

GEOMETRY

MEASUREMENT

DATA ANALYSIS

INTEGRATED TOPICS

PROBLEM SOLVING AND PROCESSES

*To Isabel, Barbara, Timothy, and Joey—may
you grow up to learn and love mathematics.*

*To my wonderfully supportive family: Roy, Carly, Bobby, Jimmy, Mom, and Dad.
And especially my grandmother, Nana—you are the reason I am in education today.*

Foreword

People who are engaged in developing standards are concerned with how the standards documents will be received and used by their readers. Whether the standards are national (such as *Principles and Standards for School Mathematics*, National Council of Teachers of Mathematics [NCTM], 2000), state (such as the new grade-by-grade objectives mandated by No Child Left Behind), or district, their authors worry that the majority of such policy documents sit, for the most part, on shelves, displaying their titles on the spine but not lending themselves to use in practice. As the chair of the Writing Group for NCTM's *Principles and Standards for School Mathematics*, I have been deeply interested in how standards are used in different educational domains and by different audiences.

Principles and Standards for School Mathematics (NCTM, 2000) explicitly makes the point that one of its intentions is to "stimulate ideas and ongoing conversations at the national, provincial or state, and local levels about how best to help students gain a deep understanding of important mathematics" (p. 6). When given the opportunity to prepare a foreword for *Mathematics Curriculum Topic Study: Bridging the Gap Between Standards and Practice*, I was delighted. I am reassured to see a publication with the premise that the content and organization of standards documents can indeed be central in a framework to guide teachers in professional learning. In an environment where legislation calls for highly qualified teachers in mathematics, where the mathematical content demands of changing workplaces and educational settings continue to escalate, and where the need to educate all students for a productive future through their mathematical preparation is increasingly greater, the pressure for teachers to continue to grow and learn is enormous. This volume provides a very important contribution to the literature and resources that can support such growth and learning.

The National Research Council's 2002 report, *Investigating the Influence of Standards: A Framework for Research in Mathematics, Science, and Technology Education* identified three "channels of influence" through which standards documents might ultimately affect outcomes in the educational system. One of these channels is teacher preparation and development. The report notes that these activities

> provide channels through which nationally developed standards might influence how teachers learn to teach initially and throughout their careers. . . . Teachers' continuing professional learning may be enhanced or constrained by the setting within which they work and by the opportunities available to them . . . If nationally developed standards are influencing the preparation

of new teachers, states would require and postsecondary institutions would create systems that enable prospective teachers to gain the knowledge and skills needed to help students meet standards-based learning goals. (p. 7)

Nonetheless, few tools and conceptual frameworks are available that would enable teachers and professional developers to move from standards documents to the day-to-day work of teaching. Research has indeed shown that such translations are not direct and that when teachers work with standards, sometimes the original meanings and intentions of the authors and policymakers are reinterpreted.

The second part of the title of this volume, *Bridging the Gap Between Standards and Practice*, is a simple and elegant description of the real contribution of Curriculum Topic Study. The book accomplishes dual purposes: as a thoughtful and careful interpretation and expansion of standards and as a concrete tool and process from which teachers can learn. The goal of helping teachers develop content knowledge, interact with local standards, examine coherence, consider learning issues, and improve pedagogy and assessment seems ideal for the contemporary educational environment. The design of Curriculum Topic Study accommodates individual teachers and groups and should also serve as a valuable resource to professional development leaders and mathematics teacher educators seeking access to current and useful materials.

A major lesson for all concerned with excellence in mathematics teaching and learning is that the process is one of continual improvement. No single set of standards will ever serve as the definitive and lasting authority for what all students should know and be able to do. Views of what mathematics are most important and of how mathematical ideas can be combined to be coherent and well connected, both mathematically and for students, will continue to evolve. Evidence and practice about effective pedagogical strategies will continue to accumulate. To process this kind of information and to make good use of it requires, at the core, interested and engaged teachers with the capacity to make connections across multiple resources, assemble ideas into forms useable in practice, and engage in serious professional dialogue, debate, and critique of others' efforts to move toward effective teaching that produces student learning for all. The tools that have been assembled in this volume, together with the framework that has been provided, are important and valuable contributions to the field.

I have already been inspired to consider how, in my own professional development work with teachers, the six outcomes that are used in the Curriculum Topic Study framework can be used productively. These are:

- Identify adult content knowledge
- Consider instructional implications
- Identify concepts and specific ideas
- Examine research on student learning
- Examine coherency and articulation
- Clarify state standards and district curriculum

This set of guiding ideas demonstrates how to integrate focus on mathematical content with some of the most current issues in pedagogy and policy.

The conceptual basis and the specific tools in *Mathematics Curriculum Topic Study* are an excellent contribution to the improvement of mathematics education. The field of mathematics education stands to learn from using this fine model and resource; the developers of standards documents can relax, knowing that creative and forward-looking tools are available to support the influence of standards by ensuring that teachers take them off the shelf.

—Joan Ferrini-Mundy
Writing Group Chair, NCTM *Principles and Standards for School Mathematics*, 1995–2000
University Distinguished Professor
Michigan State University

Preface

OVERVIEW

In today's complex society, mathematical literacy is a necessary cornerstone in schools, the workplace, and everyday life. Mathematical literacy involves more than the ability to execute a procedure. It involves a deep conceptual knowledge of mathematics and an ability to apply this knowledge in a variety of contexts. Mathematical literacy is for everyone—*all* students and *all* adults. To achieve the level of mathematical literacy that will provide students with the confidence and competence they need to be productive citizens, teachers' knowledge of mathematics and effective strategies to teach it are pivotal. Teachers must be given the tools and support they need to understand the knowledge base of mathematics that underpins the standards, the research that contributes to an understanding of how students perceive and learn mathematics, and ways to translate theory into practice.

Achieving mathematical literacy for the diverse students who make up today's classrooms is facilitated when teachers have a strong interest and desire to acquire an extensive professional knowledge base. Coupled with this desire, teachers need new tools and processes to help them access and apply this professional knowledge base in their practice. *Mathematics Curriculum Topic Study: Bridging the Gap Between Standards and Practice* provides such tools, processes, and applications.

The Curriculum Topic Study (CTS) approach was adapted from the experiences of co-author Page Keeley in working with the American Association for the Advancement of Science's (AAAS) Project 2061's procedure for the study of a single benchmark. That procedure involves a rigorous analysis of a benchmark's key ideas and the associated research, and it uses Project 2061's resources, including *Science for All Americans, Benchmarks for Science Literacy,* and *Atlas of Science Literacy,* all of which include mathematics, science, social science, and technology, under the umbrella of *science literacy.* The Project 2061 study procedure was modified and expanded for the CTS Project to create a set of topic study guides with preselected readings linked to a specific purpose used in a process called Curriculum Topic Study (CTS). CTS focuses on topics instead of a single learning goal, and it includes additional reference materials such as the *Principles and Standards for School Mathematics* (National Council of Teachers of Mathematics [NCTM], 2000), a sourcebook for cognitive research, *The Research Companion to Principals and Standards for School Mathematics* (NCTM, 2003), and an adult mathematics content trade book, *Beyond Numeracy* (Paulos, 1992), authored by a mathematician.

Mathematics Curriculum Topic Study draws on and extends the outstanding work of AAAS/Project 2061 and NCTM's national mathematics education standards development and distribution by building a bridge between the development and dissemination of standards and their purposeful use in the classroom. It is an example of how professional developers have been able to draw on the research and development work done by AAAS and the NCTM and connect it to the immediate needs of teachers and professional developers. CTS draws on the current knowledge base regarding effective professional development for mathematics teachers—addressing the need for greater focus on content, standards, and research in how students learn.

In using CTS, teachers actively seek information from standards and research to provide all students the opportunity to learn and enjoy mathematics. They see the standards and research as providing a wealth of information from highly respected individuals in the mathematics education community and capitalize on the knowledge and expertise in ways that improve the teaching and learning of mathematics.

We have facilitated educators' use of Curriculum Topic Study's practical tools and processes in a variety of contexts and schools and with teachers at various levels of experience in teaching. We have observed how teachers build a common understanding of the standards and research and bring that understanding to life in their classrooms, schools, and districts. We have learned how educators used Curriculum Topic Study to align curriculum, plan instruction, and design assessments that are congruent with the recommendations that come from renowned researchers, practitioners, and policy advocates in the mathematics community. Curriculum Topic Study has moved national standards documents, as well as state standards and frameworks, beyond rhetoric and off the shelf and into the hands and minds of education professionals, who use them routinely and purposefully in their practice.

The *Mathematics Curriculum Topic Study's* tools and processes were originally designed for and piloted with the Maine, New Hampshire, and Vermont teachers participating in the National Science Foundation (NSF)-funded Northern New England Co-Mentoring Network. We wanted to provide a common focus, by topic, to examine implications across states, each of which has a different set of standards and frameworks. The *Mathematics Curriculum Topic Study* pilot was expanded to include the Maine Governor's Academy for Science and Mathematics Education Leadership, a State Mathematics and Science Partnership Project: Mathematics: Access and Teaching in High School (MATHS), and various other mathematics professional development programs offered through the Maine Mathematics and Science Alliance.

After we saw the initial impact of using the *Mathematics Curriculum Topic Study* process with educators, and being encouraged by our national professional development colleagues, we submitted a grant proposal to the NSF's Teacher Professional Continuum Program. This grant, *Curriculum Topic Study—A Systematic Approach to Utilizing National Standards and Cognitive Research*, was awarded to the Maine Mathematics and Science Alliance (MMSA) in May 2004. The MMSA and our partner, WestEd, are working with several professional development organizations, universities, teachers, and teacher educators over the next four years to develop Curriculum Topic Study into a set of science, mathematics, and professional development materials that will be available nationally. The Science Curriculum Topic Study book, *Science Curriculum Topic Study: Bridging the Gap Between Standards and Practice*, was published in February 2005, with the National Science Teachers Association as a copublisher. It has been heralded as "the missing link" by the science education community. In addition to a science and mathematics Curriculum Topic Study book, a *Facilitator's Guide to Using Curriculum Topic Study* will be produced for science and mathematics professional developers and other facilitators of science and mathematics teaching and learning. There is also a companion Web site, www.curriculumtopicstudy.org. To learn more about this NSF-funded project, please visit the Web site.

NEED

Engaging mathematics educators in scholarly thought and purposeful use of standards and research on student learning is critical to improving student achievement. National and state standards and an expanding body of cognitive research have been available to teachers since the start of the standards-based wave of mathematics education reform. However, what has been missing is a systematic process not tied to any one project, which includes vetted readings and a set of tools to collectively and deliberately use them in practice.

In addition, the new "highly qualified teacher" requirements set by *No Child Left Behind [NCLB]* make this a critical time for teachers to have the tools and processes they need to continuously develop as professionals. In this *NCLB* age of standards and high-stakes accountability, it is not enough to be guided by a list of state standards or a topical alignment to ideas in mathematics.

To seek continuous improvement toward the goal of improving student learning in mathematics requires educators to understand the standards and use research when planning instruction. If your goal is to become a standards- and research-based educator, *Mathematics Curriculum Topic Study* provides the tools and processes needed to help you develop and draw on a common knowledge base in mathematics that can be used in a variety of curricular, instructional, and assessment applications.

AUDIENCE

The primary audience for this book is K–12 teachers, preservice teachers, preservice higher education faculty, professional developers, and mathematics education specialists. Sections of the book and the CTS process may also be useful to administrators, mathematicians working on curriculum development and education reform projects, parents (especially home-schoolers), standards revision committees, and assessment developers.

ORGANIZATION

The book is divided into six chapters. Chapter 1 provides an introduction to CTS and a description of the knowledge and research base that anchors the development and design. It includes a rationale for the importance of studying a curricular topic and why topics were chosen as the focus.

Chapter 2 takes the reader on a tour of a CTS guide. It describes the different features of a CTS guide and provides descriptions of the resources that are used in the process.

Chapter 3 describes the ways users of CTS engage in the process. It describes how to get started and defines the different purposes and outcomes a user must identify before beginning the process. It describes an instructional model for adult learning used in the process, based on the learning cycle. Individual and group use is addressed, and guiding questions are provided to accompany the resources.

Chapter 4 describes the various professional contexts in which CTS can be used. Embedded throughout this section are various examples and tools that teachers can use, such as improving content knowledge, curriculum, instruction, assessment, professional development, and leadership.

Chapter 5 describes how CTS has been used in actual practice. Real-life vignettes are described that illuminate the different ways people have used the information they derive from CTS.

Chapter 6 is the core of the book. It contains the 92 CTS guides, arranged in eight different categories. The study guides are reproducible for use with other teachers and professional developers.

The resources section contains additional resources that complement CTS, as well as some of the worksheet templates described in the chapters.

HOW TO USE THIS BOOK

The primary goal of this book is to provide mathematics educators with ready-to-use study guides that have a common format and include vetted sections in the content, standards, and research resources for reading about, studying, and reflecting on a mathematics topic. It is an essential companion to help you to use the standards to which you may already have access and to incorporate other professional mathematics education resources into your professional library. Educators who are familiar with the CTS approach can immediately access and use the guides in Chapter 6. Others will find it helpful to read Chapters 1 through 5 first to get a clear sense of how and why the guides were developed and of how they can be used effectively. This is not intended to be a "how to" book for professional developers who are interested in ways to facilitate use of CTS in their professional development settings. Such a book will be developed as part of the Curriculum Topic Study Project in 2006–2007. In the meantime, professional developers can use this book to learn about the process and practice using it. Higher education faculty can encourage their students to use this book to plan their lessons and gain a deeper understanding of standards- and research-based teaching and learning in preparation for the reality of teaching in schools and classrooms.

CTS provides tools and processes for use in improving teachers' understanding of the topics they teach. Rather than providing a step-by-step guide to designing curriculum, instruction, and assessment, CTS promotes inquiry among educators in discovering new knowledge about teaching and learning mathematics. It is an involved process that may seem complex and time consuming at first. But then again, it is complex and time consuming because learning is complex and takes time. Superficial knowledge and dabbling around with fun activities are different from developing a deep, professional knowledge of mathematics. The latter makes the CTS investment in time and intellectual energy worth it. Like any complex endeavor, it gets easier, becomes internalized, and proceeds much more quickly after multiple opportunities to practice and share strategies and learning with others. Our advice is to start small at first. Try one section and one resource in a CTS guide. Reflect on what you learned and try a new topic using two or more sections and additional resources in the CTS guide. Add a few more sections and resources, and before you know it, the training wheels will be off! You will be well on your way to cycling satisfactorily through a rich and invigorating process and body of knowledge that is sure to have an impact on you, your colleagues, and—most important of all—your students.

ACKNOWLEDGMENTS

This book would not have been possible without the keen insights, time, and energy of so many wonderful teachers and colleagues with whom we work. We are deeply indebted to all of you for sharing your wisdom and experiences along with helping us think through, pilot, and field-test various components of the book.

The first set of mathematics CTS tools and processes was developed for pilot use by the mentor teachers in the Northern New England Co-Mentoring Network (NNECN) project. We want to thank each and every one of you, and your "mentees," for your significant pioneering contribution to this project. We are especially grateful to Christine Downing and Connie Upshultz for their enthusiastic use of the material, helpful comments during pilot sessions, contributions to vignettes, and willingness to drive all the way to Maine to share their CTS classroom experiences. We also wish to thank the teacher leaders in the Maine Governor's Academy for Science and Mathematics Education Leadership for providing a teacher leadership test bed. Thank you to Governor's Academy Fellow Leslie Minton and Judy Parent for your specific feedback and contributions. A special thank you to Kathy Casparius for your help in refining the applications of CTS through your experienced eyes as an accomplished veteran teacher of high school mathematics.

Once again we are indebted to our mentors and role models, Susan Mundry and Kathy Stiles, for encouraging us to pursue this book. You inspire us with your knowledge of professional development and teacher change, and we will forever be grateful to you for helping us stretch and develop our skills and knowledge about standards- and research-based professional development. To all our National Academy for Science and Mathematics Education Leadership (NASMEL) colleagues, thank you for supporting and encouraging us!

To our MMSA colleagues, we give special thanks for finding the time in your busy schedules to support this work. Our deep appreciation goes to Carolyn Arline, who was always there to run ideas by, brainstorm topics, review guides, reflect on contexts and processes, and provide feedback on pilot sessions. Thank you to Lynn Farrin and Deb Mcintyre for their extensive review of the material and their constant words of encouragement and support. We are indebted to Chad Dorsey, who effortlessly laid out and edited graphics for us. Thank you to Jill Rosenblum and Joyce Tugel for frequent check-ins and words of encouragement. A special warm thank you goes to Brianne Van Den Bossche, our cheerful, multi-talented project assistant, who competently managed a lot of behind-the-scenes work for us, as well as Victoria Abbott, who so nicely lent us a hand when needed. Our deep appreciation goes to Janre Mullins for her remarkable ability to help us stay within our budget for developing a product of this magnitude. Thank you Nate Keeley, our web designer extraordinaire, who created and maintains our CTS Web site. We are extremely grateful to Dr. Francis Eberle, MMSA executive director and co-principal investigator for the CTS Project. Your quiet, intellectual demeanor combined with your support for innovation helps us continually shape and transform our work to meet quality standards our organization is proud to uphold. Your faith in our work is uplifting!

There are so many other professional colleagues who supported and contributed to this book in some way. In particular, we would like to thank Dr. Bill Nave, our "connoisseur of feedback." His innate ability to see things that we may have missed during the field-testing helped to strengthen the tools and processes in this book. Thank you to Dan Hupp, Tad Johnston, Kim Schroeter, and Cynthia Hillman-Forbush for helping create the first 20 guides three years ago to use in the initial piloting. We gratefully acknowledge the work of Project 2061, led by Dr. JoEllen Roseman, and the National Council of Teachers of Mathematics, led by James L. Robillo. Your national leadership efforts and the extraordinary resources developed and produced by your organizations provide the foundation for our work. Many thanks go to Soren Wheeler, our freelance "science and mathematics literacy editor," for your wonderful way with words and knack for shaping ideas.

We gratefully acknowledge our Corwin Press editor, Rachel Livsey, for supporting this second book in a series of three publications and helping us stay on course. We also wish to thank Diane Foster and Phyllis Cappello for ensuring that all the pieces of the book are intact and helping us navigate through each step in the publication process. We are deeply indebted to the National Science Foundation and all the program officers for the Teacher Professional Development Continuum Program. These talented and passionate individuals have done so much to tirelessly support mathematics and science education in the United States. In particular, we would like to give special thanks to Dr. Michael Haney, our program officer, and Dr. Carole Stearns for the dedicated and unwavering support you provide to those of us in the NSF TPC community. And a huge thank you to all the teachers who will use this book—it is through you that we can all make a difference in students' lives.

And finally, as coauthors, we want to acknowledge each other. To Cheryl Rose, I will forever be grateful to you for agreeing to work on this project with me. My knowledge of mathematics education has increased exponentially through my interactions with you! To Page Keeley, thank you for recognizing my potential and bringing me along for this wonderful adventure!

The contributions of the following manuscript reviewers are gratefully acknowledged:

Anne Roede Giddings
Assistant Superintendent
Ansonia Public Schools
Ansonia, CT

Katherine E. Stiles
Senior Research Associate
WestEd
Tucson, AZ

Cindy Bryant
Consultant
Missouri Math Academy
Salem, MO

Rhonda Naylor
Mathematics Teacher and Coordinator
Campus Middle School, Cherry Creek Schools
Englewood, CO

Cathy Carroll
Senior Project Director
WestEd
Redwood City, CA

Thomas Berger
Mathematics Professor
Colby College
Waterville, ME

John Donovan
Assistant Professor of Mathematics Education
University of Maine
Orono, ME

Fred Gross
Mathematics Project Director
Educational Development Center (EDC)
Newton, MA

Tad Johnston
State Mathematics Specialist
Maine Department of Education
Augusta, ME

Fred Prevost
Mathematics Education Professor
Plymouth State University
Plymouth, NH

We also gratefully acknowledge the following Curriculum Topic Study pilot and field test participants:

Arline, Carolyn
Maine Mathematics
   and Science Alliance
Maine

Bailey, Ellen
Windham Middle
   School
Maine

Beede, Lisa
Hussey Elementary
   School
Maine

Austin, Ann
China Primary
   School
Maine

Baker, Marshalyn
Messalonskee Middle
   School
Maine

Belisle, Mary
Greely Junior High
   School
Maine

Belmonte, Linda
Campbell High School
New Hampshire

Beloin, Frances
Nashua North
   High Shool
New Hampshire

Brasseur, Linda
North Country Union
   High School
Vermont

Bricchi, Tracy
Merrimack Valley High
   School
New Hampshire

Brown, Peggy
Mt. Ararat Middle
   School
Maine

Burns, Kay
McKelvie Middle
   School
New Hampshire

Burr, Deanne
Longfellow Elementary
   School
Maine

Casparius, Kathy
Cony High School
Maine

Coleman, Katie
Searsport Middle School
Maine

Cook, Jim
Norridgewock
   Central School
Maine

Corrado, Sue
Longfellow
   Elementary School
Maine

Cote, Jessica
Hodgkins Middle
   School
Maine

Darling, Laurette
China Primary School
Maine

Davidson, Joyce
DR Gaul Middle
   School
Maine

DeMatties, Tom
Castleton Village
   School
Vermont

Dodge, Lois
China Primary School
Maine

Dokas, Lauren
McKelvie Middle
   School
New Hampshire

Downing, Christine
Pennichuck Jr. High
New Hampshire

Drake, Joelle
Hussey School
Maine

Ellis, Martha
Maranacook
   Community
   High School
Maine

Fancher, Karen
Poland Regional High
   School
Maine

Feal-Staub, Kevin
Wilmington
   High School
Vermont

Floyd, Kathy
Poland Regional
   High School
Maine

Foley, Sally
Deer-Isle Stonington
   Elementary
Maine

Fortier, Carole
Castleton Village
   School
Vermont

Fortin, Rhonda
Westbrook High School
Maine

Fuller, Debbie
Riverton
   Elementary School
Maine

Gale, Amy
Sutton Village School
Vermont

Gallagher, Bonnie
Troy Howard
   Middle School
Maine

Gardner, Alicia
Gilford High School
New Hampshire

George, Beckee
Poland Regional
   High School
Maine

Gorden, Nancy
Dike-Newell
   Elementary School
Maine

Gott, Lauree
Veazie Community
   School
Maine

Gregory, Lynnette
Sutton Village School
Vermont

Guidi, Linda
Elm Street Jr. High
New Hampshire

Haddock, Charlie
Windham Middle
   School
Maine

Haney, Jane
G. Herbert Jewett
   School
Maine

Harriman, Nancy
Dike-Newell Elementary
   School
Maine

Henry, Renee
Farrington Elementary
   School
Maine

Houston, Julie
Vassalboro Community
   School
Maine

Hutchinson, Mary Jo
Delran Intermediate
   School
New Jersey

James, Sharon
Winooski School District
Vermont

Jeffords, Jen
Windham Middle
   School
Maine

Johnston, Rebecca
SeDoMocha Middle
   School
Maine

King, Kathleen
Noble VI
Maine

Knudson, Ellen
Bismarck Public Schools
North Dakota

Koppen, Karen
Riverton Elementary
   School
Maine

Kotros, Mary Ann
Riverton Elementary
   School
Maine

Leavitt, Diane
Burlington
   High School
Vermont

Leonard, Amanda
Windham Middle
   School
Maine

Lucas, Sarah
TC Hamlin Elementary
   School
Maine

Malloy, Janilyn
U-32 Community
   School
Vermont

Marcouillier, Barbara
Williston Central
   School
Vermont

Marriner, Anne
Riverton Elementary
   School
Maine

Matzke, Jeanne
Gilford High School
New Hampshire

McCabe, Rosemarie
Elizabeth Public Schools
New Jersey

McCaffrey, Ken
Brattleboro Union
   High School
Vermont

Minton, Leslie
Maine Mathematics
   and Science Alliance
Maine

Moody, Lyndon John
Calais High School
Maine

Morgan, Sabrina
Howard Wood
   Elementary
California

Murray, Kevin
Poland Regional
   High School
Maine

Myers, Allen
Williston Central School
Vermont

Naylor, Rhonda
Campus Middle School
Colorado

Nolan, Kathleen
North Country
   Union Jr. High School
Vermont

O'Meara, Maria
Mt. Ararat Middle School
Maine

Paine, Deborah
Pinkerton Academy
New Hampshire

Pandolfo, John
Spaulding High School
Vermont

Parent, Judy
Wiscasset High School
Maine

Parker, Michael
Farrington Elementary
   School
Maine

Pellerin, Cindy
Windham Middle
   School
Maine

Terry, Beth
Mary Williams
   Elementary School
Virginia

Poland, Gretchen
Poland Regional High
   School
Maine

Porter, Ingrid
Noble VI
Maine

Poulin, Sarah
Windham Middle
   School
Maine

Powers, Gloria
Houlton High School
Maine

Reed, Laura
Windham Regional
   Career Center
Vermont

Reichert, Jason
Winooski School District
Vermont

Richburg, Virginia
Randolph Union High
   School
Vermont

Robinson, Jan
Wheeling Public Schools
Illinois

Rogers, Heather
Mt. Ararat Middle School
Maine

Rossier, Kathy
Williston Central School
Vermont

Rumsey, Ryan
Windham Middle School
Maine

Saucier, Susan
Dike-Newell Elementary
   School
Maine

Slaski, Pete
Mt. Ararat Middle School
Maine

Slattery, Katherine
Telstar Middle School
Maine

Southworth, Meghan
Troy Howard Middle
   School
Maine

Tye, Elizabeth
Magnolia Public Schools
Arkansas

Spaulding, Darren
Rahway Middle School
New Jersey

St. Pierre, Melissa
Mt. Ararat Middle School
Maine

Testa, Susan
Nashua High School
   North
New Hampshire

Towle, Shawn
Falmouth Middle School
Maine

Treworgy, Bob
Mt. Ararat Middle
   School
Maine

Unger, Barbara
Middlebury Union
   Middle School
Vermont

Upschulte, Connie
Pennichuck Jr. High
   School
New Hampshire

Valliere, Louise
Stevens High School
New Hampshire

Violette, Nancy
Poland Regional
   High School
Maine

Walling, Jessica
Hussey Elementary
Maine

Wells, Kristen
Windham Middle
   School
Maine

Woodcock, Sarah
Windham Middle
   School
Maine

Yindra, Liz
Poland Regional High
   School
Maine

York, Dawn
Medway Middle School
Maine

About the Authors

Page Keeley is the senior program director for science at the Maine Mathematics and Science Alliance (MMSA). Her work at the MMSA involves leadership, formative assessment, professional development, and the design of materials and tools to support standards- and research-based teaching and learning. She is the principal investigator and project director of three NSF-funded projects for science and mathematics, including *Curriculum Topic Study—A Systematic Approach to Utilizing National Standards and Cognitive Research, The Northern New England Co-Mentoring Network,* and *PRISMS—Phenomena and Representations for the Instruction of Science in Middle Schools.* She is also the director of the Maine Governor's Academy for Science and Mathematics Education Leadership and directs a science and literacy initiative, Linking Science, Inquiry, and Language Literacy. She was a Fellow in the first cohort of the National Academy for Science Education Leadership. Prior to working at the MMSA, Page taught middle school science and mathematics and high school biology and applied chemistry for 15 years. During that time, she served as president of her state science teachers association and served two terms on the executive board of the National Science Teachers Association. She received the Presidential Award for Excellence in Secondary Science Teaching in 1992 and the Milken National Educator Award in 1993. Prior to teaching, she worked as a research assistant in immunogenetics at the Jackson Laboratory in Bar Harbor, Maine. She received her undergraduate degree in life sciences at the University of New Hampshire and her master's in science education at the University of Maine.

Cheryl Rose is the senior program director for mathematics at the Maine Mathematics and Science Alliance (MMSA). Her work at the MMSA is primarily in the areas of leadership, mathematics professional development, and school reform. She is currently the co-principal investigator of the mathematics section of the NSF-funded project, Curriculum Topic Study, and principal investigator and project director of a Title IIa State Mathematics and Science Partnership Project, MATHS—Mathematics: Access and Teaching in High School. Prior to working on these projects, Cheryl was the co-principal investigator and project director for MMSA's NSF-funded Local Systemic Change Initiative, BEAMM—Broadening Educational Access to Mathematics in Maine, and was a fellow in the Cohort 4 of the National Academy for Science and Mathematics Education Leadership. Before coming to the MMSA in 2001, Cheryl was a high school and middle school mathematics educator for 10 years. Cheryl received her BS in secondary mathematics education from the University of Maine at Farmington and her MEd in curriculum and instruction from City University in Seattle.

Introduction to Curriculum Topic Study

Curriculum Topic Study was extremely helpful as a cornerstone and starting point for our lesson study. As we planned our lesson, we used Curriculum Topic Study to stay grounded in the content goals for the lesson and identify potential learning difficulties.

Curriculum Topic Study has opened my eyes as to the meaning of adopting a "standards-based" program. I frequently refer to the Curriculum Topic Study Guides to help me find the information I need to understand concepts that I previously would not have considered teaching at my grade level.

Our math department meetings have changed significantly since using Curriculum Topic Study to build a common understanding and language about our state standards. Using the resources and discussing our findings has given us the confidence to make sound decisions about our common assessments and instructional strategies.

Each time our K–8 curriculum committee studies a new topic, I leave with a greater understanding of how student ideas build over time and the importance of a coherent curriculum that connects mathematical ideas.

Curriculum Topic Study has helped me design workshops for curriculum implementation support. Using Curriculum Topic Study as a lens to examine our new Connected Mathematics units has helped our teachers understand how the lessons align with standards and flow conceptually. In addition, Curriculum Topic Study has given our teachers added confidence and tools to improve their own understanding of mathematical ideas.

WHAT IS CURRICULUM TOPIC STUDY?

The above quotes came from mathematics educators who use Curriculum Topic Study (CTS) in their work as teachers, mentors, professional developers, and curriculum and assessment committee members and as part of collaborative learning communities. CTS is a methodical study process that uses a set of tools and strategies—organized around 92 curriculum topics—and is designed to help educators improve the teaching and learning of mathematics. Mathematics educators who use CTS in a deliberate and systematic way will:

- Develop a deeper understanding of the specific content they teach
- Identify and clarify the specific concepts and procedures that are important for students to know and be able to do
- Clarify learning goals from their state or local standards
- Gain a deeper understanding of the intent of national, state, and local mathematics standards
- Improve the coherency of development within and across grades and topics
- Identify potential learning difficulties, developmental considerations, misconceptions, and misunderstandings associated with a topic
- Examine essential characteristics of effective instruction and models of standards- and research-based practice
- Apply effective strategies for teaching specific ideas and procedures associated with a topic
- Take advantage of important connections between mathematics and science instruction
- Increase opportunities for students of all levels and backgrounds to achieve the learning goals articulated in district, state, and national standards
- Acquire and use a common language and knowledge base about teaching and learning in mathematics
- Provide more content focus to professional development activities

CTS helps individuals or groups of teachers study, in a systematic way, relevant readings from a core set of professional mathematics education resources. These readings are identified and screened in advance, then organized in Curriculum Topic Study Guides (see example in Figure 1.1). The specific features and uses of CTS Guides are described in Chapter 2.

There are 92 CTS Guides in Chapter 6—ranging from specific topics, such as triangles, to broader topics, such as geometric shapes—organized in seven categories. The majority of the guides address K–12 topics. Guides that address sophisticated content, such as quadratics, are designed to be used primarily with upper grade levels.

For each topic, a CTS Guide lists relevant readings from sources that include national standards documents, trade books written by mathematicians, research summaries, and K–12 conceptual strand maps (see Figure 1.2). Optional readings, videos, and Web-based material can also be used to supplement the study of a topic.

Figure 1.1   Example of a Curriculum Topic Study Guide

Standards and Research-Based Study of a Curricular Topic

PROBABILITY

Section and Outcome	Selected Sources and Readings for Study and Reflection Read and examine *related parts* of:
I. Identify Adult Content Knowledge	**IA:** *Science for All Americans* ▸ Chapter 9, *Probability,* pages 135–137 **IB:** *Beyond Numeracy* ▸ *Coincidences,* pages 38–41 ▸ *Probabilities,* pages 187–191 ▸ *Statistics – Two Theorems,* pages 227–230
II. Consider Instructional Implications	**IIA:** *Benchmarks for Science Literacy* ▸ 9D, *Uncertainty,* general essay page 226, grade span essays, pages 227–230 **IIB:** *NCTM Principles and Standards for School Mathematics* ▸ Grades PreK–12 Overview Data Analysis and Probability, page 48, *Understand and Apply,* page 51 ▸ Grades PreK–2 Data Analysis and Probability, page 109, *Understand and Apply,* page 114 ▸ Grades 3–5 Data Analysis and Probability, *Understand and Apply,* page 181 ▸ Grades 6–8 Data Analysis and Probability, *Understand and Apply,* pages 253–255 ▸ Grades 9–12 Data Analysis and Probability, page 325, *Understand and Apply,* pages 331–333
III. Identify Concepts and Specific Ideas	**IIIA:** *Benchmarks for Science Literacy* ▸ 9D, *Uncertainty,* pages 227–230 **IIIB:** *NCTM Principles and Standards for School Mathematics* ▸ Grades PreK–2 Data Analysis and Probability, page 108 or 400 ▸ Grades 3–5 Data Analysis and Probability, page 176 or 400 ▸ Grades 6–8 Data Analysis and Probability, page 248 or 401 ▸ Grades 9–12 Data Analysis and Probability, page 324 or 401
IV. Examine Research on Student Learning	**IVA:** *Benchmarks for Science Literacy* ▸ 9D, *Probability,* page 353 **IVB:** *Research Companion* ▸ Chapter 14, *Research on Students' Understanding of Probability,* pages 216–224
V. Examine Coherency and Articulation	**V:** *Atlas of Science Literacy* ▸ *Statistical Reasoning,* page 127 noting the conceptual strand "Probability"
VI. Clarify State Standards and District Curriculum	**VIA:** *State Standards:* Link Sections I–V to learning goals and information from your state standards or frameworks that are informed by the results of the topic study. **VIB:** *District Curriculum Guide:* Link Sections I–V to learning goals and information from your district curriculum guide that are informed by the results of the topic study.
Visit www.curriculumtopicstudy.org for updates or supplementary readings, Web sites, and videos.	

Figure 1.2 Types of Readings and Their Sources

Type of Resource	Source
Adult mathematics literacy description	*Science for All Americans,* AAAS Project 2061 (AAAS, 1990)
Adult mathematics trade book	*Beyond Numeracy,* by John Allen Paulos (1992)
National, state, and local standards	*Benchmarks for Science Literacy,* AAAS Project 2061, (AAAS, 1993) *Principles and Standards for School Mathematics* (NCTM, 2000) State standards or frameworks and/or local curriculum standards or frameworks
Research summaries	*Benchmarks for Science Literacy,* Chapter 15, Project 2061 *Research Companion to Principles and Standards for School Mathematics* (NCTM, 2003)
Conceptual strand maps	*Atlas of Science Literacy,* American Association for the Advancement of Science Project 2061, AAAS (2001)

CTS users may find additional material to complement the readings in a selected CTS Guide from their own collection of professional resources or on the CTS Web site at www.curriculumtopicstudy.org.

CTS provides an effective and efficient way to intellectually engage with mathematics professional readings. Typically, educators have to sift through a huge amount of unfamiliar and often daunting material from disparate sources. Indeed, many teachers may not even know where to look for the information they are seeking. CTS Guides identify the purpose of different resources and explicitly link relevant parts of the text information contained in the resources to topics of study that are useful from the teachers' perspective.

> CTS Guides do the groundwork for the busy educator, providing a one-page guide to relevant results from an enormous range of readings that have been vetted and organized in advance.

The *Principles and Standards for School Mathematics* (National Council of Teachers of Mathematics [NCTM], 2000), *Science for All Americans* (American Association for the Advancement of Science [AAAS], 1990), and *Benchmarks for Science Literacy* (AAAS, 1993) have provided a carefully crafted description of the mathematical ideas and skills all students should achieve by the time they graduate from high school. *Atlas of Science Literacy* (AAAS, 2001) further clarified those documents by providing a set of conceptual strand maps that detail how those ideas and skills connect and develop from kindergarten through high school. States and districts have modeled their own standards after these national documents, and stakeholders at every level are learning how to evaluate, modify, and develop assessments, curricula, and instructional materials to reflect this vision of mathematics for all students.

> What has been missing is a *comprehensive, systematic* process to help educators make effective use of national standards and research on student learning.

Although few mathematics teachers realize that *Science for All Americans, Benchmarks,* and the *Atlas* address student learning in mathematics as well as science, many teachers have seen or own a copy of the *Principles and Standards.* Also, the research on student learning is growing and becoming increasingly accessible to practitioners through print publications and on the Web. Yet, for all of the thought that went into national standards and all of the research on how students learn, just having the documents and research articles is not enough to truly impact student learning. In particular, this means being able to relate them to state and local standards and to their own curricular and instructional challenges. CTS is a *deliberate* process that uses a set of common, high-quality, collective resources to help mathematics educators become better informed educators who understand what the label "standards- and research-based" means.

CTS is not a replacement for formal content coursework, but it can help teachers learn new content or refresh their content knowledge at the same time that they are studying the pedagogical implications of teaching that content. This can be particularly helpful to elementary teachers, who are expected to teach all content areas and seldom have substantive coursework in mathematics. But it can also be helpful to teachers who have had upper-level mathematics coursework, helping them translate formal mathematics content into content that is appropriate for students at different grade levels. This synthesis of content and pedagogy is an essential learning experience for teachers, an experience that content courses and many professional development offerings largely overlook.

> CTS helps educators make the bridge between national standards and research and their local and state efforts to help all students learn challenging mathematics.

Educators who use CTS will realize what powerful tools the national standards and research on student learning can be for implementing their state standards and improving their students' opportunities to learn mathematics. And they will know how to use those tools effectively. CTS provides guidance and effective strategies for educators to use professional resources and research in their practice. CTS moves the mathematics standards off the shelf and into the hands and minds of teachers, leaders, and professional developers, who can use them routinely in an effective, systematic way to improve teaching and learning of mathematics.

WHY STUDY A CURRICULUM TOPIC?

By taking the time to study a topic before planning a unit or lesson, teachers build a deeper understanding of the content, connections, and effective ways to help students achieve understanding of the most important concepts and procedures in that topic. This can significantly improve instruction, regardless of the materials used. A former director of the National Science Foundation's (NSF) Elementary, Secondary, and Informal Education Division points out that teachers who are unfamiliar with the topics they teach tend to rely on textbooks and teach in a more didactic way, often failing to make connections between important ideas in mathematics:

> . . . [When] teachers cover topics about which they are well-prepared, they encourage student questions and discussions, spend less time on unrelated topics, permit discussions to move in new directions based on student interest, and generally present topics in a more coherent way, all strategies described as standards-based teaching. However, when teachers teach topics about which they are less well-informed, they often discourage active participation by students, keep any discussion under tight rein, rely more on presentation than on student discussions, and spend time on tangential issues. (Kahle, 1999)

National standards, research, and other professional tools can help teachers prepare in ways that allow them to provide the best learning experiences possible for their students. But teachers need to see the connection between those resources and tools and the topics they teach. CTS makes that connection, ensuring that those resources and tools are used in ways that are effective, meaningful, and relevant to the teacher.

A plethora of general professional tools for teachers are available in schools, districts, and professional development settings. Examples include: *Concept-Based Curriculum and Instruction* (Erickson, 1998), *Understanding by Design* (Wiggins & McTighe, 1998), *Enhancing Professional Practice: A Framework for Teaching* (Danielson, 1996), *Classroom Instruction That Works: Research-Based Strategies for Increasing Student Achievement* (Marzano, Pickering, & Pollack, 2001), *Mapping the Big Picture: Integrating Curriculum and Assessment K–12* (Jacobs, 1997), and *Differentiated Instructional Strategies: One Size Doesn't Fit All* (Gregory & Chapman, 2002). Such tools can be useful to teachers who know the content and structure of their discipline and are familiar with the research base on student learning. But the same tools may not suffice for novice teachers, elementary teachers who teach all content areas, and others who may not have a sufficient knowledge base in the area of mathematics they teach. Current reform-oriented practices in mathematics center on teaching for understanding and engaging students in the "big ideas" of mathematics. As a result, "one tool fits all" may result in "one tool fits few" if we fail to help the teacher connect general teaching resources to the specific ideas and skills they are actually teaching.

CTS extends the power of these valuable although content-generic tools. While CTS is right in line with their underlying principles, it also provides a topic-specific study process needed to make these tools more effective for use by mathematics teachers. For example, CTS builds on current thinking about designing learning experiences in approaches such as *backwards design,* used in *Understanding by Design* (Wiggins & McTighe, 1998). Backwards design begins by identifying evidence of meeting desired standards and then proceeds to plan teaching and learning experiences. This model suggests four filters for determining what is worth teaching and understanding in a topic. Three of these filters relate to the CTS process and include examining (1) the extent to which the "big ideas" in a topic are addressed, (2) the extent to which the ideas and processes in a topic reside at the heart of the discipline, and (3) the extent to which abstract and counterintuitive ideas need to be uncovered, including students' misconceptions about ideas related to the topic.

Although these three filters can be powerful, they assume that teachers are comfortable with mathematical content, know what the "big ideas" are, can make the connections that support student learning, and are aware of students' misconceptions and alternative ways of thinking. Unfortunately, this often is not the case. In reality, many good teachers missed the "big ideas" in their own mathematics education. Elementary and middle school teachers may have a limited mathematics background, and high school mathematics teachers frequently specialize in a particular area of mathematics. Teachers may not be aware of the misconceptions and alternative ideas their students hold, and sometimes, they harbor those very same misconceptions.

> CTS combines the wisdom of teacher practice with the recommendations from standards and research and serves as the essential first step in effective planning and design.

The critical and often overlooked first step in any effective instructional design process involves a clear understanding of the specific ideas and procedures that students need to learn and the pedagogical implications of helping students learn them. A careful study of a topic, using CTS, clarifies the "end in mind" and provides a framework for planning assessment and instruction that is true to the content and takes student thinking and developmental levels into account. All too often, teachers strike out on their own, even when a wealth of information and resources, carefully thought through by distinguished mathematicians and educators, sits at their fingertips.

CTS also reflects the research base on teacher knowledge and the importance of pedagogical content knowledge. Knowing the content is different from knowing how to organize and represent it in a way that encourages student learning. Indeed, an advanced understanding of content can sometimes make it harder to identify difficulties a novice learner is likely to have. Designing learning experiences and facilitating learning requires pedagogical knowledge related to mathematics content. Teachers with this special knowledge understand what makes the learning of specific topics easy or difficult for learners and can develop strategies for representing and formulating content to make it accessible to learners (Shulman, 1986). Thus, even those teachers who understand the mathematics behind the topics they teach can benefit from CTS. Through CTS, teachers with a strong mathematics content background can gain new insights about specific ideas and procedures that may have been overlooked, connections within and across topics, effective contexts for learning, developmental considerations for introducing new ideas and skills, and new instructional strategies that result in increased learning.

Outside of the work done by NCTM through regional and annual meetings, academies, and the distribution of outreach material; and AAAS's support for K–12 science literacy (which includes mathematics), there has been little systematic, widespread work to help teachers understand and use standards and research on student learning. Many pre- and inservice efforts to support teachers' content knowledge place little emphasis on helping teachers become aware of the connection between the topics they teach, the recommendations in standards, and research on students' alternative ideas and ways of thinking. Without a process to compare current practice with standards and research, teachers are likely to continue doing what they have always been doing. Recall the old adage, "If you always do what you've always done, you'll always get what you've always gotten."

> Teachers may have copies of standards or occasionally come across a research article; what has been missing is a process for using them to impact teaching practice, knowledge, and beliefs.

CTS brings this process to teachers at all levels of experience and engages them in classroom applications of standards and research. In today's climate of accountability, teachers are assuming more personal responsibility for their own learning. Rather than waiting for the system to provide more effective professional development programs, mathematics educators can use CTS to continue to grow and improve as teachers, enhancing student learning of the most important ideas in mathematics.

WHY FOCUS ON TOPICS?

To understand why this book focuses on topics, it is important to clarify what is meant by the word. In the context of CTS, *topics* are the broad organizers for ideas and skills in a curriculum; they do not describe the endpoint of instruction. Learning goals describe what students should know and be able to do after instruction, but they need to be organized and sorted into important topics within the curriculum (see Figure 1.3). Unfortunately, the research and the national, state, and local

Figure 1.3   Topics as Organizers

Topics as Organizers for Curriculum and Instruction

- Teachers design instruction by organizing the mathematics concepts and procedures they teach by unit topics.
- Curriculum materials and district curriculum guides are often organized by topics. Yet, the standards and results of research describing the cognitive difficulties students face are organized by broad conceptual strands.
- Topics provide a framework for understanding the nature of mathematics, connections among mathematical ideas, problem-solving processes, applications to other disciplines, and implications of mathematics and technology.

---

standards that drive curriculum, instruction, and assessment often are not organized in the same way as the mathematics content in school curricula. Educators must make a bridge between the way they organize mathematics topics and the specific, research-based ideas and procedures laid out in national, state, and local standards. CTS provides a methodical way to make this bridge.

> Because curriculum and instruction are organized around topics, CTS uses topics as the entry point for looking at important and related ideas and procedures taught within a single lesson or a broader curricular unit.

Making this distinction clear, while highlighting the relationship between learning goals and topics, is one of the main goals of CTS. Rather than focusing on teaching a topic per se, CTS helps teachers think about the organization of curriculum, instruction, and assessment around a connected set of specific ideas and skills. When teachers focus solely on topics without drilling down into the specific key ideas, they risk losing the benefits of standards and research, which make critical distinctions within topics about what is important to teach and how best to teach it. Topics provide a framework for understanding the nature of mathematics, connections among mathematical ideas, problem-solving processes, applications to other disciplines, and implications of mathematics and technology.

CTS Guides range in grain size from a specific idea or skill, such as addition and subtraction, to a broader topic, such as computation and operations (within which addition and subtraction is a subtopic). For a topic to be included in a CTS Guide, it must be considered critical content in mathematics, and it must be linked to specific learning goals articulated in national standards.

There are 92 topics included in this book (see Chapter 6), but this does not imply that all of these topics should be taught in the K–12 mathematics curriculum. The Third International Mathematics and Science Study suggests that American curricula suffer from being a "mile wide and an inch deep," resulting in little conceptual understanding for students (Schmidt, McKnight, & Raizen, 1997). CTS is meant to help teachers provide students with a deeper conceptual understanding of the learning goals in a selected topic, not to ensure that they cover every possible topic superficially.

The intent of CTS is to provide enough examples of common topics so that teachers can find CTS Guides that address the topics they are currently teaching, consolidate topics for deeper understanding, and improve their understanding of how students best learn the ideas and skills in the topics they teach. To this end, the CTS Guides include both traditional topics that might appear in textbooks, standards-based curriculum materials, district scope and sequence curriculum guides, and content categories used to organize national and state standards and frameworks. Many of these topics have overlapping concepts and procedures, and some are completely

Figure 1.4   Characteristics of Expert Teachers

Expert Teachers

- Know the structure of the knowledge in their disciplines
- Know the conceptual barriers that are likely to hinder learning
- Have a well-organized knowledge of concepts and inquiry procedures and problem-solving strategies (based on pedagogical content knowledge)

SOURCE: Bransford et al., 2000.

subsumed in others. Furthermore, because each CTS Guide examines a topic from a K–12 perspective, teachers eliminate unnecessary redundancy while planning purposeful reiteration of ideas that need to be revisited in different contexts or at increasing levels of sophistication. This careful examination of a topic, in contrast to the "checklist of standards or objectives," promotes the coherence that may be lacking in current attempts at standards-based curriculum, instruction, and assessment.

THE UNDERLYING KNOWLEDGE AND RESEARCH BASE

Teachers need to develop a personal understanding of the reform recommendations articulated in *Principles and Standards for School Mathematics* and other documents. Clearly, translating standards into classroom practice is a challenge yet to be overcome. At the same time, there is a shift toward providing transformative professional development and supporting resources that reflect the current knowledge base on how teachers and students learn. The NRC reports, *How People Learn* (Bransford, Brown, & Cocking, 2000) and *How Students Learn Mathematics in the Classroom* (Donovan & Bransford, 2005) are raising awareness among mathematics educators of the need to understand the preconceptions and alternative ideas students bring to their learning. CTS—by virtue of its focus on the structure of mathematics content, research into students' learning, and pedagogical strategies linked to specific ideas and skills—reflects the findings from *How People Learn*, which distinguish expert teachers from novices (see Figure 1.4). There is a strong link between teacher expertise, which involves both content and pedagogical content knowledge, and student achievement. Because teacher expertise has such a demonstrated impact on student learning, it stands to reason that processes that develop mathematics teachers' knowledge and skills, such as CTS, are a sound investment toward improving student achievement in mathematics.

> National standards have been around for almost a decade, yet studies such as *Investigating the Influence of Standards* (National Research Council [NRC], 2002) show that standards have not made a significant impact where it matters most—the classroom.

THE ORIGIN OF CURRICULUM TOPIC STUDY: FROM SCIENCE TO MATHEMATICS

The CTS approach was first adapted for use in science education from AAAS Project 2061's study of a benchmark, a powerful approach to understanding the intent of a specific goal for student learning and seeing how that learning goal can impact

Figure 1.5   Parallel Resources Used in Science and Mathematics Curriculum Topic
Studies (CTS)

Science CTS Resources	Mathematics CTS Resources
Science for All Americans (AAAS, 1990)	*Science for All Americans* (AAAS, 1990)
Science Matters (Hazen & Trefil, 1991)	*Beyond Numeracy* (Paulos, 1992)
Benchmarks for Science Literacy (AAAS, 1993)	*Benchmarks for Science Literacy* (AAAS, 1993)
National Science Education Standards (National Research Council [NRC], 1996)	*Principles and Standards for School Mathematics* (NCTM, 2000)
Making Sense of Secondary Science (Driver, Squires, Rushworth, & Wood-Robinson, 1994)	*Research Companion to Principles and Standards for School Mathematics* (NCTM, 2003)
Atlas of Science Literacy (AAAS, 2001)	*Atlas of Science Literacy* (AAAS, 2001)
State standards, frameworks, or curriculum guides	State standards, frameworks, or curriculum guides

teachers' knowledge and practice. Although it is important to examine a single
learning goal in certain cases, the authors' work with teachers throughout New
England revealed that they often need to examine collections of learning goals and
relate them explicitly to the topics they teach. It was also clear that teachers benefited
from working with a range of standards documents, including both *Benchmarks
for Science Literacy* (AAAS, 1993) and the *National Science Education Standards* (NRC,
1996), and from looking beyond standards documents to resources for learning
content and research on how students learn specific ideas and skills. Based on these
experiences, CTS expanded the Project 2061 benchmark study procedure to include
examination of additional content resources such as *Science Matters: Achieving Scientific Literacy* (Hazen & Trefil, 1991), *Making Sense of Secondary Science* (Driver, Squires,
Rushworth, & Wood-Robinson, 1994), and topic-specific supplementary resources
such as videos, journal articles, Web sites, and content material.

Our experience suggested that mathematics teachers would benefit from a
similar topic study approach. Draft versions of the mathematics CTS were developed
to be used in the NSF-funded Northern New England Co-Mentoring Network
(www.nnecn.org) to help mathematics mentors use national standards and cognitive
research in their work with novice teachers. Subsequently, a mathematics version of
Science Curriculum Topic Study: Bridging the Gap Between Standards and Practice (Keeley,
2005) underwent development, piloting, and national field-testing after receiving
funding in 2004 from NSF's Teacher Professional Continuum Program. Figure 1.5
shows the parallel collection of resources used in science and mathematics CTS.

National, State, and Local Standards

The term *standards* (sometimes referred to as benchmarks, learning results,
performance indicators, and so on) conveys different meanings to different people.
CTS defines *standards* as a set of outcomes that individually define the mathematical ideas and procedures that students should know and be able to do and that

collectively provide a vision for achieving mathematical literacy for all students. A misperception by many educators and school systems is that the standards themselves are, or imply, a curriculum. Curricular decisions at the state and local level should be *informed* by standards, but there is a variety of ways to organize the ideas and skills in standards into a curriculum.

The national content standards used in mathematics CTS include the *Principles and Standards for School Mathematics* and *Benchmarks for Science Literacy.* NCTM, an international professional organization committed to excellence in mathematics teaching and learning for all teachers and students, first developed standards for mathematics in 1989, including *Curriculum and Evaluation Standards for School Mathematics.* After 10 years of ongoing efforts by a group of teachers, teacher educators, administrators, researchers, and mathematicians to examine, monitor, and evaluate the NCTM standards, a revised and retitled document was released in 2000. The major components of *Principles and Standards for School Mathematics* establish a foundation for school mathematics programs and articulate content and process standards that describe what students should know and be able to do as they progress through the grades.

The NCTM documents were the first set of standards to promote mathematical literacy for all students. Mathematical literacy can be defined as "an individual's capacity to identify and understand the role that mathematics plays in the world, to make well-founded judgments, and to engage in mathematics in ways that meet the needs of that individual's current and future life as a constructive, concerned, and reflective citizen" (De Lange, 1999, p. 76). Since the release of the first document, most states and local districts have developed their own content standards or are revising their existing content standards. In addition, multiple curriculum materials and instructional programs have been developed and aligned to the standards described in the NCTM documents.

Fewer mathematics educators realize that the standards documents developed by AAAS also address mathematical literacy. AAAS, a prestigious private organization of scientists, mathematicians, engineers, and educators, led the first national effort to define goals for adult science literacy in the late 1980s, with the development of *Science for All Americans* by Project 2061. Rather than a list of standards, *Science for All Americans* provides a narrative description of the interconnected web of understanding that every adult American should possess after a K–12 education, including concepts and procedures in mathematics. This narrative account reflects a strong consensus among respected scientists, mathematicians, and educators. Based on cognitive research and the expertise of teachers and teacher educators, specific mathematics learning goals were developed for the K–2, 3–5, 6–8, and 9–12 grade spans—steps along the way to achieving the vision of science literacy, which includes mathematics as its own discipline, laid out in *Science for All Americans.* These steps along the way were published in *Benchmarks*, along with rich descriptions of the context and instructional implications of those learning goals, and they were later depicted in a collection of conceptual strand maps in *Atlas of Science Literacy.*

Each of these AAAS documents includes chapters on the nature of mathematics, the mathematical world, common themes, and habits of mind, providing a rich description of the mathematical knowledge and skills all children and adults should attain. The term *science literacy* can be misleading, and many mathematics educators may assume that the only mathematics included is used to support science. Although this is a part of science literacy, the AAAS Project 2061 documents treat mathematics as both a separate discipline and as knowledge that supports and relates to science. Consider the National Science Foundation (NSF). While the name refers only to science, NSF provides significant support for mathematics (including this book). It also supports initiatives in technology and engineering. In this sense, *science* is a broad umbrella term that encompasses all of these disciplines, including mathematics. Throughout the rest of this book, we will use the term *mathematical literacy* within the broader context of *science literacy* when referring to AAAS Project 2061 resources used for CTS.

> CTS provides a more valid and reliable way to interpret standards, resulting in teaching that actually reflects the intent of the standards.

Mathematics educators continue to face numerous challenges in the current standards-based teaching and learning environment, ranging from implementing new curricula to the high-stakes accountability requirements mandated by the No Child Left Behind legislation. Educators face the daunting task of applying local, state, or national standards in their own curricular, instructional, and assessment context. Local districts and states have spent considerable funds, time, and energy in developing their standards. There has been a flurry of activity in attempting to align curriculum, instruction, and assessment to standards. But there is a missing link in the chain that connects standards to efforts to implement new policies, programs, and practices. Little time has been spent helping educators interpret the content, curricular, and instructional meaning of the standards. Interpretation has been left to individual teachers. As a result, consistency and coherency—and what counts as "alignment"—vary across classrooms, districts, and states.

CTS will help educators to use standards, both national and state, and to recognize their role as central pieces in their local mathematics education system. Through CTS, teachers will develop a better understanding of standards and become personally involved in their use. Standards can then become living documents translated into classroom practice.

Cognitive Research

Research into student learning—both in general and with regard to specific ideas—is another fundamental feature of CTS. Recommendations from *How People Learn* (Bransford et al., 2000) emphasize the need to build on existing knowledge and to engage students' preconceptions—particularly when they interfere with learning. Certain preconceptions about mathematics in general, which may even be fostered in school settings, can be counterproductive to student learning. Three of these preconceptions are (1) the idea that mathematics is about learning to compute, (2) the idea that mathematics is about "following rules" to guarantee correct answers, and (3) the preconception that some people have the ability "to do" math and some don't (Donovan & Bransford, 2005). For teachers using CTS, knowledge of the conceptions about mathematics that students bring to the classroom has proven a powerful learning experience.

CTS also helps teachers to identify students' preconceptions about particular concepts and procedures. The research literature on these specific conceptions has been growing, even since the publication of *Benchmarks* and the *Principles and Standards*. However, much of the literature has been difficult for teachers to find and access. In fact, many teachers are not aware that useful summaries of the research base are available. Each CTS Guide links the mathematics topic to relevant research summaries. CTS uses two research compendia to provide concise, accessible summaries of the research that has been done around specific concepts and procedures in different curricular topics. *Benchmarks'* Chapter 15 contains research summaries linked to specific learning goals in other mathematics chapters. In Section 2 of the *Research Companion to Principles and Standards for School Mathematics* (NCTM, 2003), research findings are arranged by the five content and process standards of the *Principles and Standards* document. New research articles, linked to specific CTS Guides, are also posted and updated in a searchable database on the CTS Web site at www.curriculumtopicstudy.org.

CTS is also informed by research on adult learning. In constructivism, learners construct knowledge by modifying or rejecting existing ideas (Bransford et al., 2000). Engaging teachers in CTS by surfacing their initial ideas related to a topic, followed by a systematic study and discussion of standards and research, reflects the constructivist theory of learning. Furthermore, when teachers engage together in CTS, they create a collaborative learning environment, interacting with one another so that they can make sense of new concepts and ideas (Jonassen, 1994). Another important aspect of learning is personal reflection. Effective teacher learners use metacognitive strategies during a topic study to monitor their own ideas and thought processes, compare and contrast them with those of others, and provide reasons why they accept them (Loucks-Horsley, Love, Stiles, Mundry, & Hewson, 2003). CTS is designed to take account of all these insights into adult learning.

> In CTS, teachers interact with the information in the standards and research and filter that information through their everyday experiences with students.

Effective Professional Development

A seminal publication for professional development in science and mathematics, *Designing Professional Development for Teachers of Science and Mathematics* (Loucks-Horsley et al., 2003) has informed CTS as a tool for transformative teacher learning. This book describes changes in mathematics education and professional development that reveal an urgent need for new teacher learning tools and materials focused on content. Some of these changes, and the way CTS responds to them, are described below:

1. The knowledge base about learning, teaching, the nature of mathematics, and professional development is growing. Our current knowledge base about teaching and learning has expanded exponentially since the rise of standards. The findings from *How People Learn* (Bransford et al., 2000) and recent papers in professional journals have increased our knowledge of how students learn specific ideas, of the misconceptions students are likely to hold, and of the developmental implications for introducing ideas in different grades. This literature reveals more about transformative learning for teachers and the importance of developing both content knowledge and pedagogical content knowledge. Consequently, teachers need tools such as CTS so that they can develop the kind of knowledge that will allow them to implement new practices successfully. CTS helps teachers access this knowledge.

2. Standards are more widely consulted as school districts shape their vision of teaching and learning. Standards are now commonplace in most schools, but implementation is still a struggle. Most state standards consulted the learning goals in national standards but also rewrote them, using performance verbs and broader descriptions of content. Like a game of telephone tag, by the time these standards reached the teachers, their clarity and specificity were lost. Consequently, many state standards leave enough ambiguity so that teachers may continue doing the same things they were doing before while claiming that they meet the standards. There is growing recognition that national mathematics standards are essential to understanding the specific intent of state standards. Through CTS, teachers can clarify the meaning and intent of their state standards, recognize the authentic changes they demand, and increase the coherency and consistency of their implementation.

3. Content and pedagogical content knowledge are playing a greater role in professional development programs. Professional development for mathematics teachers has shifted from a schoolwide focus on discipline-generic opportunities to learning experiences that are directly connected to the mathematics content they teach as well as the instructional materials they use. CTS reflects this shift by helping individuals and groups of teachers study the content and pedagogical implications of the mathematics topics they teach. "In order for teachers to demonstrate the highest levels of pedagogical content knowledge, they must have sufficient subject matter knowledge. With limited mathematical understanding, teachers' pedagogical content knowledge is restricted" (Loucks-Horsley et al., 2003, p. 40).

> Teachers who experience CTS together draw on the same knowledge base and use common language in their professional conversations about teaching and learning mathematics.

4. "Job-embedded," "practice-based," and "collegial" forms of professional development are more widely accepted, researched, and practiced. Teachers can embed CTS into their daily practice and preparation for instruction, including their preparation to implement new instructional materials and assessments. Furthermore, CTS is well-suited to collegial structures such as study groups, lesson study, and collaborative analysis of student work. By using CTS up-front, teachers socially construct their understanding and ground their professional development in a common knowledge base.

RESEARCH ON READERS' INTERACTION WITH TEXT

The CTS process involves a substantial amount of reading and analysis. This may appear to contradict the principle of active learning in professional development. An NSF *Foundations Series* research monograph, however, has examined ways in which a constructivist paradigm can facilitate teachers' learning from and with text material as part of a strategy called "Gathering and Making Sense of Information" (National Science Foundation, 2002). This strategy provides a theoretical rationale and empirical support for CTS as an effective strategy for both individual learning and learning within a community.

Selected readings can be an integral part of constructing a personal understanding of content, standards-based reform, and the use of cognitive research findings. And recent research on reading shows how CTS readings can also become part of an active and socially constructed process:

Reading researchers have argued that reading does not need to occur as an isolated, or even individual activity. First, reading should be purposeful. In other words, teachers should read either to address questions that *they* feel the need to know more about or because their concerns could not be resolved through discussion. Reading can also be a catalyst for other experiences. Indeed, reading can fulfill many functions while teachers inquire into any topic. (Siegel, Borasi, & Fonzi, 1998). Readings can provide background information, raise questions for further inquiry about a topic, synthesize different points of view, and offer models for teachers' own practice. Reading is not a passive or straightforward matter of decoding or extracting information from text (e.g., Pearson & Fielding, 1991; Rosenblatt, 1994). Rather, readers construct meaning in interaction with the text, their own background and interests, and their purposes for reading the text. Furthermore, such construction of meaning can be even more productive when it is augmented by interactions with other learners so that different interpretations can be shared and discussed. (NSF, 2002, p. 000)

> Readings in the CTS Guides reflect research studies and the collective wisdom of the hundreds of researchers, scientists, mathematicians, and educators who contributed to national standards and of mathematics trade books authored by highly respected mathematicians. Thus they are automatically grounded in research and accurate mathematics.

Reading and analyzing text in a social context led by a skilled facilitator is preferred, but CTS can also be useful as a stand-alone process for individual teachers, particularly teachers in isolated areas or those constrained by limited release time for workshops. Through CTS, those teachers can still take charge of their own professional development through a self-directed study.

MATHEMATICS TEACHERS AND TEACHING

Standards and research provide a sound theoretical foundation and vision for student and teacher learning, but the rubber meets the road in the classroom. What does it take to be effective in this new vision of mathematics teaching? What do teachers need to know and be able to do to be effective?

Content Knowledge

Research studies have found that high school mathematics teachers with a standard certification in their field of instruction (usually indicating coursework in both subject matter and education methods) had higher-achieving students than teachers teaching without certification in their subject area (Darling-Hammond, 2000; Monk, 1994). However, the current reality is that many classrooms lack a highly qualified teacher. Many of the nation's teachers are not adequately prepared to teach mathematics using standards-based approaches and in ways that bolster student learning and achievement (NRC, 2001). Data from *The Status of High School Mathematics Teaching* (Whittington, 2002) reveal that only 40% of

> Mathematics content—including an understanding of central facts, principles, concepts, ideas, procedures, and important generalizations within the discipline and how they are organized—is at the heart of effective teaching, and thus student learning.

secondary mathematics teachers have taken coursework in all areas recommended by NCTM: abstract algebra, geometry, calculus, data analysis and statistics, applications of mathematics/problem solving, and history of math. The data also show that although teachers reported the importance of emphasizing concepts and reasoning, the highest percentage of class time was spent solving textbook problems, reviewing homework, and practicing routine algorithms. The NRC (2001) addresses this area of concern in the publication, *Adding It Up: Helping Children Learn Mathematics:*

> The preparation of U.S. preschool to middle school teachers often falls short of equipping them with the knowledge they need for helping students develop mathematical proficiency. Many students in grades Pre-K to 8 continue to be taught by teachers who may not have appropriate certification at that grade and who have at best a shaky grasp of mathematics. (p. 4)

Teachers cannot effectively promote learning beyond their own mathematical content knowledge (Ma, 1999). However, one of the myths about the need for teachers to learn content is that merely taking a content course or having other learning experiences that focus solely on content will help teachers become better mathematics teachers. Some teachers pursue content studies for their own enjoyment through less formal venues such as immersions in a scientific or engineering setting that requires use of mathematics, solving challenging mathematics problems on their own, or attending seminars and presentations led by mathematicians. Although all these experiences are valuable and may increase teachers' content knowledge, they do not always link the content adults learn to the classroom where they teach. Content learning that is disconnected from the content taught in the classroom, including strategies for making the content accessible to learners, will not necessarily result in improved student learning. Ongoing opportunities for teacher learning—especially professional development programs that focus on content and how to teach it—coupled with tools like CTS can close the gap between what teachers know and what they need to know to teach effectively. (Loucks-Horsley et al., 2003).

Effective teaching reflects an understanding not only of the content but also of how concepts and procedures relate to and build on one another. For example, before most students are able to understand a given computational algorithm, they must have the chance to develop, explore, and explain their strategies, comparing them to others' strategies. Furthermore, developing computational fluency can both enable and be enabled by investigating data, identifying and generating patterns, and conducting explorations with shapes (NCTM, 2000). Teachers who know how the content builds from understanding and relating ideas within and across topics are better able to diagnose and address learning difficulties. They know what questions to ask when students are engaged in mathematical inquiry and which learning pathways will help students the most.

CTS is designed to help teachers identify the content they need to understand as mathematically literate adults. Two resources used in CTS that can improve teachers' adult content knowledge are *Science for All Americans* (AAAS, 1990) and *Beyond Numeracy* (Paulos, 1992). The former describes the specific mathematical ideas and skills that are important for adults who will encounter mathematics in their daily lives, including teachers of every subject area and grade level. Reading *Science for All Americans* is also helpful for teachers who already have a background or major in mathematics or science, as it describes how ideas come together in an integrated picture of science and mathematics.

Beyond Numeracy (Paulos, 1992) is a mathematics adult trade book written by a mathematician. Often when teachers do not understand a topic they need to teach, they turn to a textbook. But textbook language is stilted and technical and is often more focused on procedures. Trade books, such as *Beyond Numeracy,* explain mathematics to adults in vivid, comprehensible ways.

Teacher content knowledge is also linked to the research base on students' ideas. Providing opportunities for teachers to examine their own mathematical ideas can help them change instructional strategies that may unintentionally convey inaccurate content.

> Many of the same misconceptions and alternative ways of thinking that research has documented for K–12 students can be found in prospective and practicing mathematics teachers.

Pedagogical Content Knowledge

Teaching for understanding requires more than content knowledge:

[Teachers] also must be skilled in helping students develop an understanding of the content, meaning that they need to know how students typically think about particular concepts, how to determine what a particular student or group of students thinks about those ideas, and how to help students deepen their understanding. (Weiss, Pasley, Smith, Banilower, & Heck, 2003, p. 28)

These skills constitute a teacher's specialized professional knowledge, called pedagogical content knowledge. Pedagogical content knowledge is an understanding of what makes the learning of specific topics easy or difficult for learners, and it includes knowledge of ways of representing and formulating subject matter to make it comprehensible to learners (Cochran, DeRuiter, & King, 1993; Fernández-Balboa & Stiehl, 1995; Shulman, 1986; Van Driel, Verloop, & De Vos, 1998). What is the important content, and what should children at the different grade or age levels know with respect to the content? What common misunderstandings do students have with respect to the content? Knowing the answers to these questions sets the course for making important pedagogical choices in the classroom to guide learning. A recent NRC (2001) report on K–8 mathematics emphasizes the importance of this type of knowledge:

Effective teaching—teaching that fosters the development of mathematical proficiency over time—can take a variety of forms, each with its own possibilities and risks. All forms of instruction can best be examined from the perspective of how teachers, students, and content interact in contexts to produce teaching and learning. The effectiveness of mathematics teaching and learning is a function of teachers' knowledge and use of mathematical content, of teachers' attention to and work with students, and of students' engagement in and use of mathematical tasks. Effectiveness depends on *enactment*, on the mutual and interdependent interaction of the three elements—mathematical content, teacher, students—as instruction unfolds. (p. 9)

This is why CTS is called the "missing link." It helps teachers think about how to create meaningful and appropriate learning opportunities for students. Examining the essays in *Benchmarks* and *Principles and Standards* and using the research summaries help teachers identify topic-specific strategies that support student learning in mathematics. These strategies can include use of particular representations, tools, and investigative activities that directly challenge students' preconceptions. Such strategies also include knowing how to sequence those experiences in such a way as to scaffold students' developing understanding. In a similar vein, *Atlas of Science Literacy* provides a graphic representation for teachers to examine students' growth of understanding as ideas and skills begin in K–2 grades and become increasingly sophisticated by the end of high school. It also provides a way for teachers to think about the connections within and between the various topics they teach in mathematics as well as the connections to science.

Beliefs About Teaching and Learning

Research documents the impact of teachers' beliefs about mathematics on their curricular decisions and instructional practices. Teacher beliefs have a strong impact on their understanding of the nature of mathematics as a discipline; what constitutes legitimate mathematical procedures, results, and justifications; and what constitutes desirable goals and acceptable outcomes for K–12 mathematics instruction (Thompson, 1992).

> Most teachers, regardless of whether they are generalists or specialists, never had the opportunity to make their beliefs explicit in traditional teacher preparation. Readings and discussions about the discipline of mathematics are notably absent from school mathematics and even college level courses. Nevertheless, because they studied in traditional mathematics classes, most teachers hold deep-seated beliefs that mathematics is a body of absolute truths with little room for creativity or personal judgment. This means that, as teachers, they are likely to value correct answers over tentative conjectures, standard procedures over personal approaches to solutions, and facts and algorithms over inductive problem solving and reasoning skills. (NSF, 2002, p. 13)

New materials and strategies for teacher learning must provide opportunities for teachers to critically examine their personal beliefs about mathematics teaching and learning and offer ways to help them develop new beliefs grounded in a reform vision.

The common teacher beliefs described above conflict with the current vision of mathematics teaching and learning reflected in the standards. CTS provides a mechanism to confront and alter existing beliefs. The CTS approach draws out teachers' knowledge and beliefs about a topic and how students learn it, and it helps them connect new ideas with their previous ideas and beliefs.

One way teachers change or reinforce their beliefs is through discourse in a social setting. Having an opportunity to present one's own ideas after studying a topic and hearing and reflecting on the ideas of others is an empowering experience. CTS encourages discourse with others that facilitates meaning-making and leads to changes in long-held beliefs. This kind of learning is highly personal. Perhaps most important, it can resolve the dissonance between long-held beliefs and new thinking, resulting in changed practice (Mezirow, 1997).

The cognitive research on how people learn has also begun to influence beliefs about teaching and learning. Mathematics teachers who have used CTS display a significant shift in how they perceive their own role. More and more, teachers are moving away from seeing teaching as telling to seeing it as facilitating learning.

They are moving from the idea that only some children can learn to the belief that all children can learn challenging content, a central premise of the standards movement.

Having a Professional Knowledge Base

A teacher's role as facilitator of learning for all students is complex and demanding (Loucks-Horsley et al., 2003). Teaching is enhanced when teachers operate from a body of specialized professional knowledge that is based on research about how to teach and how people learn (Stigler & Hiebert, 1999). In the section of *Principles and Standards of School Mathematics* (NCTM, 2000) titled, Working Together to Achieve the Vision, the use of current research is included as an important component of improving mathematics teaching and learning:

> [Teachers] must adjust their practices and extend their knowledge to reflect changing curricula and technologies and to incorporate new knowledge about how students learn mathematics. . . . Teachers must develop their own professional knowledge using research, the knowledge base of the profession, and their own experiences as resources. (p. 370)

CTS helps teachers develop such a professional knowledge base. Teachers who use CTS can describe and support their choices of instructional strategies by citing the research or national standards. Conversations among teachers who have used CTS become more deliberate and grounded in a common body of professional knowledge. For example, in observations of teachers during the CTS process, they were frequently heard to say, "According to the research it is common for students to have trouble with this concept. What can we do differently to help them?" As they engaged in conversations about what is important to teach, they would say, "Let's look at the research and standards." This language reflects the fact that those teachers were making evidence-based decisions that move them beyond their personal opinions while still respecting practitioner wisdom and experience.

THE TEACHER PROFESSIONAL CONTINUUM

Traditionally, preservice and inservice mathematics teacher education was expected to produce and support teachers competent in the knowledge and skills they would need to sustain their learning over the period of their mathematics teaching career. However, with new legislation regarding teacher quality, standards-based reform of mathematics teaching and learning, and the diverse knowledge and experience of teachers, it is now recognized that teachers' professional development needs to be differentiated and continuous—building from their undergraduate education into a lifelong career of learning.

Learning to teach can be regarded as a continuum of professional experiences (Bransford et al., 2000). Research on professional development is linked to this concept of a professional continuum (see Figure 1.6). This continuum begins with teachers' experiences as they progress through their K–12 education,

> As teacher characteristics change, their needs for professional development change accordingly.

Figure 1.6 The CTS Mathematics Teaching Continuum

Preservice Mathematics Teachers	Novice Mathematics Teachers	Experienced Mathematics Teachers	Accomplished Mathematics Teachers	Mathematics Teacher Leaders	Mathematics Teacher Educators
Students learning to be teachers	Teachers in the induction stage or new to teaching mathematics	Teachers with professional certification with several years of teaching	Experienced teachers who have achieved expert status	Master teachers who lead mathematics education improvement efforts	Professional developers and others who teach teachers

and it builds to include preservice programs, induction, professional development for experienced teachers, and professional leadership activities. Studies show that teachers develop differently and have different attitudes, knowledge, skills, and behaviors at various points during their career. Their concerns about teaching, their instructional behaviors, their mathematical content knowledge, their understanding of how students learn mathematics, and their perceptions of themselves, their work, and their profession all change over time. Teachers with different levels of expertise use and engage in CTS in different ways that are meaningful to them. In addition, CTS provides a process and set of tools that teachers can use to lead professional development and support the learning of their less experienced colleagues.

NSF's Teacher Professional Continuum Program, which provided funding for the development of CTS, is designed to provide support for a comprehensive, coherent, and integrated sequence of lifelong learning for teachers (NSF, 2002). In response, CTS is designed to consider teachers' professional development, inservice, and professional growth opportunities in light of their career stage. CTS supports personalized learning targeted toward the unique needs of an individual teacher as well as members of a learning community and moves them along a professional learning pathway. CTS is a tool designed to address continuous learning, both inside and outside of the classroom, by helping educators at all career stages evolve in the mathematics teaching profession.

2

Examining the Components of a Curriculum Topic Study Guide

THE CTS GUIDE

At the core of the Curriculum Topic Study (CTS) process is the CTS Guide. Figure 2.1 shows an example of a CTS Guide on the topic of decimals. There are 92 CTS Guides in Chapter 6, representing a full range of specific to broad content and skill-based topics across the discipline of mathematics. Teachers select, study, analyze, and reflect on prescreened readings contained in a guide to improve their understanding of teaching and learning related to a particular mathematics topic. Teachers may choose any of the sections contained in a guide, or they may choose all of them, depending on their purpose. Teachers interested in using standards and research remark that they can quickly and easily find readings relevant to the topics they teach when they use the guides. CTS Guides save busy teachers the time-consuming work of searching for the right information.

> Each CTS Guide identifies a particular topic in mathematics and links six purposeful outcomes to selected readings from the nationally available resources.

Sections and Outcomes

Each CTS Guide uses a standard template divided into two corresponding parts. The left-hand side, labeled "Section and Outcome," contains the section number

Figure 2.1 Example of a CTS Study Guide

Standards and Research-Based Study of a Curricular Topic

DECIMALS

Section and Outcome	Selected Sources and Readings for Study and Reflection Read and examine *related parts* of:
I. Identify Adult Content Knowledge	**IA:** *Science for All Americans* ▸ Chapter 9, *Numbers,* pages 130–131 ▸ Chapter 12, *Computation,* pages 187–190 **IB:** *Beyond Numeracy* ▸ *Computation and Rote,* pages 52–55 ▸ *Rational and Irrational Numbers,* pages 205–208
II. Consider Instructional Implications	**IIA:** *Benchmarks for Science Literacy* ▸ 9A, *Numbers* general essay, page 210, grade span essays, pages 212–214 ▸ 12B, *Computation and Estimation* general essay, pages 288–289 **IIB:** *NCTM Principles and Standards for School Mathematics* ▸ Grades K–12 Overview Number and Operations, *Understand numbers,* page 33, *Understand meanings,* page 34, *Compute fluently,* page 35 ▸ Grades 3–5 Number and Operations general essay, page 149, *Understand numbers,* pages 149–151, *Compute fluently,* page 152, pages 155–156 ▸ Grades 6–8 Number and Operations general essay, page 215, *Understand numbers,* pages 215–217, *Understand meanings,* pages 218–219, *Compute fluently,* pages 220–221 ▸ Grades 9–12 Number and Operations general essay, page 291, *Understand numbers,* pages 291–292, *Compute fluently,* page 294
III. Identify Concepts and Specific Ideas	**IIIA:** *Benchmarks for Science Literacy* ▸ 9A, *Numbers,* page 211, pages 212–214 ▸ 12B, *Computation and Estimation,* pages 290–291 **IIIB:** *NCTM Principles and Standards for School Mathematics* ▸ Grades 3–5 Number and Operations, page 148 or 392 ▸ Grades 6–8 Number and Operations, page 214 or 393 ▸ Grades 9–12 Number and Operations, page 290 or 393
IV. Examine Research on Student Learning	**IVA:** *Benchmarks for Science Literacy* ▸ 9A, *Rational Numbers,* page 350 ▸ 12B, *Operations with Fractions and Decimals,* pages 358–359, *Converting Between Fractions and Decimals,* page 359, *Number Comparison,* page 359
V. Examine Coherency and Articulation	**V:** *Atlas of Science Literacy* ▸ *Mathematical Processes,* page 27 noting the conceptual strand "computation and operations" ▸ *Ratios and Proportionality,* page 119 noting the conceptual strand "computation"
VI. Clarify State Standards and District Curriculum	**VIA:** *State Standards:* Link Sections I–V to learning goals and information from your state standards or frameworks that are informed by the results of the topic study. **VIB:** *District Curriculum Guide:* Link Sections I–V to learning goals and information from your district curriculum guide that are informed by the results of the topic study.
Visit www.curriculumtopicstudy.org for updates or supplementary readings, Web sites, and videos.	

(I through VI) and the user outcome for that section. The six sections in a guide may be used in any order. The CTS Guides need not be used in a linear process. The following describes each of the sections and their outcomes:

- **Section I. Identify Adult Content Knowledge:** This section helps users identify what all adults (including teachers) should know and be able to do to be considered literate in mathematics, regardless of the career path they have chosen. It also provides explanations of mathematical ideas encountered in the media, public issues, and other popular venues.

- **Section II. Consider Instructional Implications:** This section helps users identify important considerations for instruction across K–12 education or within a particular grade span, suggests effective instructional strategies and contexts, and provides a broad overview of the big ideas, concepts, and procedures for K–12 students related to the topic.

- **Section III. Identify Concepts and Specific Ideas:** This section helps users identify the concepts, specific ideas, procedures, level of sophistication, and appropriate terminology related to a topic at particular grade levels.

- **Section IV. Examine Research on Student Learning:** This section identifies relevant research so that users can examine developmental considerations, including misconceptions and their sources, intuitive rules, ways of thinking, and difficulties encountered by students in understanding the specific ideas within the topic.

- **Section V. Examine Coherency and Articulation:** This section helps users examine the K–12 conceptual growth in understanding as a coherent flow of ideas and skills that builds in sophistication over time. Studying the K–12 growth of understanding will help users identify important prerequisites for learning and examine connections within and across topics that can promote student understanding.

- **Section VI. Clarify State Standards and District Curriculum:** This section helps users clarify the meaning and intent of their state standards or the learning goals in their district curriculum or mathematics curriculum programs by linking the information in the previous five sections to the local context in which the users work. It also helps users to identify important ideas in mathematics that may be missing at the state or local level but should be addressed along with their standards.

Selected Readings

The right-hand side of a CTS Guide, titled "Selected Sources and Readings for Study and Reflection," lists vetted readings from the CTS set of resources for study and reflection. Each section provides relevant selections from two choices of resources. The order of the resources within each section does not imply that the first one is the primary source material. Users may choose to read both choices or focus on only one. For example, in Sections II and III, the user may decide to use only the *Principles and Standards for School Mathematics* (National Council of Teachers of Mathematics {NCTM}, 2000) instead of *Benchmarks for Science Literacy* (*Benchmarks*) (American Association for the Advancement of Science [AAAS], 1993), or vice versa. Figure 2.2 shows the links between the outcomes and the source material for reading, study, analysis, and reflection.

Figure 2.2 Links Between Outcomes and Source Material

If your outcome for studying a topic is to:	Then you would read the related parts of:
I. Identify adult content knowledge	*Science for All Americans* (AAAS, 1990) and/or *Beyond Numeracy* (Paulos, 1992)
II. Identify instructional implications	*Benchmarks for Science Literacy* (AAAS, 1993) essays and/or *Principles and Standards for School Mathematics Standards* (NCTM, 2000) content standard essays and vignettes
III. Identify concepts and specific ideas	*Benchmarks for Science Literacy* bulleted learning goals and/or *Principles and Standards for School Mathematics Standards* bulleted learning goals
IV. Examine research on student learning	*Benchmarks for Science Literacy* Chapter 15 research summaries and/or *Research Companion to Principles and Standards for School Mathematics Standards* (NCTM, 2003) summaries
V. Examine coherency and articulation	*Atlas of Science Literacy* (AAAS, 2001) strand maps and narratives
VI. Clarify state standards and district curriculum	Your state standards or frameworks document and/or Your district curriculum guide or the guide to your curriculum materials

CTS Supplementary Material

At the bottom of each study guide is a link to the CTS Web site, www.curriculum topicstudy.org, where users can find optional readings and media resources to supplement individual CTS Guides.

The CTS Web site (see Figure 2.3) is a dynamic, updated source of additional CTS source material. A searchable database on the Web site allows the CTS user to search by topic for videos, journal articles, books, professional development resources, DVDs, CD ROMs, and Internet sites that supplement sections of a specific CTS Guide. For example, if users search the database for supplements to the CTS Guide, Geometric Shapes, they will see a chapter from Edwin A. Abbott's (1964) classic book, *Flatland,* titled "Of the Nature of Flatland," which can be used with Section I to improve adult understanding of the one-dimension perspective of a two-dimensional shape. Users will also find a link to the Improving Measurement and Geometry in Elementary Schools (IMAGES) Web site, which incorporates findings from educational research that can be used to supplement Section IV. The CTS Web site also contains a blank template of a CTS

Figure 2.3   CTS Web Site

CTS Supplementary Resource Site

www.curriculumtopicstudy.org

Figure 2.4   CTS Mathematics Source Material

**Bibliography of Source Materials for
Mathematics Curriculum Topic Study**

American Association for the Advancement of Science. (2001). *Atlas of science literacy.* Washington, DC: Author; Arlington, VA: National Science Teachers Association.

American Association for the Advancement of Science. (1993). *Benchmarks for science literacy.* New York: Oxford University Press.

American Association for the Advancement of Science. (1990). *Science for all Americans.* New York: Oxford University Press.

National Council of Teachers of Mathematics. (2000). *Principles and standards for school mathematics.* Reston, VA: Author.

National Council of Teachers of Mathematics. (2003). *Research companion to principles and standards for school mathematics.* Reston, VA: Author.

Paulos, J. (1992). *Beyond numeracy.* New York: Vintage.

Guide in the CTS Resources section, which can be customized for use with a specific audience—say, if a professional developer is working with teachers in a particular grade level and wants to focus on a specific selection of resources or to combine two related topics into one. Additional study guides may be developed after this publication, and they will be posted on the Web site when available.

COMMON RESOURCES FOR STUDY AND REFLECTION

All professionals—lawyers, doctors, mechanics, accountants—have their own career-specific reference tools that inform their practice. Mathematics educators need their unique professional libraries as well. The set of books used for CTS can be considered mathematics teachers' tools of the trade. The six resources for CTS, listed in Figure 2.4, make up the suite of tools used for CTS, and many of them are commonly used by the mathematics education community.

A special feature of the CTS approach is that it uses a common collection of nationally available resources, including several that are considered essential "tools of the trade" in the mathematics teaching profession.

Building a Professional Collection: Experts at Your Fingertips!

The resources used in CTS have been available to mathematics educators for several years. In a perfect world, every teacher of mathematics would be provided with a set of national standards and the other common resources used in CTS. Yet, in our experience, many teachers do not even know about some of these materials (often, it is only this lack of awareness that prevents teachers from owning their own copies). Several mathematics state and national organizations, as well as departments of education, have made considerable efforts to get the standards into the hands of teachers and administrators. Preservice teachers are often required to purchase some of these books for their courses. Teachers who do not own their own copies and may not have funds available can find several of these materials online (see Resource A and links to online versions provided through the CTS Web site).

In our experience, teachers and school districts that have used CTS usually purchase selected resources or the full set, realizing how important and useful the CTS process can be for supporting curriculum, instruction, and assessment. The importance of these professional resources to teachers' ongoing professional growth often convinces administrators to provide copies for each teacher or, at the least, several sets to be shared within a school. CTS not only gets the standards and research documents into the hands of teachers and into schools but also provides a process through which they are deliberately and routinely used. The advantage of the CTS design is that teachers can select only those resources they need, based on purpose and availability.

> On the other hand, many teachers and schools have the national standards, but they collect dust on the shelf because teachers have never had a process for using them.

If you have the resources used in CTS, you have experts at your fingertips at all times. Teachers who have used CTS refer to the use of the tools as "standing on the shoulders of giants." Because the standards and resources such as *Atlas of Science Literacy* (*Atlas*) (AAAS, 2001) were developed through peer review, discussion, and consensus by leading mathematicians, researchers, and educators from K–12 schools, universities, organizations, and governmental agencies, they reflect the best thinking available about what is important to learn in mathematics and how and when to teach it effectively. The research summaries have been put together by some of the world's leading mathematics education researchers, who have dedicated their work to understanding how students learn mathematics. The mathematics section of *Science for All Americans* (AAAS, 1990) and *Beyond Numeracy* (Paulos, 1992) were both developed by respected mathematicians devoted to mathematics literacy for all. CTS shifts the burden from an individual's biases, intuition, and experience to sound recommendations and information that users can combine with the wisdom of their own practice. Teachers we have worked with remark, "Now that I have these resources and CTS to help me use them, I can't imagine being a mathematics teacher without them!"

> Imagine being able to vicariously turn to leading experts for advice whenever you need it! That is what CTS does—it provides users with an external perspective derived from some of the best thinking in the mathematics education world.

Descriptions of the Common Resources Used in CTS

Some of these resources, such as the *Principles and Standards for School Mathematics,* are more familiar to teachers than others. *Benchmarks* and *Science for All Americans* are less familiar to the mathematics community. The *Atlas* has been published more recently, and it may not be as familiar to the mathematics community as it is to the science community. However, this does not imply that they are only peripherally connected to mathematics. The mathematical ideas in *Science for All Americans, Benchmarks,* and *Atlas* highlight both the integrity of mathematics as a unique discipline and its important connections to the scientific world. Resources used in CTS are available through the NCTM bookstore (see Chapter 7) or major booksellers such as Amazon.com or Barnes and Noble. You can check the CTS Web site at www.curriculumtopicstudy.org to find links to some of the books or to get suggestions for ordering them. The following is a description of the collection of resources used in the CTS Guides and the corresponding section(s) in which they are used:

> A key feature of CTS is its flexibility—you can use as many or as few of the resources as your purpose demands and your access allows.

IA: *Science for All Americans* **(AAAS, 1990):** Written by James Rutherford and Andrew Ahlgren for AAAS, this book was first published in 1989. It represents the first phase of AAAS's science literacy reform initiative, Project 2061. To AAAS, which is a prestigious private organization made up of scientists, mathematicians, educators, and engineers, *science literacy* is a general term that includes science, mathematics, technology, and social science, as well as the interconnections among them. *Science for All Americans* defines the enduring, interconnected knowledge that *all adults* should have acquired after their K–12 education to ensure a knowledge-literate society. The book reflects the belief that a literate person is one who is aware that science, mathematics, social science, and technology are interdependent human enterprises with strengths and limitations; understands key concepts and principles; is familiar with the natural world and recognizes both its diversity and unity; and uses knowledge and ways of thinking for individual and social purposes.

Science for All Americans softens the boundaries between traditional content domains and emphasizes the big ideas and connectedness of mathematics topics. The mathematics technical terminology it uses is the terminology with which all adults are expected to be familiar to understand mathematics in their everyday lives. Chapters 2, 9, 11, and 12 address mathematical ideas for adult literacy.

Teachers who have used *Science for All Americans* praise its eloquent and easy-to-read prose. One teacher remarked, "This is as close to poetry as one can get in science and mathematics." Teachers who have never used it before quickly embrace it and have commented that it is a book you can open up and start reading anywhere, for pleasure as well as professional use. It is also a resource that opens up rich and engaging discussions between mathematics and science educators who are striving to ensure that their students are prepared for a future increasingly dependent on understanding both mathematics and science, as well as connections to technology and social science.

IB: *Beyond Numeracy* **(Paulos, 1992):** Written by John Allen Paulos in 1991, this book provides an explanation of mathematics topics ranging from numbers and computation to chaos theory and differential equations. It differs from *Science for All Americans* because it describes more than the knowledge that accrues by the end of a K–12 education. Several of the concepts described in *Beyond Numeracy* exceed mathematical literacy but are useful and interesting for developing an appreciation of how mathematics is used in our everyday lives. According to the author, "Remembering this formula or that theorem is less important for most people than the ability to look at a situation quantitatively, to note logical, probabilistic, and spatial relationships and to muse mathematically" (p. 6). The text is interesting and comprehensible, even to those who have limited or no math background. *Beyond Numeracy* avoids the stilted, fragmented descriptions typical in the textbooks that are often the only option for novice teachers who are looking to enrich their understanding of mathematics. *Beyond Numeracy* gives meaning to abstract ideas through rich examples and analogies. Additional mathematics content trade books that can be used with Section I of selected CTS Guides can be found on the CTS Web site.

IIA, IIIA, IVA: *Benchmarks for Science Literacy* **(AAAS, 1993):** *Benchmarks* followed *Science for All Americans,* and the chapters and sections in *Benchmarks* correspond to the chapters and sections in *Science for All Americans. Benchmarks* describes the specific steps along the way to achieving the mathematical literacy described in *Science for All Americans* by listing specific mathematical ideas and skills that all students should learn at Grades K–2, 3–5, 6–8, and 9–12. The chapters in *Benchmarks* that are focused on mathematics (2, 9, 11, and 12) were based on the work of six different school-district teams, with input from hundreds of educators, scientists, mathematicians, university faculty, and mathematics education specialists. Each section within a chapter begins with a general essay that gives a broad overview of the ideas students should learn and the types of instructional opportunities and contexts that would effectively impact learning. Essays for each grade level discuss difficulties students might face and offer suggestions for instruction. Chapter 15 in *Benchmarks* contains summaries of research on student learning that are linked to the other sections in *Benchmarks.*

> Until using CTS, many mathematics teachers weren't even aware of the mathematics sections in *Benchmarks* or the Chapter 15 research summaries; now they use them on a regular basis.

In our experience, teachers have found *Benchmarks* to be an invaluable resource because of the clarity of the goals for learning it describes. See Resources A for additional mathematics resources developed by Project 2061 that complement *Benchmarks* and *Science for All Americans.*

IIB and IIIB: *Principles and Standards for School Mathematics* **(NCTM, 2000):** Released in 2000, this document is more detailed than *Benchmarks* in presenting a vision of mathematics literacy for all students. The NCTM previously released three separate documents in the 1990s, including the *Curriculum and Evaluation Standards for School Mathematics, Professional Standards for Teaching Mathematics,* and *Assessment Standards for School Mathematics.* From the beginning, NCTM recognized that to remain realistic, the standards must periodically go through a cycle of implementation, evaluation, and revision. From 1995 through 1999, NCTM worked on revising and updating the original standards through an extensive process aimed at engaging the entire mathematics community. As a result, the *Principles and Standards for School Mathematics* was released in 2000 in both print and electronic formats. The document includes six principles, five content standards, and five process standards for math education; of these, only the content and process standards are used in CTS. Since the original and revised standards were published, many schools have used them to design their curriculum and course syllabi, and the NCTM standards have informed the development and revisions of state standards and frameworks, as well as numerous curriculum programs.

Principles and Standards for School Mathematics divides grade spans by PreK–2, 3–5, 6–8, and 9–12, and it includes the content standards of numbers and operations, algebra, geometry, measurement, and data analysis and statistics. Each content standard has a descriptive essay that describes student learning, experiences, and potential misconceptions and learning difficulties. There are numerous examples of student work that demonstrate student knowledge and thinking.

IVB. *Research Companion to Principles and Standards for School Mathematics* **(NCTM, 2003):** Released in 2003, this book is a comprehensive summary of the research that was used to guide and assist those involved in revising the original standards. The *Research Companion* is arranged by sections, including research on *Principles and Standards for School Mathematics* topics and research on teaching and learning. The *Research Companion* contains nine chapters, which "survey the literature on curriculum topics associated with the content standards" (p. 2), serving as a useful resource that helps teachers deepen their understanding of how students think about major ideas in mathematics and how these ideas affect their learning.

> Teachers who are aware of the importance of identifying students' potential misconceptions as a way to build from students' ideas to correct mathematical ones have found the *Research Companion* to be a powerful new resource.

V. *Atlas of Science Literacy* **(AAAS, 2001):** A joint publication of AAAS and the National Science Teachers Association (NSTA), *Atlas* is a collection of conceptual strand maps, based on *Benchmarks* and *Science for All Americans*; the conceptual strand maps show how students' ideas and skills develop from K through 12. The current volume of the *Atlas* used in the CTS Guides includes 11 strand maps within the following categories: mathematical inquiry, communication and information, mathematical representation, proportional reasoning, and statistics. Mathematics educators are now embracing this powerful tool for depicting the development of and connections among the ideas and skills in *Benchmarks*. For any particular topic, a map depicts the strands or "storylines" that are part of that topic and important connections to other topics. For any individual idea or skill, the maps show both the prerequisites and the later ideas or skills that build on it. The maps can be very helpful in clarifying what level of sophistication is appropriate at different grade levels. The *Atlas* maps referenced in the CTS Guides cover about half of the mathematical ideas and skills that are laid out in *Benchmarks* and *Science for All Americans.* For this reason, some topics do not have an associated map in Section V. A second volume of *Atlas*

> Graphically depicting ideas and skills as part of students' K–12 growth of understanding helps educators see where students are coming from, where they are now, and where they are headed next.

is currently in development and expected to be released in 2006. The CTS Web site at www.curriculumtopicstudy.org will provide updated links to Section V of the CTS Guides when the next volume of *Atlas* becomes available.

VI. State Standards or District Curriculum Guides: These are your own individual state standards or frameworks, your K–12 scope and sequence guides, curriculum program manuals, and teacher guides. Through these resources, CTS allows you to connect your insights and findings from the study process with your local and state context, including accountability factors. In this way, educators in each state and across districts can combine the CTS national resources with ones that are unique to their state, district, or school settings.

3

Engaging in Curriculum Topic Study

GETTING STARTED

The CTS Guides are at the heart of the CTS approach, so understanding how to use the guides is a critical first step. How do you get started using CTS? Educators who are familiar with the CTS resources and process can go directly to Chapter 6, select a CTS Guide, and get started with minimal direction. If you are new to CTS, we suggest starting with a few introductory steps that will acquaint you with the resources and the process.

Gathering Your Resources

Figure 2.4 in the previous chapter lists the complete set of common resources used in CTS. Your access to the resources will determine which CTS purposes and outcomes you can focus on. If you do not have your own personal copies of these resources, check with your colleagues, mathematics department, or school or district professional library to see if you can borrow them. In our work, we have found that new users of CTS are surprised to find that several of these resources, *Principles and Standards for School Mathematics* (National Council of Teachers of Mathematics [NCTM], 2000) and *Benchmarks for Science Literacy* (American Association for the Advancement of Science [AAAS], 1993) in particular, are often "gathering dust" somewhere on a shelf in their school or district. In addition, you can access *Science for All Americans* (AAAS, 1990), *Benchmarks for Science Literacy,* and several *Atlas of Science Literacy* (AAAS, 2001) maps for free online if you can't locate a hard copy.

Principles and Standards for School Mathematics can also be accessed online permanently if you are an NCTM member or temporarily if you are not yet a member. To link to these sites, visit the CTS Web site at www.curriculumtopic.org.

> There is growing recognition that access to professional literature, tools, and resources is part of what makes a professional mathematics educator.

To get the most out of the CTS process, it is critical that you have at least one of the resources used in Sections II and III of the CTS study guides—*Benchmarks* or *Principles and Standards for School Mathematics*. In many schools where we have worked, administrators have recognized the power of these tools and purchased sets for their schools, committees, and even individual teachers. These resources are one of the best professional development investments in mathematics teaching and learning a school administrator or educator can make. The use of a personal, professional library—when combined with professional development and the chance to apply learning in the classroom—can move novice teachers more quickly toward becoming knowledgeable practitioners.

If you are using CTS in a group setting, it is not necessary for each individual to have copies of all the books. Furthermore, you may decide to use either *Benchmarks for Science Literacy* or *Principles and Standards for School Mathematics*, or both. If you are using *Benchmarks*, we strongly recommend that you also use *Science for All Americans*. We recommend the following set of shared books for every group of five teachers:

- one copy of *Science for All Americans* and/or one copy of *Beyond Numeracy* (Paulos, 1992)
- two copies of *Benchmarks for Science Literacy* and/or two copies of *Principles and Standards for School Mathematics*
- one copy of *Research Companion for Principles and Standards for School Mathematics* (NCTM, 2003)
- one copy of *Atlas of Science Literacy*
- one or more copies of your state standards or frameworks and/or local district curriculum guide

In addition to gathering the resources you have available, a few basic materials are helpful: Post-It notes™ for inserting page markers or making notes, highlighters for marking handouts, paper and pen for recording your notes, and chart paper and markers for recording group ideas. If you are doing CTS as a group, prepare copies of the CTS Guide and any necessary worksheet templates for the participants in your group (see Resource B). You might want to have at least one computer to transcribe ideas. If you have a computer connected to the Internet, you can download the worksheet templates contained in Resource B from the CTS Web site at www.curriculum topicstudy.org. This allows you to enter CTS results in an expanding Word document. Access to the Web site also allows you to copy and paste information from the online resources, saving the time and effort of rewriting important information.

Experienced CTS users may wish to include additional supplementary material. For example, you might include a recent journal article about student learning to supplement Section IV, or you may view an Annenberg video of instruction targeted at a specific idea for Section II. Supplementary materials are listed in a searchable database and can often be accessed from the CTS Web site. New supplementary resources are added regularly, so check often.

Becoming Familiar With the CTS Guides and Resources

If you are new to CTS, we recommend you become familiar with the CTS Guide and resources before you begin a topic study. This book provides all the materials you need to familiarize yourself with CTS. Read Chapter 2 to become familiar with the features of a CTS Guide and to get a sense of the content, origins, and uses of each of the resources. Then select a guide from Chapter 6 and examine how the resources are linked to the outcomes. Open one of your resources and try locating the identified section for reading listed on the guide. Choose a vignette from Chapter 5 to get a sense of how CTS relates to the various types of work of mathematics educators.

> If you are new to CTS, we recommend you become familiar with the CTS Guide and resources before you begin a topic study.

You can read the Chapter 2 summaries to become familiar with the resources, or refresh your knowledge of their origin and use. Spend some time examining each of the resources to see how it is arranged. Read the introductions or prefaces in each book to learn more about their underlying philosophy or purpose and how their contents are arranged. If you are new to *Science for All Americans, Benchmarks,* and *Principles and Standards for School Mathematics,* we recommend using Richard Audet and Linda Jordan's (2003) book, *Standards in the Classroom: An Implementation Guide for Teachers of Science and Mathematics,* to become better acquainted with these national standards resources (see Resources Section). The book contains Discovery Guides that introduce the features of the CTS resources. This can be particularly useful for the AAAS publications, which may be less familiar to mathematics educators. Figure 3.1 shows an example of a Discovery Guide for *Science for All Americans* (Audet & Jordan, 2003, p. 19).

Defining Your Purpose and Choosing Your Outcomes

At this point, you are ready to start the study of a curriculum topic. What is your purpose for using CTS? There are three general purposes: (1) to learn how to use the CTS process, (2) to learn more about a particular mathematics topic, or (3) to apply findings from CTS to a particular aspect of your work as a mathematics educator. Various ways of using CTS are listed in Figure 3.2. Examples of the various ways CTS can be applied in your work are described in more detail in Chapter 4 and illustrated through actual case examples in the Chapter 5 vignettes.

> The outcomes you choose will determine the resources you will need and the sections you will read.

The first step is to choose the topic that addresses your learning needs. Do you want to narrow it down to a fairly specific topic, or would a broader topic serve your purpose better? Which guide most closely matches the content you are targeting? Once you have chosen a curriculum topic and the appropriate CTS Guide, you should decide on your desired outcome. What do you want to learn? What do you need to get out of the process? What will you do with the information? The specific outcomes of the CTS study process are listed by section in the left column of the CTS Guide. The selected readings listed in the right column of the guide are matched to the outcomes. Do you want to improve your content knowledge of the topic? Gain a better understanding of effective, topic-specific

Figure 3.1   Science Discover Guide: *Science for All Americans*

19	Chapter 2: Exploration

E**XPLORATION** 2.3   Science Discovery Guide: *Science for All Americans*

These are sources of information that you need to complete the Discovery Guide. You should complete each of the discovery tasks and identify the page(s) where you located the information.

- American Association for the Advancement of Science. (1990). *Science for all Americans.* New York: Oxford University Press.
- www.project2061.org

PAGE(S)	1. What national organization spearheaded the preparation of this document? Who participated in writing it? When was it published?
PAGE(S)	2. Why do you think that the particular title, *Science for All Americans (SFAA)*, was chosen for this book?
PAGE(S)	3. When *SFAA* uses the expression "science literacy," what is the intended meaning?
PAGE(S)	4. Each chapter of *SFAA* is built around a set of Recommendations. Select a single idea from a chapter that relates directly to what you teach. Summarize the major points in the section. Do you agree with what *SFAA* recommends all high school graduates should know about this concept? Explain.
PAGE(S)	5. Find the chapter titled Common Themes. Describe the four big ideas that pervade all of science, mathematics, and technology.
PAGE(S)	6. Which of the Principles of Learning do you regard as the most important? Why?
PAGE(S)	7. What are the major differences between the type of teaching and learning suggested in this document and what you typically see and use in your school?
PAGE(S)	8. What chapters in *SFAA* would be of special interest to a person with an interest in the history of science, mathematics, and technology?

Figure 3.2   Examples of the Variety of CTS Applications

- Learning new content or refreshing an existing knowledge base
- Deepening understanding of mathematical thinking
- Choosing content to design course syllabi
- Translating university course content into appropriate K–12 experiences
- Developing or reviewing a K–12 curriculum scope and sequence
- Making relevant interdisciplinary connections
- Selecting or analyzing curriculum materials
- Implementing new curricula
- Developing instructional materials or lessons
- Examining or choosing instructional strategies
- Clarifying learning goals, including goals in state standards documents
- Structuring knowledge in a topic to identify big ideas, concepts, procedures, skills, specific ideas, facts, terminology, and formulas
- Developing formative and summative assessments
- Analyzing assessment tasks and student work
- Designing content-specific professional development using various formats such as lesson study, case discussions, looking at student work, study groups, action research, and so on.
- Mentoring new teachers
- Content-coaching of colleagues
- Designing preservice courses, practicums, and inservice opportunities
- Reviewing and revising state or district standards
- Identifying connections between informal and formal learning experiences
- Preparing for meetings with parents or other stakeholders to discuss mathematics teaching and learning

instructional strategies? Gain a K–12 "big picture" of the topic? Understand the meaning and intent of the learning goals that make up the topic? Identify students' misconceptions or developmental issues associated with the topic? Look for connections among ideas in a topic? You might choose one, several, or all of the outcomes.

It is also important to keep the grade or grade span relevant to your work in mind. If your overall purpose demands a K–12 perspective, then you should read all of the grade-level sections. If your overall purpose is focused on a specific grade, you might read only the sections that include that grade. Or, if you are an elementary mathematics specialist, you might focus on the K–5 sections. However, examining the specific ideas and skills that come before and after the grade or grade span you are targeting can provide valuable insights and give you a more coherent picture of how learning builds over time.

Processing Information From CTS Sections

If you are doing CTS for the first time or you are studying an unfamiliar topic, we recommend doing a full study of all six sections. You do not need to have all of the resources at the start, but for the purpose of explaining the outcomes, we will assume that all of the books are available to you. Begin by recording your initial ideas about the topic, based on your grade or grade-span focus.

Activation and Processing Strategies

Figure 3.3 lists examples of your prior knowledge about the topic that you should activate and record before you begin CTS. Establishing your baseline knowledge about the topic is a critical part of engaging in a topic study. It provides focus for your study and a record of initial understandings and beliefs for an individual or group that you can reflect on later. It also activates your thinking about the topic, so that during the readings you can connect new ideas with old.

Another method to activate prior knowledge of a topic, focus the study, and reflect on results, is the K-W-L strategy (see Figure 3.4). Using a sheet of paper with three columns or chart paper for group recording, brainstorm a list of what is already known about the topic under K. Generate questions about things you want to learn about the topic under the W. Use these questions to guide your investigation of the topic as you study the readings. After you complete the study, compare the K column with results from the study and record new ideas under the L. After you complete your study, it can be useful to examine the K list and decide if there is anything you would change based on your results. For example, you may have found that ideas that were listed as important ideas for students to learn actually exceed the developmental level of your students. The K-W-L method can also be used with each individual section (I-VI) of a CTS Guide. A Word document template for K-W-L can be downloaded from the CTS Web site.

Additional strategies suggested by users for activating prior knowledge, focusing reading, extracting meaning, and reflecting on results will be added to the CTS Web site. The third book in this series (to be published in 2007) will include a discussion of strategies for facilitators to use in group professional development, preservice education, and committee work.

Figure 3.3   Initial Activation Questions

What important ideas or skills make up this topic?

What is important for students to know or be able to do?

What learning opportunities or teaching strategies are effective with this topic?

What difficulties or misconceptions are you aware of that are associated with this topic?

What relevant connections can be made within mathematics or with other disciplines?

Figure 3.4   K-W-L Strategy

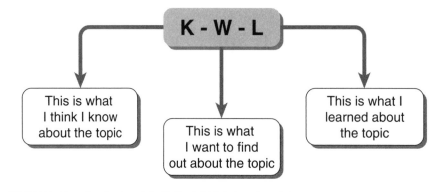

Reading the CTS Sections

CTS is designed to be flexible. You don't have to use *all* the resources or do every section. Also, you can begin your study with any section—it is not necessary to go through from Section I to Section VI. For example, one way of using CTS is to start with Section I, which defines adult literacy. From there, you might choose to go to Section III to trace back the grade-level learning goals that lead up to adult literacy. Once the learning goals are clear, you might decide to focus on the instructional implications and research on student learning in Sections II and IV (these often overlap). After gaining a clearer understanding of the content and pedagogical considerations, you might choose to continue with Section V to examine how connections are made and get a clearer picture of how teaching and learning builds over time. And last, although it can be done at any time, it is useful to look at your state or local standards and reflect on how all the previous sections bring clarity to these documents or suggest additions to them.

> There is no defined sequence to a topic study; it all depends on your purpose.

As you read the parts identified for each section, be aware that not *everything* you read will apply to the topic. At the top of each CTS Guide, users are alerted to read only the related parts of the vetted readings (see Figure 3.5). To the extent possible, we narrowed the selected readings to the pages with relevant information, but some information on those pages will still likely be outside of the topic. For example, one page in an essay in *Principles and Standards of School Mathematics* about fractions also includes information about negative integers, even though the latter is not directly relevant to the Fractions CTS Guide. In Section III, you may have to focus your attention on the learning goals that relate directly to the topic, even though others in the section might appear to be connected to the topic. As you read, you will have to scan continuously for and extract the information that is directly related to the topic. Sometimes the relevant information may be only a paragraph or a single sentence. To save time and maintain focus, use the filter of the topic as you read, and be aware that you may need to draw some boundaries.

As you become experienced in using CTS, you will probably find additional information that was not included in the CTS Guide but that contributes to an understanding of the topic. The CTS Guides have to put a boundary around the topic to remain manageable and readable, but there are always more relevant connections and threads to follow. The *Atlas* is very helpful in linking other ideas that may not be included in CTS Sections I–III.) The selected readings in a CTS Guide are not exhaustive, but they are central to the topic. The third book in the CTS series, a *Facilitator's Guide to Curriculum Topic Study* (anticipated date of publication in 2007), will describe in more detail some reading strategies that can help you extract information and make meaning from your readings.

Figure 3.5 An Important Consideration While Reading Selected Parts

Guiding Questions
for Individual Sections of a CTS Guide

As you are becoming familiar with CTS, we suggest you use guiding questions to help focus on connecting relevant parts of the reading to the outcome for that section. Figure 3.6 provides suggestions for general and resource-specific questions to guide reading, study, and analysis. Select the questions that are most relevant to your purpose and the resources you have available. Feel free to develop, modify, and add your own questions to this list.

THE CTS LEARNING CYCLE:
INQUIRY, STUDY, AND REFLECTION

Various instructional models have grown out of the principle that students learn by building on information they already know. These models allow time for students to grapple with solutions to challenging problems, make connections, develop mathematical ideas and conjectures, analyze patterns, extend their understanding, and apply what they have learned to new contexts. A prominent example of this kind of instructional model is the "launch, explore, summarize" process used in *Getting to Know Connected Mathematics* (Lappan, Fey, Fitzgerald, Friel, & Phillips, 1996). In the early 1960s, J. Myron Atkin and Robert Karplus proposed an instructional model called the learning cycle, which stressed a guided discovery approach for science instruction and which has undergone several adaptations for use in mathematics education. The learning cycle helps teachers organize and facilitate learning by determining students' prior knowledge and guiding them to explore new ideas, construct new understandings, discard ideas that are no longer useful, and apply their learning in a meaningful context.

This attention to students' prior ideas and the process of constructing new ideas is also important for adult learners. CTS uses the learning cycle to create a learning

> CTS is, in essence, an inquiry. The topic is the object of the investigation.

environment that helps teachers modify their ideas and personal beliefs about teaching and learning. What are the essential learning goals related to a topic? What ideas and skills are developmentally appropriate? What common misconceptions are students likely to have? How does the topic connect to other mathematics topics? How do state or local standards match findings from national standards and research? Through these questions, a CTS user investigates a topic and discovers new knowledge about mathematics teaching and learning. Because CTS is an inquiry into a topic, it uses a research-validated instructional model compatible with the inquiry approach. The CTS learning cycle of "inquiry, study, and reflection" is an instructional model that can be used to go through the phases of learning associated with a CTS. Figure 3.7 compares the learning cycle used for student investigation of a mathematics problem to the learning cycle used for adult investigation of a mathematics curriculum topic.

Although the learning cycle is not required in order to engage in CTS, our work with teachers has shown that the cycle (see Figure 3.8) provides a structure for teachers to investigate a topic effectively and make sense of the information they uncover. The CTS learning cycle can be used by individuals or groups, and it can be applied to some or all of the sections of a CTS Guide. In the following, the six stages in the CTS learning cycle are described, along with the embedded processes of reflection

Figure 3.6   Guiding Questions

Section I: Identify Adult Content Knowledge

General Questions to Use With Both Resources (IA and IB):

1. What "big ideas" and major concepts make up this topic?

2. What new content did you learn or improve your understanding of?

3. What examples were used to understand the ideas?

4. What other new insights about the topic did you gain from this reading?

Additional Questions to Use with IA: *Science for All Americans*	Additional Questions to Use with IB: *Beyond Numeracy*
1. What enduring understandings should all adults, including teachers, know about this topic?	1. How does the reading clarify the content of the topic? What content knowledge did you gain from this reading that exceeds or is not included in the standards?
2. What rich interconnections within the topic emerge from the reading?	2. How does the reading help you identify the basic ideas underlying a math topic?
3. How does the reading help you see what a K–12 education is aiming toward?	3. Are there explanations or vivid examples you can use with students to explain concepts in an interesting, comprehensible way?
4. What technical terminology used in the reading implies the mathematical vocabulary every adult should be familiar with?	4. Did you find anything that helped you understand mathematics in current events or everyday situations?

Section II: Consider Instructional Implications

General Questions to Use with Both Resources (IIA and IIB):

1. What suggestions are provided for effective instruction of the topic?

2. What student learning difficulties, misconceptions, or developmental considerations are mentioned?

3. Does the reading suggest representations or everyday experiences that are effective in learning the ideas in the topic?

4. What other new insights about the topic did you gain by reading this section?

Additional Questions to Use with IIA: *Benchmarks for Science Literacy*	Additional Questions to Use with IIB: *Principles and Standards for School Mathematics*
1. How does the general essay help you gain a K–12 "big picture view" of the topic?	1. How do the essays, tasks, and student work help you think about the instructional implications of the topic?
2. How do the grade-level essays illustrate an increasing sophistication in the content and the ways concepts and skills in the topic are taught?	2. What linkages do you find among student learning, teaching, and classroom contexts?
	3. How do the grade-level essays compare in sophistication of ideas and contexts for learning?

Figure 3.6 (Continued)

Section III: Identify Concepts and Specific Ideas

General Questions to Use with Both Resources (IIIA and IIIB):

1. Which learning goals align well with the topic?

2. What concepts, procedures, specific ideas, or skills make up the learning goals in this topic?

3. How do these goals help you determine what you can eliminate or place less emphasis on?

4. How does the sophistication or cognitive complexity of the learning goals change from one grade span to the next?

5. How do the learning goals in the *Benchmarks* compare to the ideas in *Principles and Standards for School Mathematics*?

6. What other new insights about learning goals related to this topic did you gain from reading this section?

Additional Questions to Use with IIIA: *Benchmarks for Science Literacy*	Additional Questions to Use with IIIB: *Principles and Standards for School Mathematics*
1. How specific or broad is the benchmark?	1. What facts, concepts, principles, and broader generalizations are embedded in the standards?
2. Can the benchmark be broken up into smaller ideas?	2. How do the expectations listed help clarify what the standard involves?
3. How does the language in the benchmark help you decide what technical terminology in the topic is important?	3. How do the standards and expectations increase in sophistication from one grade span to the next?

Section IV: Examine Research on Student Learning

General Questions to Use with Both Resources (IVA and IVB):

1. What specific misconceptions or difficulties might a student have about ideas in this topic?

2. Are there any suggestions as to what might contribute to students' misconceptions and how to address them?

3. Is there an age or grade when students may be more likely to learn certain ideas in the topic?

4. How does the research draw attention to important prerequisite knowledge?

5. What other new insights about the topic did you gain by reading this section?

Additional Questions to Use with IVA: *Benchmarks for Science Literacy*	Additional Questions to Use with IVB: *Research Companion to* and *Principles and Standards for School Mathematics*
*Note: We suggest you first read "The Role of Research" on pp. 327–329 to understand the use of the research base.	*We suggest you first read "What Research Says About the NCTM Standards" on pp. 6–20.
1. How can the research be used to complement the benchmark ideas?	1. Are there questions or tasks that might be helpful to use to find out what students know about the topic?
	2. Are there suggestions for helping students avoid or overcome misconceptions?
	3. What implications for teacher practice and learning are indicated by the research?

Section V: Examine Coherency and Articulation

Questions to Use with the *Atlas of Science Literacy* (V)

1. How does a map help you trace a concept or skill from its simple beginning in K through 2 to a culminating, interconnected, sophisticated idea attained by the end of Grade 12?

2. What connections can you identify among ideas or skills in the topic?

3. What connections can you identify to different content areas within or outside of mathematics?

4. How does the map help you see the K–12 vertical articulation of student learning in the topic?

5. What prerequisite ideas can you identify that are necessary for learning the topic?

6. How do the storylines or conceptual strands in a map help you think about the way to coherently organize the concepts and skills in a topic?

7. How do the map and its narrative section improve your overall understanding of the topic?

8. What other new insights about the topic did you gain by examining the map?

Section VI: Clarify State Standards and District Curriculum

Questions to Use with Both Resources (VIA and VIB)

1. Which suggestions from Sections II–V align well with your state or district standards or frameworks? Where do you see gaps that need to be addressed?

2. How does the addition of cognitive performance verbs affect the learning of the ideas in the topic? Are the verbs in your state or district standards appropriate for the nature of the content and research-identified difficulty of the ideas in the topic?

3. How can the research findings inform the placement of your state or district standards? Are they appropriately placed, or are there some that may need to be reconsidered?

4. How do the readings improve your content understanding of the concepts and skills associated with the topic in your standards, curriculum guide, or materials?

Additional Questions to Use with VIA: *State standards or frameworks*	Additional Questions to Use with VIB: *District Curriculum Guide*
1. Which learning goals in your state standards are integral to learning the ideas in the topic?	1. Which concepts or skills essential to developing a coherent understanding of the topic are included in your district curriculum guide or curriculum materials? What gaps would you fill, based on your study?
2. How did reading Sections I through V help you better understand the meaning and intent of your standards or frameworks?	
3. How can the study help make a bridge between a broad content standard and a learning goal?	2. How do the study results help you see why certain lessons in your curriculum program need to be taught and not skipped over?
4. How can the study results help improve K–12 articulation of your standards?	3. How do the results help you identify the appropriate sequence of instructional opportunities in your curriculum?
5. How do the endpoints in the Grades 9–12 section of your standards related to the topic compare with the adult literacy ideas in Section I?	4. How do the results help you recognize that some topics need to be revisited within or at different grade levels with new contexts and increasing sophistication of concepts?
6. How does a comprehensive study of Sections I through V help you consider students' "opportunity to learn and demonstrate" your state standards?	

Figure 3.7 Comparing and Contrasting a Learning Cycle Model of a Student Mathematics Investigation and an Adult CTS Investigation

Student Learning Cycle Investigation of a Mathematics Problem	Adult Learning Cycle Investigation of a Curricular Topic
• Students are engaged around a purpose for investigating a problem • Students surface their existing ideas about the concepts involved in the problem • Students explore ideas by manipulating materials or numbers and gathering evidence • Students clarify findings, resolve dissonance, and develop an acceptable mathematical conjecture • Students use their findings to solve a new problem, provide further explanations, or apply to a novel situation	• Adults are engaged around a purpose for investigating a topic • Adults surface their existing knowledge and beliefs related to the topic • Adults explore ideas by interacting with text and gathering evidence • Adults clarify readings, resolve dissonance, and develop a standards- and research-based understanding of the topic based on evidence from their readings • Adults apply their findings from the CTS to an aspect of their work in order to improve student learning

and self-assessment (Figure 3.11, at the end of this section, describes what CTS users and facilitators would do in each stage):

Topic Engagement

The topic engagement stage requires individuals or groups to think about why they want to engage in a curriculum topic study. What is your purpose? What grade levels will you focus on? What are you interested in learning? What topic or topics will you examine? What outcomes (sections of the CTS Guide) will fit your purpose? The engagement stage helps reinforce the purpose for the study, encourages readiness, and generates interest before beginning the study.

Topic Elicitation

The topic elicitation stage asks learners to activate and identify their current knowledge and beliefs about the topic. It draws on teachers' previous experiences, their beliefs about teaching and student learning, and their prior knowledge. It uses the central question: What do you know about the topic before engaging in the study? Depending on whether you decide to do a full topic study or select particular sections, the ideas you might elicit related to the topic include:

- content knowledge
- content or skills important for all students to know
- effective instructional strategies
- common student difficulties or misconceptions
- precursor or prerequisite ideas
- technical terminology and facts
- connections within and across the content areas of mathematics

Figure 3.8   The CTS Learning Cycle

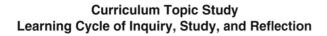

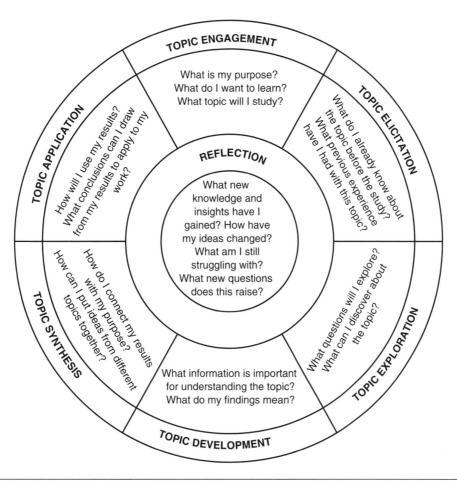

A four-square template may be useful in organizing this information visually (see Figure 3.9). A worksheet copy for duplication is provided in Resource B, or you can download a Word version off the CTS Web site.

Topic Exploration

In the topic exploration stage, teachers use the CTS Guide to focus on selected readings. This stage is characterized by a preliminary scan of the readings. In-depth reading for meaning comes in the next stage. For now, the purpose is to get a taste of what is in the readings, to gain some new ideas to use as a start for further development and thinking, to raise questions, and to acquire a broad perspective of the topic. This is the stage where you might note something that resonates or conflicts

Figure 3.9   Four-Square Elicitation Organizer

Prior Knowledge Related to the Topic

Adult Content Knowledge	Student Knowledge
Misconceptions or Difficulties	Connections

with your current understandings that you want to investigate further. By previewing the material, users are, in a sense, testing the ideas they generated during the elicitation stage. You can record thoughts, information, questions, and observations in different forms. One possibility is to add information to the four-square graphic provided in Figure 3.9. The exploration stage is also a time to begin constructing a sense of the topic. What is your initial interpretation of what you are reading? This stage is still personal to the learner. Because this is only a preliminary scan, the suggested time limit for this stage is 15 minutes for all six sections, or even less if you focus only on particular sections.

Topic Development

In the topic development stage, the CTS user is carefully reading and analyzing all of the appropriate sections in the guide. Teachers process the information and construct meaning from the text as they read. They jot down notes on ideas that are important to understanding the topic. The guide emphasizes that you should read the *related* sections. Readers should be aware that some information included on the pages provided for the resources may not be directly related to the topic being studied. As you read, you need to continually filter out information that is not relevant to the topic. For example, if you are exploring the topic of "measures of center and spread," you would read the essay in the Data Analysis section of *Principles and Standards for School Mathematics.* That section includes text related to correlation, but you would focus only on the parts that are relevant to measures of center and spread.

If you are working in a group, this stage of the study is a time to clarify your ideas with others and the facilitator. In this way, the group can develop a shared understanding that can provide common ground for discussions. What does this information mean? Do I interpret it the same way as others in my group do? This is where engaging in collegial discussion and having a skilled facilitator can help participants make formal meaning out of their study. It is also a time when the separate sections of the CTS Guide can come together to form a complete picture of the topic. This is especially important for groups that decide to engage in a jigsaw, with one person taking responsibility for each particular section. After studying their assigned section, members of the group should come back together to share what they have learned and, as a group, construct a full and complete understanding of the topic.

We recommend creating a summary sheet at this stage. The summary concisely organizes the information from the study following the outline of the CTS Guide. It can be used with a full topic study or selected sections. Figure 3.10 shows an example of a Grades 6–12 CTS Section II, III, and IV summary on the topic of integers. These summary sheets can be filed as a collection that teachers can use for future applications.

Topic Synthesis

In this stage, teachers synthesize their summary results from all six sections or selected sections and relate the findings from their study back to their original purpose. For example, if the purpose of the study was to develop a set of diagnostic assessments that reveal students' misconceptions, the CTS user would probably focus on combining findings primarily from Sections III and IV. Questions that may guide the synthesis work at this stage include: What is the purpose we started with? What information from the study will address our original purpose?

If two or more topics are being studied by a group of teachers, this is the stage where they can make connections between the two. For example, the study of perimeter, area, and volume may be combined with the study of nonlinear relationships to explore the idea of maximizing area when given a fixed perimeter. This stage is also an opportunity to combine topic studies focused on content with topic studies focused on cross-cutting categories from the CTS Guides in the problem solving and processes and unifying themes strands. For example, study results on the topic of addition and subtraction might be combined with results from studying the topic of proof and justification to refine an elementary grades unit that has students develop addition algorithms. In this way, the unit can effectively integrate ideas about generalization, examples and nonexamples, and conjectures with instruction focused on addition and subtraction.

Topic Application

In the topic application stage, individuals or groups decide how they are going to apply the information from their study. The central question is: How can I apply these findings to my work? This stage draws on evidence gathered from CTS to construct a plan for addressing a particular purpose. Based on evidence from CTS, users will draw conclusions, make inferences, and revise their hypotheses about the best ways to improve teaching and learning. For example, the purpose of a group's

> Applying findings from a CTS helps district curriculum committees identify redundancy or gaps and arrange the ideas in the curriculum for a more coherent flow of instruction.

Figure 3.10 Curriculum Topic Study Summary for Integers

Section II. Overview of Context, Content Overview, and Instructional Implications

General Essay:

- School experiences with numbers should "foster an appreciation of the beauty and versatility of numbers and contribute to the development of number sense" (*Benchmarks,* AAAS, 1993, p. 220).
- Development of number sense is of critical importance because it gives students confidence to solve problems using mathematics and leads to viewing mathematics as a way to communicate ideas.
- Numbers should be genuinely encountered in all curricular areas with ample time allotted to allow students to examine "fascinating" mathematical ideas.
- Problem-solving, inquiry, and student design projects are all engaging strategies which strongly contribute to the development of number sense.
- "Making judgments about answers is as much a part of computation as the calculation itself" (*Benchmarks,* p. 288).
- "It is not sufficient for students to learn how to perform mathematical operations in the abstract if they are to become effective problem solvers and to be able to express their arguments quantitatively whenever appropriate" (*Benchmarks,* p. 288–289).
- Problem solving that requires students to make calculations and check their answers against their estimates and their knowledge of whatever the problem pertains to should be a part of experiences at every grade level and content area.
- Experiences should include use of calculators and computers, which can vastly extend the mathematical capabilities of everyone.

Elementary School Essay:

- Negative integers should be introduced at this level through the use of familiar models such as temperature or owing money.
- The number line is an appropriate and helpful model, and students should recognize that points to the left of 0 on a horizontal number line can be represented by numbers less than 0.

Middle School Essay:

- Described as "the most important period of all in helping students develop an understanding of numbers" (*Benchmarks,* p. 213). Students begin to encounter negative numbers and fractions in the activities they do in science and technology.
- Practical introduction of negative numbers and fractions should be balanced with opportunity for students to relate these new ideas to other mathematical ideas including relationships between operations, number systems, and abstract number patterns (*Benchmarks,* p. 213).
- Build upon/link students' prior experiences with whole number concepts and skills to deepen understandings of integers.
- Students should be given opportunity to develop proficiency using integers to solve problems.

High School Essay:

- Elaboration of middle school ideas. Encounters with numbers and computations are primarily through problem solving or learning more advanced mathematics.
- Students at the high school level deepen and refine their understanding, working with number relations, operations, ratios, estimations, measurement, graphs, etc.
- "Students should enter high school with an understanding of basic operations and fluency on using them on integers, fractions, and decimals" (*Principles and Standards,* NCTM, 2000). (foundation for their understanding of algebra)

Section III: Examine National Learning Goals and Specific Ideas at Different Grade Spans

Elementary School:

- Numbers less than 0 can be explored by extending the number line and through familiar applications.

Middle School:

- A number line can be extended on the other side of zero to represent negative numbers. Negative numbers allow subtraction of bigger numbers from a smaller number to make sense and are often used when something can be measured on either side of a reference point (time, ground level, temperature, budget).
- The operations of + and − are inverses of each other: One undoes what the other does; likewise x and ÷.
- Use, interpret, and compare numbers in several equivalent forms such as integers, fractions, decimals, and percents.
- Students should develop meaning for integers and represent and compare quantities with them.
- Students should understand the meaning and effects of arithmetic operations with fractions, decimals, and integers.
- Students should use the associative and commutative properties of addition and multiplication and the distributive property of multiplication over addition to simplify computations with integers, fractions, and decimals.
- Students should understand and use the inverse relationships of addition/subtraction and multiplication/division to simplify computations and solve problems.
- Students should develop and analyze algorithms for computing with fractions, decimals, and integers and should develop fluency in their use.
- Extend students' initial (familiar) understandings of negative numbers to include the idea that positive and negative integers can be used to note relative changes or values.
- Develop the idea that integers are "useful," especially when solving (algebraic) problems.
- Expand exploration of the inverse relationships between operation pairs (addition/subtraction, multiplication/division) with middle school students.

High School:

- Find answers to problems by substituting numerical values in simple algebraic formulas and judge whether the answer is reasonable by reviewing the process and checking against typical values.
- Make up and write out simple algorithms for solving problems that take several steps.

Section IV: Examining Cognitive Research Findings

- Students may have formed their initial conceptions of negative numbers in "inappropriate ways" using everyday experiences such as below-zero temperatures, lost yards in football games, etc. (*Principles and Standards,* pp. 214–15).
- Limited research on the difficulties experienced by students when working with negative numbers (NCTM, 1993).
- Some studies have indicated that introduction of negative numbers to students at an earlier age is beneficial. (NCTM, 1993)
- Using a "zero-pairs" using chips to model positive and negative number operations (NCTM, 1993, p. 194).
- Researchers have questioned using number lines, thermometers, and countdowns as introductory lessons to integers because these do not aid in the teaching of operations using integers. Preliminary studies have indicated that students do not think in terms of these models when calculating answers to problems such as −5 −3 and make errors (NCTM, 1993, p. 194).
- Because two symbol systems are used simultaneously in algebra, many students think of −x as a negative number. Teachers need to alert students to the uses of the − sign and refer to −x as "the opposite of x" rather than "negative x" (Research Ideas, High School).

study might be to improve the current curriculum. After studying the topic of place value, a district curriculum committee might decide to use its results to examine the articulation of K–8 learning goals in their curriculum.

Study Reflection and Self-Assessment

This is a critical part of the process, whether the study is undertaken by an individual, a pair, a team, or a large group of educators. It is embedded throughout CTS and is connected to the elicitation of prior ideas described above. Figure 3.11 shows an example of a reflection summary sheet that can be used to organize information, thoughts, questions, and ideas generated through reflection and self-assessment. A worksheet copy is provided in Resource B and is available on the CTS Web site. Questions used to guide reflection and self-assessment might include:

> Reflection and self-assessment is at the center of the CTS learning cycle of inquiry, study, and reflection.

- What important knowledge have I gained from this process?
- What new insights about teaching and learning have I gained?
- How have my ideas or understandings about content changed?
- Are there ideas I am still struggling with?
- How has this CTS changed my beliefs about teaching and learning?
- Are there beliefs I hold that I am still resistant to change?
- What will I do differently as result of CTS?
- What other questions does this raise for me?

USING CTS ALONE OR WITH A GROUP

> The flexibility of CTS allows it to be used alone by an individual, anytime and anywhere, or with a group for a designated purpose.

CTS can serve many purposes for both individual teachers and for groups of teachers in a professional growth setting. Ultimately, the decision of how to use CTS depends on what you want to accomplish. Do you want to build your own capacity for using standards and research, or are you building the capacity of the group with which you work? Do you learn best when you have an opportunity to interact and share ideas with a group? Are you addressing the learning needs of the students you have, or are you working with other teachers across grades to impact all students and gain a multigrade picture? Are you intent on using CTS as the focus on which to build a learning community? Are you intent on helping others change long-held beliefs and practices? The answers to these questions will help you determine whether you want to use this book for your own individual purposes or as a partner in the learning of a collaborative group.

Using CTS on Your Own

Individual teachers use CTS on their own to inform lesson planning and implementation, to examine student work or ideas, to help them address confusions that come up in their classroom, or to select the most effective instructional materials and

Figure 3.11   Examples of What CTS Users and Facilitators Do During a Group CTS Using the CTS Cycle of Inquiry, Study, and Reflection

Stage	What the CTS User Does	What the CTS Facilitator Does
Topic Engagement	Asks: • What is my purpose? • What grade level(s) will I focus on? • What do I want to find out? • What topic(s) will I study? • What outcomes will I focus on? Thinks about purpose for doing CTS, shows interest in the topic, and encourages readiness	• Uses a hook to engage the group in the topic (video, student work, presents a dilemma, etc.) • Defines purpose and outcomes • Generates questions • Charts groups' responses • Generates interest and curiosity from the group • Ascertains readiness to proceed
Topic Elicitation	Asks: • What adult mathematics knowledge should a literate adult have? • What content or skills are important for all students to know? • What instructional strategies or contexts are effective? • What difficulties or misconceptions related to the topic am I aware of? • What technical terminology, facts, or formulas are important? • What connections exist within and across the content areas of mathematics? Activates and records current knowledge and beliefs about the topic	• Asks elicitation questions • Provides recording worksheets for individual responses • Asks group to share initial ideas • Observes and listens carefully • Safely uncovers knowledge and beliefs of the group • Records ideas on chart • Suspends judgment
Topic Exploration	Asks: • What predictions can I make about what I will learn from this study? • What do I see that I want to dig deeper into? • What is resonating with me or causing conflict that I need to revisit? • What questions do I want to explore further? Does a quick scan to get an initial taste of the topic and what it involves, records ideas and questions, begins to formulate some initial ideas that will be further explored.	• Directs group to the CTS Guide and selected readings • Provides time for a quick scan • Keeps group on task and encourages them to do a "quick read" and not get bogged down in details • Encourages them to pay attention only to related parts, providing sticky notes to mark relevant portions • Encourages interaction among the group • Observes and listens during interactions • Suspends judgment
Topic Development	Asks: • What information relates to the topic I am studying? • What are the important ideas? • What do these findings mean? Processes information for meaning, jots down important notes, filters information as to what is most relevant, clarifies ideas with others, listens critically to others' ideas, suspends own opinions and experiences and focuses on the data from the text, listens to and comprehends clarifications offered by the facilitator, reflects on initial ideas and outcomes, summarizes groups' findings	• Assigns the groups' tasks • Uses jigsaws and other strategies to provide time for reading and processing • Monitors time • May provide optional additional supplements for reading or video • Encourages collaboration • Asks probing and clarifying questions during group sense-making • Provides time and support to work through dissonance • Encourages explanations based on evidence citing • Provides clarifications when needed • Connects new ideas to old and helps reflect on the outcomes • Helps group construct the summary

(Continued)

Figure 3.11 (Continued)

Stage	What the CTS User Does	What the CTS Facilitator Does
Topic Synthesis	Asks: • What is my purpose for using these results? • What information from the CTS results will help me with my purpose? • How do I combine findings from the selected sections? • How can I put ideas from different topic studies together? Synthesizes results and extracts relevant information, prepares to apply findings	• Reminds group of their purpose. • Encourages group work to extract meaningful information • Helps group connect CTS findings to their purpose • Provides examples
Topic Application	Asks: • How will I use the findings in my work? • What can I draw from the findings to help me apply them to my work? Thinks about how to use the findings, draws conclusions, makes solid inferences, revisits hypotheses, and applies CTS results to the particular problem or work unique to the user's context	• Refers users to the evidence in drawing their conclusions • Helps support users in thinking about ways to implement findings • Shares examples of ways findings have been applied in the particular curricular, instructional, or assessment context • Encourages reflection and self-assessment after task is completed
Reflection and Self-Assessment	Asks: • What new knowledge and insights have I gained? • How have my ideas or beliefs changed? • What will I do differently now? • How will this help others I work with? • What am I still struggling with? • What new questions does this raise for me? Reflects back on initial ideas recorded during the elicitation stage and considers how ideas have changed, how results can inform actions of others, and considers new questions to investigate.	• Refers individuals or group back to their initial ideas generated during the elicitation stage • Provides time and structures for participants to reflect on their learning • Helps individuals or groups identify next steps for further investigation

strategies. As teachers study a topic as part of their own self-directed learning, they increase their understanding of what is important to teach about the topic, what their students might find difficult, and how they might effectively address the various ideas and ways of thinking students have.

Maybe you are switching to teach a different grade level or have just encountered some students who are having difficulty learning a mathematical idea. You might be asking yourself: What is blocking these students from learning? This is a good time to use CTS to get some insights from the standards and research that can help you make well-informed instructional decisions.

In developing CTS, we encountered many teachers who thought they knew and taught to the standards. Although they knew a lot about standards, they discovered through CTS that they could do a much better job of making connections between the topics they teach and the "big ideas" in mathematics. They also found that by studying the common misconceptions students face, they could probe and assess understanding far better than they had been doing. With this book and the suggested resources, individual teachers have access to the professional knowledge base needed to enhance or advance their own understanding of the standards and how to teach to them. For example, medical professionals constantly read medical literature to stay current and to refresh their knowledge of areas in which they lack experience or want to further their knowledge so that they can stay current with the latest research and clinical findings. This type of learning challenges the paradigm that professional development always involves coming together with a group led by a facilitator. Although those experiences are crucial and highly encouraged, valuable professional development can also include the type of self-directed learning that occurs through CTS.

> In many ways, individual teachers are doing what other professionals do—turning to the literature to deepen their knowledge of their practice.

Teachers with strong mathematics backgrounds have found CTS to be a useful resource in bridging what they know about the content with what is appropriate for their students. It helps them to see that what they perceive as simple ideas may be stumbling blocks for students. For example, a middle school algebra teacher may know that students are struggling with understanding equations but not know why or what to do about it. CTS can help that teacher to trace those difficulties back to their source. By reading the standards and research, the teacher may find that students often think that = stands for "and the answer is . . ." rather than a sign of equivalence. The teacher might also find strategies for addressing this preconception in the classroom.

Professional developers also find CTS useful to their work. Professional developers of mathematics who are excellent staff developers and facilitators but lack a strong math content background—or are specialized in a particular grade level—find that CTS grounds them in the content-specific issues that may come up in a professional development session. Professional developers also need to be able to cite current research or standards recommendations that relate to the specific needs of the teachers with whom they work.

Group Use of CTS

CTS is often used in settings with groups of teachers who are engaged in professional development, teacher induction/mentoring, curriculum selection, and committees for school improvement in mathematics. Group use of CTS can involve two teachers engaged in a topic study or a large professional development audience. Groups of mathematics and science teachers can also engage in CTS together, finding common ground and establishing connections between their curricula. For example, mathematics and science teachers might identify graphs as a topic of study. The science teachers could study the science CTS topic, graphs and graphing, while the mathematics teachers study the mathematics CTS topic, graphic representation. Each

> Learning is enriched through the social engagement with mathematics content that comes with a collegial, collaborative environment supported by CTS.

group could select resources specific to its subject area, then identify common ideas and skills in integrated groups. In this way, teachers could increase their awareness of how and when these ideas and skills are taught in the other subject area and discuss ways of working together to improve students' understanding of that topic.

School- and district-based study groups, along with other teacher networks, are also a good context for CTS. Typically, such study groups will identify goals for improved student learning in a particular area, and then they will use CTS to establish expectations for students at each grade level. Through CTS, the study group can develop a shared vision of appropriate and effective instruction and assessment practices, and they can set goals to try out and discuss the impact of new practices based on what they learned.

Mentor teachers or instructional coaches can also use CTS to help novice teachers plan their lessons and deepen their mathematics content and pedagogical content knowledge. CTS can provide a way for mentors or coaches and novice teachers to discuss goals of the lesson and make adjustments in the lesson plan as they study the topic together. CTS provides professional resources that mentors or coaches and novice teachers explore as a team, so that the mentoring and coaching relationship becomes collaborative rather than didactic.

CTS can be embedded in virtually any professional development session that seeks to increase teachers' understanding of what content is important, when it should be taught, what common misconceptions students hold about the topics, and what is important to assess. In particular, CTS is a valuable tool to use on district inservice days, where teachers often have a say in planning their day of learning. Through CTS, teachers have an effective way to explore a topic that fits the needs of the students in their school and provides teachers with a clear focus and goal. CTS transforms an inservice day from a general learning experience for all to a content-specific experience that meets the particular needs of mathematics teachers.

The third book in the CTS series, *Facilitator's Guide to Curriculum Topic Study* (anticipated release in 2007), will address facilitating the CTS process with professional development groups. It will describe various group structures, facilitation techniques for engaging learners, group learning strategies and tools, learning designs for CTS, examples of CTS used with various professional development strategies, and vignettes that illuminate group use of CTS.

4

Contexts for Using Curriculum Topic Study

This chapter presents examples of ways the Curriculum Topic Study (CTS) process and tools are used in the different contexts that mathematics educators encounter in their work.

CTS can be used in these contexts, among others:

- Mathematics content knowledge
- Curriculum
- Instruction
- Assessment
- Preservice and inservice education and professional development
- Leadership

> CTS is not a rigid, lock-step, linear process. It is meant to be molded and shaped to fit the unique context of each user.

This list is not exhaustive. As you become familiar with CTS, you may find other ways to use CTS. As part of the CTS project funded by the National Science Foundation (NSF), we will continue to work with educators nationwide. In the process, we will document the various ways educators use CTS in their contexts and the new tools the CTS users develop. The CTS Web site will be continually updated with these new examples and tools.

In Chapter 5, we have provided illustrative vignettes based on actual applications of CTS by mathematics educators; these illuminate how CTS has been used in different contexts. The vignettes illustrate the use of several of the tools and suggestions that are discussed in this chapter. Figure 4.1 lists the specific vignettes that correspond to the contexts described in this chapter (many vignettes address more than one context—the figure identifies the contexts that are most central to the vignette). After you read and examine the suggestions and examples in this chapter, it may be helpful to read a corresponding vignette to get a more complete picture of what CTS looks like in practice.

Figure 4.1 Context Examples of Vignettes

Context	Vignette
Content Knowledge	Vignette #2: A High School Teacher Uses CTS to Guide Implementation on Functions Vignette #5: A Middle School Teacher Uses CTS to Understand Concepts of Surface Area and Volume
Curriculum	Vignette #1: A Team of Primary Teachers Uses CTS to Clarify District Curriculum Goals for Addition and Subtraction Concepts Vignette #2: A High School Teacher Uses CTS to Guide Implementation on Functions Vignette #3: A Department Chair Uses CTS to Help Guide Discussion on Quadratic Factoring Vignette #4: A Multi-Grade Elementary Team Uses CTS to Examine Alignment of Curriculum, Instruction, and Assessment Vignette #6: A Team of Middle and High School Teachers Uses CTS to Identify Goals for Learning About Decimals, Fractions, and Percents
Instruction	Vignette #2: A High School Teacher Uses CTS to Guide Implementation of Unit on Functions Vignette #3: A Department Chair Uses CTS to Help Guide Discussion on Quadratic Factoring Vignette #5: A Middle School Teacher Uses CTS to Understand Concepts of Surface Area and Volume Vignette #6: A Team of Middle and High School Teachers Uses CTS to Identify Goals for Learning about Decimals. Fractions and Percents
Assessment	Vignette #4: A Multi-Grade Elementary Team Uses CTS to Examine Alignment of Curriculum, Instruction, and Assessment Vignette #7: An Intermediate Teacher Uses CTS to Prepare for a Unit on Probability Vignette #8: Teachers Use CTS to Analyze Student Thinking on Area Measurement
Professional Development	Vignette #9: A Teacher Leaders Uses CTS to Prepare for a Professional Development Session on Proportionality
Leadership	Vignette #3: A Department Chair Uses CTS to Help Guide Discussion on Quadratic Factoring Vignette #8: Teacher Leaders Use CTS to Analyze Student Thinking Using a Diagnostic Probe on Area Measurement

CTS AND MATHEMATICS CONTENT KNOWLEDGE

Mathematics educators recognize the critical importance of having a strong, broad base of mathematical knowledge—the big ideas, concepts, procedures, and fundamental facts of mathematics. This knowledge base plays a critical role in education, allowing teachers to make conceptual connections within and across topics and disciplines. Teachers can benefit from interactions with other teachers in which they explore problems of practice and engage in continuing discussion that enriches their knowledge of subject matter, students, and teaching (National Research Council, 2002). Many teachers pursue content learning for their own enjoyment, to increase their confidence, and to meet requirements for certification. Content learning experiences—such as engineering immersions, research in science that uses mathematics, or mathematics courses at universities—are valuable, but they can at times be impractical due to scheduling and geographic constraints. Furthermore, these experiences do not conscientiously relate the content covered to teachers' specific needs. It is critical that teachers have opportunities to learn the particular content they need to teach and that they learn it in ways that are directly linked to classroom practice.

> Content that is learned disconnected from how to teach it may provide teachers with more mathematical understanding but will not necessarily result in improved student learning. Standards and accountability systems have made us more aware that the content teachers need to learn is the content they will teach. (Loucks-Horsley et al., 2003, p. 333)

In addition, the timing and depth of learning experiences teachers need may vary considerably. Some teachers may need immediate content support focused on a specific idea or skill whereas others may simply need a refresher on a given topic. Teachers need just-in-time, just-for-me opportunities to learn content that relates directly to the classroom. CTS is a scholarly, versatile process that can provide just those kinds of opportunities for teachers.

CTS is not meant to replace formal mathematics content coursework. Instead, it offers a systematic way for teachers to increase their knowledge of mathematics, understand how mathematical knowledge is structured, and identify specific ideas and skills appropriate to different grade levels. CTS not only provides an added value to traditional coursework but also serves a larger range of teacher needs. Furthermore, CTS can actually support formal coursework. Teachers can identify the content they need to know more about through CTS, then be better equipped to find university courses, content institutes, or research experiences that fit their particular needs.

CTS is particularly helpful to elementary teachers or other generalists who teach multiple subjects and have not had coursework in all the areas of mathematics they teach. While many high school teachers specialize in a particular area of mathematics such as geometry, algebra, or calculus, they are often faced with teaching a new class that includes topics outside their area of specialty (for example, statistics or discrete mathematics). In some schools, teachers are using mathematics curricula that integrate across mathematics topics, such as Interactive Mathematics Program™ (IMP). In addition, science teachers often embed mathematics in their science lessons. All of these teachers can benefit from using CTS to enhance their content knowledge.

Figure 4.2 Recording Information From the CTS Guide for Content Knowledge of a Topic

Section and Purpose	Resource Used	Content Information to Record as You Read
Section I	*Science for All Americans*	• Culminating big ideas in the topic • Important concepts and specific ideas related to the topic • Illustrative examples that clarify the content
	Beyond Numeracy	• Information that contributes to understanding the topic in a real-world context • Basic facts, vocabulary, principles, generalizations, or laws associated with the topic • Illustrative examples or analogies that clarify the content
Section II	*Benchmarks for Science Literacy*	• Big ideas that span grade levels • Grade-level concepts and ideas important for understanding the topic
	Principles and Standards for School Mathematics	• Big ideas that span grade levels • Grade-spanning concepts and ideas important for understanding the topic
Section III	*Benchmarks for Science Literacy*	• Specific math ideas in the goal statements • Technical terminology used in the goal statements
	Principles and Standards for School Mathematics	
Section IV	*Atlas of Science Literacy*	• Connections between ideas that provide clarification for the content

Using CTS to Identify the Knowledge Needed to Teach a Topic

An old adage says "You don't know what you don't know if you don't have the knowledge to begin with."

Section I of the CTS Guides includes readings from *Science for All Americans* (American Association for the Advancement of Science, 1990), *Beyond Numeracy* (Paulos, 1992), and optional supplementary content readings or videos. These resources describe what mathematically literate adults know about a particular topic. (Optional content reading supplements are listed on the CTS Web site at www.curriculumtopicstudy.org.).

Sections II, III, and V provide further clarification of the content at different grade levels. For teachers engaged in formal coursework at the university level, these sections can help to extend and transform their content knowledge into the kind of knowledge they need to be able to teach students at different grade levels.

Figure 4.3   K-W-L Strategy

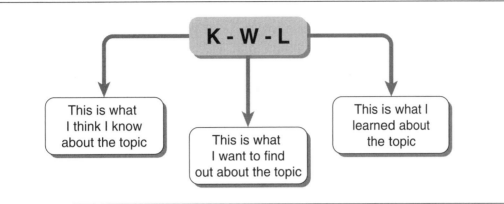

Figure 4.2 shows how selected readings can be used to identify the relevant content in a topic that teachers need to know and that students should be learning.

When using CTS to build your own content knowledge, it is important to start with what you already know about the topic you are studying. K-W-L is a strategy used with students to identify the prior knowledge they bring to their learning (K), what they would like to learn (W), and what they learned after an instructional opportunity (L). The important point is to compare prior thinking to new ideas and new ways of seeing the content. This reflection is an important part of the learning process. We have adapted the K-W-L strategy (see Figure 4.3) for adult learners using CTS. (Guidelines for using the K-W-L strategy are provided in Chapter 3.)

Figure 4.4 shows an example of a teacher's use of K-W-L to examine content ideas about volume and surface area. (This example is illuminated in Vignette 5, in Chapter 5.) Notice how the teachers' knowledge about surface area and volume of three-dimensional objects was enhanced, and in some instances modified, after using CTS to compare initial ideas with new understandings.

Using CTS to Examine the Structure of Conceptual Knowledge in a Topic

Understanding the content of a topic by itself is not enough. Lynn Erickson's 1998 book, *Concept-Based Curriculum and Instruction*, defines *structure of knowledge* and *topic* this way:

Structure of Knowledge: A schema (visual or verbal) that specifies a cognitive hierarchy and relationship between facts, topics, concepts, generalizations and principles, and theories. (p. 168)

Topic: A category of study that implies a body of related facts to be learned. Study that is focused on topics, without a conceptual lens, results in memorization and surface understanding rather than integrated thinking and deep understanding. (p. 168)

Figure 4.4 Example of a Teacher Using K-W-L With a Surface Area & Volume CTS

What I think I **K**now about the content in the topic	• Three-dimensional (3-D) objects have many sides • *Faces* and *vertices* are words used to describe 3-D objects • *Volume* is how much room inside a 3-D object • There is a difference between the dimensions of the object, how many units fill an object, and the amount of material it takes to make or cover the object • Surface area is found by adding the area of all the faces • Volume is found by multiplying the base and height
What I **W**ant to learn about the content in the topic	• What is the relationship between the surface area and the volume of a 3-D figure? • What is the definition of a *net*? • Are there multiple formulas and methods for finding surface area and volume?
What I **L**earned about the content in the topic	• The volume of a rectangular prism or cylinder can be found by multiplying the area of the base and the height • Surface area of a 3-D object can be determined by finding the area of the object's net (a two-dimensional representation of a 3-D object) • Volume does not generally determine surface area • Surface areas of similar objects are proportional to the squares of the lengths of their corresponding sides, but their volumes are proportional to the cubes of those lengths • A cube-like rectangular prism has nearly equal linear dimensions • Rectangular prisms that are more cube-like have less surface area than other rectangular prisms with the same volume • Area and volume can be found by breaking an object into known reference shapes such as rectangles and rectangular prisms

These two definitions underscore the importance of understanding the structure of conceptual knowledge in a topic. This is further supported by the research on expert knowledge in *How People Learn* (Bransfod, Brown, & Cocking, 2000):

> [Experts'] knowledge is not simply a list of facts and formulas that are relevant to their domain; instead their knowledge is organized around core concepts or "big ideas" that guide their thinking about their domains. (p. 36)

In CTS, the structure of conceptual knowledge in a topic is represented by the three-level schema in Figure 4.5. Procedural knowledge is not included in this schema.

The terms used in this schema may have different meanings to different people. To be clear about our intent, we use the following operational definitions and accompanying examples:

Top Level:

Broad content and process standards. Fundamental and comprehensive concepts that provide connections between content standards in mathematics (e.g., algebra, measurement, and representation).

Big ideas. Generalizations, theories, or broad ideas that show relationships among concepts. Big ideas are the essential understandings that often cut across grade spans

Figure 4.5   Structure of Conceptual Knowledge in a Topic

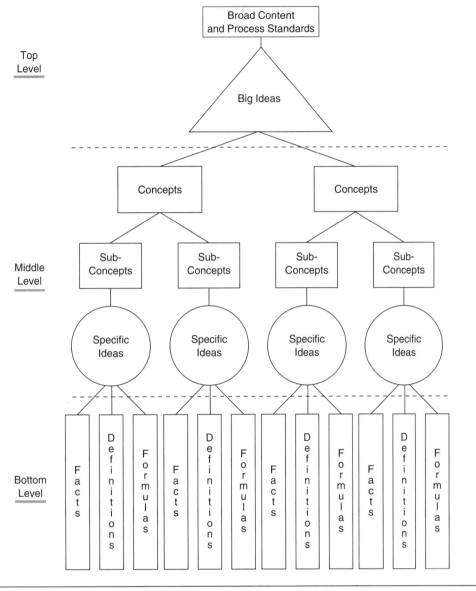

and inform adult literacy. In *Principles and Standards for School Mathematics* (National Council of Teachers of Mathematics, 2000), the big ideas are referred to in the goals that apply across all grade spans (e.g., the relationship between quantities can be represented).

Middle Level:

Concepts. Mental constructs made up of one to three words that can be broad or topic specific. Even though factual knowledge may evolve and change, concepts remain universal and timeless. Concepts can begin with basic ideas and culminate in sophisticated understanding. Students refine and enhance their thinking about concepts over the course of their K–12 experience. Several of the CTS topics are also concepts (e.g., measures of center and spread, linear rates, or transformations).

Subconcepts. Concepts broken down into more specific mental constructs that relate to a broader concept (e.g., mean, slope, or translation).

Specific ideas. Mathematical statements about a concept or subconcept that articulate the conceptual knowledge at a given developmental level. Specific ideas lend clarity and exactness to a broad local, state, or national learning goal. In *Principles and Standards,* specific ideas are embedded in the grade-span expectations (e.g., there are techniques and tools to accurately find length, area, volume, and angle).

Bottom Level:

Facts, definitions, and formulas: Definitions, formulas, fragments of specific knowledge, and technical vocabulary. Although certain facts and terminology are necessary, when taught and learned in isolation, they are less likely to contribute to conceptual understanding (e.g., the perimeter of a square is four times the length of a side).

This schema is useful in unpacking learning goals in a topic by identifying the concepts linked to the topic, the specific ideas that describe the concepts, and the important facts, definitions, or formulas associated with the topic. Examining national standards helps educators tease out concepts and specific ideas as well as identify the terminology that is important for students to use with the topic. The opposite of unpacking is "building up." The schema shows how concepts and specific ideas in a topic can be combined to build up to fundamental and comprehensive "big ideas." These big ideas make up the broad content and process standards that span several different topics or even disciplines.

Figure 4.6 shows an example of how the different levels of knowledge about measures of center and spread at a high school level were identified using CTS. Readings from Section I and III helped extract the big ideas. Sections II, III, and V helped the users identify the concepts, subconcepts, and specific ideas. The terminology used in the Section III and VI learning goals was combined with relevant factual knowledge. Overall, the process helped teachers deepen their understanding of the basic concepts related to a learning goal in their district curriculum document. Figure 4.7 shows an example of how the teachers used the CTS Structure of Knowledge to construct questions that reflect the structure of the knowledge in the topic, ranging from overarching essential questions to specific elicitation of facts, definitions, and formulas. These questions can guide and focus both adult and student content-learning and assessment so that the emphasis is not on lower level knowledge such as facts, definitions, and formulas.

> Using CTS to establish the structure of conceptual knowledge in a topic helps educators shift the emphasis from lower level facts, definitions, and formulas to the important middle- and upper-level conceptual ideas needed to develop deeper understanding.

CTS AND CURRICULUM

It is not easy to design a K–12 mathematics curriculum that is aligned with standards. It is even more difficult when committee members lack the necessary tools

Figure 4.6   Example: Structure of Conceptual Knowledge in a Topic

---

Structure of Conceptual Knowledge in a Topic

Topic: Measures of center and spread
Grade Level: High school

Content and Process Standards:

- Data analysis
- Representation

Big Ideas:

- Questions can be formulated and addressed by collecting, organizing, and displaying data
- Statistical methods can be used to analyze data

Related Concepts and Subconcepts:

- Univariate data
- Bivariate data
- Summary statistics
    Center
    Spread
- Shape of a data set
- Transformations

State/District Learning Goal: Predict and draw conclusions from charts, tables, and graphs that *summarize data* from practical situations

Specific Ideas:

- Describing center, spread, and shape is essential in analyzing univariate and bivariate data
- Several statistical methods can be used to analyze averages and distributions
- Graphic representations of data sets are useful in analyzing the shape of the data
- Linear transformations of data may or may not affect shape, center, or spread
- There are limitations to using summary statistics when comparing two or more data sets

Facts, Definitions, and Formulas:

- Measures of spread including standard deviation and interquartile range can be calculated using an algorithm
- Technology can be used to quickly calculate measures of spread
- The mean and median can differ greatly for a skewed distribution
- Adding a constant to all observed values in a data set changes the measure of center by that constant but does not change the measure of spread or the shape of the distribution
- Multiplying each observed value in a data set by the same constant multiplies the mean, median, range, and standard deviation by the same factor
- The shape of a distribution of a single measurement variable can be analyzed using histograms, box plots, dot plots, stem-and-leaf plots, and scatter plots
- Parallel box plots, back-to-back stem-and-leaf plots, or same-scale histograms can be used to compare data sets

---

and resources to undertake this arduous work. A curriculum scope and sequence can be compared to a jigsaw puzzle.

Imagine that we are faced with a pile of jigsaw puzzle pieces and told to put them together. Our first reaction might be to ask for the picture. When we put

Figure 4.7 Levels of Questioning

Topic: Measures of Center and Spread	
Structure of Knowledge	**Sample Question**

Big Ideas:
 	
 • Questions can be formulated and addressed by collecting, organizing, and displaying data
 • Statistical methods can be used to analyze data
 	
 State/District Learning Goal: Predict and draw conclusions from charts, tables, and graphs that *summarize data* from practical situations
 	
 Related Concepts and Subconcepts:
 	
 • Univariate data
 • Bivariate data
 • Summary statistics
     Center
     Spread
 • Shape of a data set
 • Transformations
 	
 Specific Ideas:
 	
 • Describing center, spread, and shape is essential in analyzing univariate and bivariate data
 • Several statistical methods can be used to analyze averages and distributions
 • Graphic representations of data sets are useful in analyzing the shape of the data
 • Linear transformations of data may or may not affect shape, center, or spread
 • There are limitations to using summary statistics when comparing two or more data sets
 	
 Facts, Definitions, and Formulas:
 	
 • Measures of spread including standard deviation and interquartile range can be calculated using an algorithm
 • Technology can be used to quickly calculate measures of spread
 • The mean and median can differ greatly for a skewed distribution
 • Adding a constant to all observed values in a data set changes the measure of center by that constant but does not change the measure of spread or the shape of the distribution
 • Multiplying each observed value in a data set by the same constant multiplies the mean, median, range, and standard deviation by the same factor
 • The shape of a distribution of a single measurement variable can be analyzed using histograms, box plots, dot plots, stem-and-leaf plots, and scatter plots
 • Parallel box plots, back-to-back stem-and-leaf plots, or same-scale histograms can be used to compare data sets
	• What types of questions can be formulated and addressed with data?
	 • What statistical methods can be used to analyze data?
	
	 • What does the shape of the data set tell you about the set as a whole?
	 • How is a linear transformation of data similar to transformations with functions?
	 • How is a linear transformation of data similar to transformations of geometric figures?
	
	 • What is the importance of using measures of center and spread when analyzing data?
	 • What is the difference between univariate and bivariate data?
	 • What is meant by a summary statistic?
	 • What are the limitations of using only one summary statistic when describing a data set?
	 • What are the limitations of using summary statistics to compare two data sets?
	 • How does the shape of a data set relate to the set's summary statistics?
	 • Describe a situation that would result in a transformation of a data set
	
	 • How do you calculate the mean and mean absolute deviation of the set of data?
	 • What types of linear transformations affect the mean?
	 • What types of linear transformations affect the median?
	 • What types of linear transformations affect the spread?
	 • What is the effect of outliers on the measures of center?
	 • What is the effect of outliers on the spread?
	 • How do you find an interquartile range?
	 • What types of graphic representations are appropriate for displaying univariate and bivariate data?
	 • For each type of graphic representation, what characteristic(s) of the data set can be easily examined?

together a jigsaw puzzle, we usually have a picture to guide us. None of the pieces means anything taken alone; only when the pieces are put together do they mean something. (Beane, 1995, p. 1)

CTS provides the picture educators need to put the pieces together in a way that makes sense for students. Examining the concepts and ideas in a topic (Sections III and VI), coupled with recommendations from the standards and the research on student learning (Sections II and IV), is like holding a jigsaw puzzle piece up to see roughly what area of the puzzle you should put it in. After getting some of the initial pieces laid out, studying the ideas in Section V can add more connections from other topics to the developing curriculum, bringing us closer to completing the puzzle.

> Without an overall picture, putting together curriculum pieces is a struggle that often results in a disconnected curriculum that fails to form a complete and coherent whole in the minds of students.

"A 'coherent' curriculum is one that holds together, that makes sense as a whole; and its parts, whatever they are, are unified and connected by that sense of the whole" (Beane, 1995, p. 3). This involves carefully thinking through the flow of ideas to the following:

- The important core set of ideas students should learn and how they combine to form the big ideas in mathematics
- How ideas develop and connect within and between content domains and disciplines
- Cross-cutting themes and processes, including problem solving, reasoning, communication, and representation
- The development of increasing sophistication across and within grades through which students build their understanding of the important ideas in mathematics

These multifaceted considerations for coherence and articulation within a K–12 curriculum are represented in Figure 4.8. The facets that make up a coherent curriculum are like the cut faces of a diamond. A single facet does not reflect the sheer brilliance of the entire diamond. However, when all of the facets are considered, the diamond stands out clearly and brilliantly as a precious gem used to create beautiful jewelry. In this same regard, when all of the facets of a mathematics curriculum are considered and put together as a whole, a "polished curriculum" stands out as a guide that will lead to effective teaching and learning.

Common practices that contribute to a lack of coherence in K–12 mathematics curriculum development include the following:

- Using standards that are too broad—lacking specific learning goals that make clear exactly what students should learn and at what grade levels
- Misinterpreting the meaning and intent of state standards that guide the local curriculum
- Failing to draw on professional tools and resources and expertise in using them to guide quality and consistency
- Adopting state standards as the curriculum
- Establishing developmental levels without reference to cognitive research
- Rushing the curriculum development and alignment process without taking the time to study, analyze, reflect, revisit, and revise

Figure 4.8   Topic Coherence and Articulation

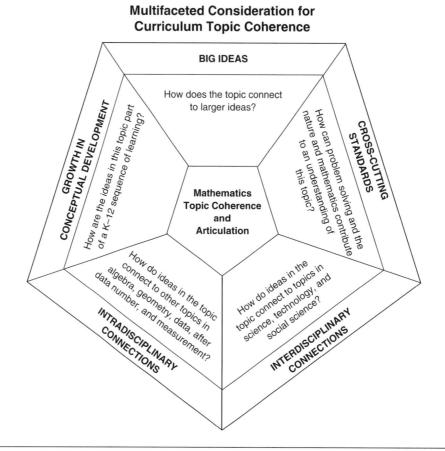

Curriculum developed through these common practices will usually exhibit the following characteristics:

- Too much unnecessary content—a curriculum that mirrors a textbook
- A vague design that can be interpreted and implemented in multiple ways by different teachers
- Topical alignment—lacking depth or focus on the most fundamental ideas and skills in a topic or discipline
  - Procedures and processes delineated and learned in isolation
  - A mix and match of curriculum materials that fail to take prior learning into account
  - A lack of relationships that enable students to connect mathematics with other ideas they are studying

> Identifying relevant topics and studying them carefully can help educators shape a curriculum for all students that does not sacrifice substance and content integrity.

Figure 4.9 provides an example of questions that can be used with CTS to guide development or revision of a mathematics curriculum. Each question includes the section in the CTS Guides that addresses that question.

Figure 4.9   CTS Curriculum Considerations

K–12 Mathematics Curriculum: Questions to Use With CTS to Guide Curriculum Decisions

1. Does your curriculum address all the required state standards (Section VI)?

2. Does your curriculum also address important national standards (Sections III and V)?

3. Does your curriculum reflect a deliberate and careful study of each curricular topic (Sections I–VI)?

4. Does your curriculum break the standards down into *specific* learning goals (Section III)?

5. Is the curriculum organized by relevant mathematical topics (list of CTS guides)?

6. Does the curriculum carefully align instruction to the learning goals (Sections II, III, IV, V)?

7. Does the curriculum provide opportunities to learn and demonstrate learning of concepts and procedures in different contexts (Sections II and V)?

8. Does the curriculum eliminate wasteful repetition (Sections III and V)?

9. Was deliberate thought given to vertical (K–12) articulation that builds from basic fundamental ideas to increasing sophistication (Section V)?

10. Was deliberate thought given to horizontal (across grade level) articulation (Section V)?

11. Does the curriculum make connections across mathematics (i.e., algebra, geometry, data, etc.) each year (Section V)?

12. Does the curriculum take into account and reflect research on developmental, age-appropriate concepts, common misconceptions or difficulties students have with certain concepts and procedures (Section IV)?

13. Are the learning goals carefully sequenced? Was the decision arbitrary or based on prerequisite and connecting ideas (Section V)?

14. Does the curriculum emphasize both conceptual and procedural understanding (Section I and III)?

15. Does the curriculum include problem solving as both a means to learn content and an ability/skill (CTS Guides on Problem Solving and Processes)?

16. Does the curriculum attempt to make connections to contexts outside the discipline such as science, social science, and technology? (Section V)

17. Is process linked to content, as opposed to teaching process skills in isolation (Section II)?

18. Does the curriculum emphasize depth over breadth (Sections I, II, III)?

19. Is the curriculum designed for ALL students (Sections I-VI)?

- **If a beginning teacher were handed the curriculum, how easy would it be to implement it as designed? Is it explicit enough? Is sufficient guidance provided for teachers?**

Note: Sections to refer to in a CTS Study Guide are referenced in the parentheses.

Curriculum committees often spend enormous amounts of time and energy preparing curriculum documents for their school or district that describe what should be taught at each grade level. "The problem with curriculum is often the 'Dusty Binder Effect.' This happens when we create elaborate notebooks full of information about what we should teach. We hand this to new teachers or vaguely refer to the existence of such materials" (Gregory & Kuzmich, 2004, p. 78). Educators can use CTS in their curriculum committees as they work to create short summaries that describe concepts and ideas for teachers and students, instructional considerations, research findings, and links to state standards. As an addition to an existing curriculum guide, these summaries can be helpful in giving teachers a sense of cross-grade curriculum topics. In this way, teachers can see how a topic develops over time without having to search and read through all the pages in their curriculum binders. These summaries can be provided in the front of school or district curriculum guides before each grade level section. Figure 4.10 shows an example of a guide that was created to show how the topic of fractions develops over multiple grade spans.

Curriculum Selection

CTS can be helpful for reviewing and selecting curriculum materials. Results from CTS can be used as a lens to examine instructional materials to determine if they are informed by standards and research. Publishers will usually claim their materials are aligned with national standards, but close examination often reveals only topical alignment, meaning the materials cover the topics that appear in standards but fail to address the important conceptual ideas within that topic. Furthermore, materials often address ideas and skills that go beyond what is developmentally appropriate for students, or they fail to consider common preconceptions or difficulties that students are likely to have. Even a quick review of relevant research will usually make clear whether a material has taken development levels and student conceptions into account.

> Through CTS, educators can apply an initial filter to determine if materials address standards and research beyond a topical match.

Although CTS can help curriculum committees to recognize important qualities of standards-based and research-informed materials, it does not provide a thorough analysis of those materials. Such analysis, an important part of the selection process, can establish the extent of alignment and the instructional quality of the lessons with more rigor and detail (see the Resource Section for information about materials analysis procedures that can be used to extend CTS).

An example of how CTS was used to examine an elementary school mathematics curriculum unit is shown in Figures 4.11 and 4.12. The review committee used the CTS Guide, Addition and Subtraction, to focus its screening of the instructional materials from Math Trailblazers. The committee used a CTS tool called the CTS Content Summary Guide for Instructional Materials Review to summarize findings from each of the CTS sections (I–VI) that would be useful in examining the unit (a worksheet copy of this tool is available in Resource B and on the CTS Web site). The summary includes CTS results such as:

- Adult concepts that could be explained in the teachers' guide
- Content knowledge for students described in the standards
- Instructional strategies and implications described in the standards and research
- Research-identified difficulties and misconceptions
- Important prerequisites to consider
- Connections to other CTS topics

Figure 4.10 Example of a District's Curriculum Clarification Guide to a Topic

Clarification of a Curricular Topic—Fractions

K–12 Content Knowledge from *Benchmarks* and *PSSM*	Related Research on Student Learning	Implications for Teaching Ideas in the Topic	Connections to NH Grade Level Expectations
Grades K–2: • Young students have experiences with simple fractions through everyday situations • Students should know that in sharing and measuring, there is a need to use numbers between whole numbers • Use whole numbers and simple, everyday fractions in ordering, counting, identifying, measuring, and describing things and experiences **Grades 3–5:** • Students should be discussing fractions as parts of a whole and as division • Students should be using various models of halves, thirds, fourths, fifths, sixths, eighths, and tenths • Students should be using area models to order and compare fractions • Students should be able to use a calculator to demonstrate understanding that a fraction can be expressed as a fraction, division and related decimal (1/2 = 1 ÷ 2 = 0.5) • Use fractions and decimals, translating when necessary between decimals and commonly encountered fractions—halves, thirds, fourths, fifths, tenths, and hundredths	• Upper elementary and middle school students may exhibit limited understanding of the meaning of fractional number. (example: 51/4 is the same as 5 + 1/4) • Elementary students may have problems perceiving a fraction as a single quantity, but rather see it as a pair of whole numbers • Elementary and middle school students make several errors when they operate on decimals and fractions. This is due to a lack of essential concepts about decimals and fractions and having memorized procedures that they apply incorrectly • Upper elementary and middle school students have difficulties comparing fractions as they tend to treat the numerator and denominator separately • Most students understand "a/b" as representing a part to whole relationship. However, this understanding becomes problematic when the fraction is either improper or complex • Textbooks or teachers do not discuss the difference between thinking of 3/5 as "three out of five" and thinking of it as "3 one fifths" • An understanding of fractions relies heavily on relationships among measure, multiplication, and division	**Grades K–12:** • School experience with numbers should contribute to the development of 'fraction' sense. Curricula should include the role that fractions play in different activities and the fractions used in problem solving come from actual measurements **Grades K–2:** • Students should develop a preference for numerical comparisons • There should be two kinds of experiences with numbers: The first experience should be with counting (How many?); the second should involve measurement (How much?) **Grades 3–5:** • If students are to learn the meaning of numbers, then what they do must be based on solving problems in which the answers matter and the numbers used are measured quantities • Students are able to make more precise and varied measurements. The realities of numbers based on measurement should be discussed	**Grades K–2:** M(N&O)–1–1 & 2–1Conceptual understanding of positive fractional numbers (benchmarks include 1/2, 1/3, and 1/4) **Grades 3–5:** M(N&O)–3–1 Conceptual understanding of positive fractional numbers (benchmark fractions: 1/2, 1/3, 1/4, 1/6, 1/8) and decimals within a context of money M(N&O)–3–2 Relative magnitude of numbers by comparing or identifying equivalent positive fractional numbers (benchmarks include 1/2, 1/3, 1/4) M(N&O)–4–1 Conceptual understanding of positive fractional numbers (benchmark fractions: 1/2, 1/3, 1/4, 1/5, 1/6, 1/8, or 1/10) and decimals as hundredths within the context of money, or tenths within the context of metric measurements M(N&O)–4–2 Relative magnitude of numbers by ordering, comparing, or identifying equivalent proper positive fractional numbers or decimals M(N&O)–4–3 Describing or illustrating the addition or subtraction of positive fractional numbers with like denominators. M(N&O)–4–4 Accurately solves problems involving addition or subtraction of decimals and positive proper fractions with like denominators M(N&O)–5–1 Conceptual understanding of proper fractions, mixed numbers, and improper fractions (including twelfths and powers of ten), decimals to thousandths, and benchmark percents (10%, 25%, 50%, 75% or 100%) M(N&O)–5–2 Relative magnitude of numbers by ordering, comparing, or identifying equivalent positive fractional numbers, decimals, or benchmark percents, or integers

(Continued)

Figure 4.10 (Continued)

Clarification of a Curricular Topic—Fractions

K–12 Content Knowledge from *Benchmarks* and *PSSM*	Related Research on Student Learning	Implications for Teaching Ideas in the Topic	Connections to NH Grade Level Expectations
Grades 6–8: • Students should work flexibly with fractions, be able to compare and order them, and find their location on the number line • Students should understand the meaning and effect of operations with fractions • Students should be able to select appropriate methods for computing with fractions • Student should be able to develop and analyze algorithms for computing with fractions and develop fluency in their use • Numbers can be written in different forms, depending on how they are being used. How fractions based on measured quantities should be written depends on how precise the measurements are and how precise an answer is needed • The expression a/b can mean different things: a part of size 1/b, a divided by b, or a compared to b **Grades 9–12:** • Use ratios and proportions in appropriate problems	• Students of all ages misunderstand multiplication and division. Commonly held misconceptions include "multiplication always makes larger," and "division always makes smaller" • Upper elementary and middle school students often do not understand that decimal fractions represent concrete objects that can be measured by units, tenths of units, hundredths of units, and so on • Lower middle school students have difficulties understanding the relationship between fractions and decimal numbers. Instruction that focuses on the meaning of fractions and decimals forms a basis on which to build an understanding of the relationship between the two. Instruction that merely shows how to translate between the two forms does not provide a conceptual base for understanding the relationship • Students have little understanding of the value represented by each of the digits of a decimal number or know the value of the number is the sum of the value of its digits when each digit is weighted by its place value • Students of all ages have difficulties choosing the largest or smallest in a set of decimals with different numbers of digits to the right of the decimal point	**Grades 6–8:** • Most important grade span in helping students to develop an understanding of proportionality • Teachers should insist that students think about the numbers they used in solving quantitative problems **Grades 9–12:** • Students should understand the relationship between arithmetic and algebraic fractions	M(N&O)–5–3 Conceptual understanding of operations and meaning of remainder with respect to division of whole numbers. Addition and subtraction of fractions with unlike denominators M(N&O)–5–4 Problem solving using addition or subtraction of proper fractions **Grades 6–8:** M(N&O)–6–1 Conceptual understanding of ratios and rates M(N&O)–6–2 Relative magnitude of numbers by ordering and comparing rational numbers M(N&O)–6–3 Effect on the magnitude of a whole number when multiplying or dividing by whole number, decimal, or fraction. Operations with fractions and decimals M(N&O)–6–4 Problem solving using single or multiple operations on fractions M(N&O)–7–1 Conceptual understanding of percents as a means of comparing the same or different parts of the whole, when the whole varies in magnitude M(N&O)–7–4 Solves problems involving proportional reasoning and percents involving discounts, tax, or tips M(N&O)–7–6 Mentally calculates parts of a number using benchmark percents and related fractions M(N&O)–8–2 Relative magnitude of numbers by ordering or comparing numbers with fractional bases **Grades 9–12:** Grade Span Expectations for Grade 9–12 are currently being developed

A summary review sheet was used to cite preliminary evidence that the unit was standards based and informed by research on student learning. The summary review sheet covers six categories:

- concepts for teacher background information
- students' content knowledge
- instructional implications
- student difficulties and misconceptions
- prerequisite knowledge
- connections to other topics

Each of the six categories was then given a rating indicating the extent to which the material matched the results from the CTS. The comments in each category provide evidence to support the rating and describe the match between a preliminary scan of the material and the CTS summary guide (Figure 4.11).

The summary review points out that Math Trailblazer's Second Grade Unit 11 appears to be well matched to the CTS results in all areas. An example of the summary review is included in Figure 4.12. (A worksheet template for the summary review can be found in Resource B and on the CTS Web site.)

CTS tools are not meant to replace rigorous and thorough curriculum analysis. Instead, they help teachers determine if the development of the instructional material was informed by standards and research. This is a critical part of the process determining whether claims that a material is "standards- and research-based" are valid.

Supporting Curriculum Implementation

Curriculum implementation is the use of new materials—materials that have been selected and organized by a school or district for a particular grade level—for developing student understanding of specific concepts and skills (Loucks-Horsley et al., 2003). Effective implementation involves knowing the key features of a new curriculum program and its materials, knowing the mathematics content in the program, and knowing why the program is presented and sequenced the way it is.

The CTS process can be used before implementing new curricula to improve understanding of the content, the meaning and intent of the curricular goals, and research that may impact student learning. Used in this way, the CTS process builds on and extends information usually presented in a teacher's guide; depending on the program and the teacher's background, the guide may or may not provide adequate support for the teacher. CTS work relevant to implementing new curriculum can be done by an individual teacher or by groups of teachers who are learning how to implement new curricula together. Figure 4.13 shows an example of a customized CTS Guide used by a MathThematics teacher leader, which combines the fractions and the customary measurement topic studies. This study was used to support a group of sixth-grade teachers. The teachers were in their second year of implementing the MathThematics material, but it was their first year incorporating Module 5, Creating Things, a unit that combines topics related to fractions with topics of measurement. The teachers were led through the CTS process with the goal of developing a common understanding of the content, instructional practices, and research and of determining how their CTS findings related to the module.

Figure 4.11 Subtraction CTS Content Summary Guide for Grade 2 Materials Review

---

CTS Content Summary Guide for Instructional Materials Review

CTS Topic: Addition and Subtraction of Whole Numbers   **Grade Level:** K–2

Concepts for Teacher Background Information (Sections I, II)	Students' Content Knowledge (Sections III, V, VI)
• Habits of mind • Computation • Estimation	• There are various meanings of subtraction • Addition and subtraction are inverse relations • A variety of methods, strategies, and tools can be used to subtract, including objects, algorithms, mental computation, estimation, paper and pencil, and calculators • Fluency (efficient and accurate) is needed with basic number combinations for subtraction

Instructional Implications (Sections II, IV)

- There are many meanings of subtraction-compare, take-away, difference, etc.
- Appropriate contexts can arise through student-initiated activities, teacher-created stories, and in many other ways
- Focus on two-digit numbers
- Student explanations of written work, solutions, and mental processes can help teachers gain insight into students' thinking
- Teachers can help students increase their understanding and skill in single-digit addition and subtraction by providing tasks that (a) help them develop the relationships within subtraction and addition combinations and (b) elicit counting on for addition and counting up for subtraction and unknown-addend situations
- Teachers should also encourage students to share the strategies they develop in class discussions; students can develop and refine strategies as they hear other students' descriptions of their thinking about number combinations
- Invented strategies often rely on composing and decomposing numbers
- Teachers need to become familiar with the range of ways that students might think about numbers and work with them to solve problems
- Practice should be purposeful and should focus on developing thinking strategies and a knowledge of number relationships rather than drill isolated facts
- Students should be encouraged to use calculators to aid in problem situations in which computations are more cumbersome or tedious

Research on Student Learning (Sections II, IV)

- Student errors suggest students interpret and treat multidigit numbers as single-digit numbers placed adjacent to each other, rather than using place-value meanings for the digits in different positions
- There is a developmental progression of concepts and skills that students use for addition and subtraction
- With specially designed instruction, second graders are able to understand place value and to add and subtract four-digit numbers more accurately and meaningfully than third graders receiving traditional instruction
- Students who used invented strategies before they learned standard algorithms demonstrated a better knowledge of base-ten concepts and could better extend their knowledge to new situations

Prerequisite Knowledge (Sections III, V)	Connections to Other Topics (Sections II, V)
• Initial understanding of base-ten system • Sense of whole numbers	• Addition • Division • Patterns • Modeling • Data

Figure 4.12 Summary Review of Grade 2 Unit 11 of Math Trailblazers

---

CTS Content Summary Review Match for Instructional Materials

Unit 11: Ways of Subtracting Large Numbers   **Grade Level: 2**

Developer: *Math Trailblazers*

Please rate the summary categories, on a scale of 1 to 5, to the extent that the material showed evidence of matching the findings and recommendations in the CTS Summary Guide: **1** = No evidence; **2** = Minimal evidence; **3** = Sufficient evidence; **4** = Strong evidence; **5** = Strong evidence that includes relevant material that exceeds the CTS findings and recommendations

Concepts for Teacher Background Information   Evidence: 1   2   3   4 $\boxed{5}$

Comments: The TIMS Tutor in the Teacher Implementation Guide addresses the needed content information on computation including both conceptual understanding and procedural knowledge. The types of subtraction problems are referred to as take-away, comparison, part-whole, and missing addend problems with clear reference to the content pedagogy needed to incorporate the problem types in instruction. Connections are made to addition, estimation, basic facts, problem solving, and representation. The materials provide a learning path continuum extending from kindergarten to fifth grade.

Students' Content Knowledge   Evidence: 1   2   3 $\boxed{4}$ 5

Comments: The second-grade unit follows the content aligned to the standards in all four areas indicated. First, the different meanings of subtraction, as indicated above, are embedded in the multiple contexts and problems used throughout. Second, the connection between addition and subtraction is discussed in the Background note and incorporated into fact family cards; "thinking addition" is incorporated as a possible strategy. Third, students use a variety of methods, strategies, and tools including base-ten pieces, estimation, student-developed strategies, calculators, and a standard algorithm. And fourth, fluency of basic number combinations is an expectation and incorporated through fact family cards and the Daily Practice and Problems (DPP).

Instructional Implications   Evidence: 1   2   3 $\boxed{4}$ 5

Comments: The instructional focus of this unit is on subtraction of two-digit numbers. Throughout the unit, the lessons incorporate multiple techniques to allow for student sharing of thought processes as individuals, with partners, in small groups, and as a class. Techniques include journal prompts, activity pages, partner work, whole class sharing, and a seminar. Contexts include money and number of items such as food, children, and baseball cards, and problems are written to address the idea of subtraction as take-away, difference, and compare, although there is no evidence of using the same numbers in multiple contexts. Practice is provided through games and DPP, calculators are used as a tool in several activities, and estimation is incorporated throughout. Practice with basic facts encourages fluency.

Student Difficulties and Misconceptions   Evidence: 1   2 $\boxed{3}$ 4   5

Comments: Although some of the "Content Notes" callouts directly point out possible student difficulties, the Unit Resource Guide is not explicit in its attention to identifying misconceptions at the lesson or unit level. The Teacher Implementation Guide does include all of the CTS summary indicators in the rationale for the structure and instructional methods within Math Trailblazers.

(Continued)

Figure 4.12 (Continued)

Prerequisite Knowledge   Evidence: 1   2   3   4   ⑤

Comments: The Background section of the Unit Resource Guide includes information identifying previous skills and concepts covered in prior Grade 2 units, and the Lesson Guides for Lessons 1 and 4 include information on the curriculum sequence. In addition to these areas, many of the lessons engage students in activating prior knowledge and building on that knowledge. As indicated in the CTS summary of Research on Student Learning, a developmental progression of concepts and skills for subtraction has been identified. The Teacher Implementation Guide aligns this progression with the scope and sequence of the material.

Connections to Other Topics   Evidence: 1   2   3   ④   5

Comments: The multiple strategies instructional method allows for multiple connections to be made to addition concepts and the use of patterns. Modeling of the subtraction process is accomplished through use of base-ten pieces.

CTS can also support curriculum implementation by helping teachers develop a curricular learning path—a one-page summary of the conceptual flow of a curricular unit. *How Students Learn: Mathematics in the Classroom* describes learning paths as "the knowledge networks that appear to be central to children's mathematics learning and achievement, and the ways those networks are built in the normal course of development" (NRC, 2005, p. 258). A study by Remillard and Geist on the use of curriculum materials suggests that "teaching with curriculum guides can be improved as teachers recognize and embrace their role while navigating openings in the curriculum to determine learning paths for students" (NRC, 2005, p. 245). By determining the learning path of a particular curriculum unit, teachers are able to see how the individual activities of the unit form a cohesive whole designed to increase student understanding of a particular topic. A CTS Curricular Learning Path includes the following:

- Broad content and process standards
- Big Ideas
- Concepts and subconcepts
- Specific Ideas
- Facts, definitions, and formulas
- The primary CTS Guide
- Related CTS Guides
- State standards

To create a learning path, teachers begin by selecting the CTS Guide most closely related to the topic of their choice and then conducting a topic study. The teachers compare the topic study results to their curriculum material to extract a set of concepts and ideas common to both the topic study and the curriculum materials. Teachers arrange this focused set of concepts and ideas into the levels of conceptual knowledge, as shown in Figure 4.5. This process produces a focused hierarchy that neatly summarizes the structure of knowledge vital to the chosen curriculum unit. Figure 4.14 shows an example of the summarized structure of knowledge for the Math in Context curricular unit, Triangles and Beyond.

Figure 4.13   Combined CTS Guide for MathThematics Grade 6 Module 5 Implementation

Standards- and Research-Based Study of a Curricular Topic

FRACTIONS AND CUSTOMARY MEASUREMENT

Section and Outcome	Selected Sources and Readings for Study and Reflection Read and examine *related parts* of:
I. Identify Adult Content Knowledge	**IA:** ***Science for All Americans*** ▸ Chapter 9, *Numbers,* pages 130–131 ▸ Chapter 12, *Computation,* pages 187–190; *Estimation,* pages 190–191; *Manipulation and Observation,* page 191
II. Consider Instructional Implications	**IIA:** ***Benchmarks for Science Literacy*** ▸ 9A, *Number,* grade span essay, pages 213 ▸ 12B, *Computation and Estimation,* general essay, pages 288–289 **IIB:** ***NCTM Principles and Standards for School Mathematics*** ▸ Grades 6–8 Number and Operations, pages 215–221 ▸ Grades 6–8 Measurement, pages 241, 243–244
III. Identify Concepts and Specific Ideas	**IIIA:** ***Benchmarks for Science Literacy*** ▸ 9A, *Numbers,* pages 213 ▸ 12B, *Computation and Estimation,* pages 291 **IIIB:** ***NCTM Principles and Standards for School Mathematics*** ▸ Grades 6–8 Number and Operations, page 214 ▸ Grades 6–8 Measurement, page 240
IV. Examine Research on Student Learning	**IVA:** ***Benchmarks for Science Literacy*** ▸ 9A, *Rational Number,* page 350 ▸ 12B, *Operations with Fractions and Decimals, Converting Between Fractions and Decimals,* and *Number Comparison,* pages 358–359 ▸ 12C, *Manipulation and Observation,* page 360 **IVB:** ***NCTM Research Companion:*** Read the *related* research in: ▸ Chapter 7, *Fractions and Multiplicative Reasoning,* pages 95–113
V. Examine Coherency and Articulation	**V.** ***Atlas of Science Literacy:*** Examine the *related* strands and their preceding narratives from the maps: ▸ *Mathematical Processes,* page 27 ▸ *Ratios and Proportionality,* page 119
VI. Clarify State Standards and District Curriculum	**VIA:** ***State Standards:*** Link Sections I–V to learning goals and information from your state standards or frameworks that are informed by the results of the topic study. **VIB:** ***District Curriculum Guide:*** Link Sections I–V to learning goals and information from your district curriculum guide that are informed by the results of the topic study.
Visit www.curriculumtopicstudy.org for updates or supplementary readings, Web sites, and videos.	

Next, the activities in the unit are examined for their flow of ideas, are briefly described, and are grouped into concept clusters. A flowchart layout helps teachers see at a glance, without having to scour numerous pages of teachers' guide notes, how the facts, definitions, and formulas are related to the ideas and concepts and how they form a scaffold throughout the unit. The path shown in Figure 4.15 is an

Figure 4.14 Structure of Knowledge Summary for a CTS Curriculum Storyline

CTS Structure of Conceptual Knowledge Summary for Triangles and Beyond

Content and Process Standards

Geometry
Measurement
Reasoning and proof

Big Ideas

Shapes can be classified by characteristics and properties
Shapes can be transformed
Visualization, spatial reasoning, and geometric modeling can be used to solve problems

Concepts and Subconcepts

Angles
    Obtuse, acute, right, straight
    Interior, exterior, corresponding, vertical

Polygons
    Triangles, quadrilaterals, *n*-gons,

Circles

Transformations and symmetry
    Line of symmetry
    Rotations, reflections, translations

Similarity and congruency

Specific Ideas

Special relationships exist among side and angle measures of the different classes of shapes
Angles and side lengths can be measured indirectly using defining properties and similar figures
Two-dimensional shapes can be constructed using a variety of different tools
Transformations may change a shape's size, position, and/or orientation

Facts, Definitions, and Formulas

Special types of quadrilaterals have specific features
A square is a special case of a rhombus and rectangle
A rhombus and rectangle are special cases of a parallelogram
Diagonals of parallelograms bisect each other
Diagonals of a rhombus are perpendicular
Diagonals are of equal length in rectangles
The corresponding sides of similar shapes are related by a constant scale factor
The corresponding angles of similar shapes are congruent
The ratio of the perimeters of similar figures is the same as the scale factor relating the side lengths, and the ratio of the area is the square of the scale factor
The sum of the measures of the interior angles of a polygon can be found by $(s - 2) * 180$ where s is the number of sides
Angles can be directly measured using a protractor
Side lengths can be directly measured using a ruler
Shapes can be constructed using a tool such as a ruler, straightedge, protractor, compass, etc.
Rotations, reflections, and translations produce congruent shapes but different positions and/or orientations
Dilations (magnifications and contractions) produce similar figures
Rectangles, squares, and isosceles trapezoids have a line of symmetry containing the midpoints of the parallel opposite sides
With rotational symmetry of a regular polygon, a rotation can be found such that the original shape matches the image but its vertices map to different vertices

Figure 4.15 Example of a Curricular Learning Path

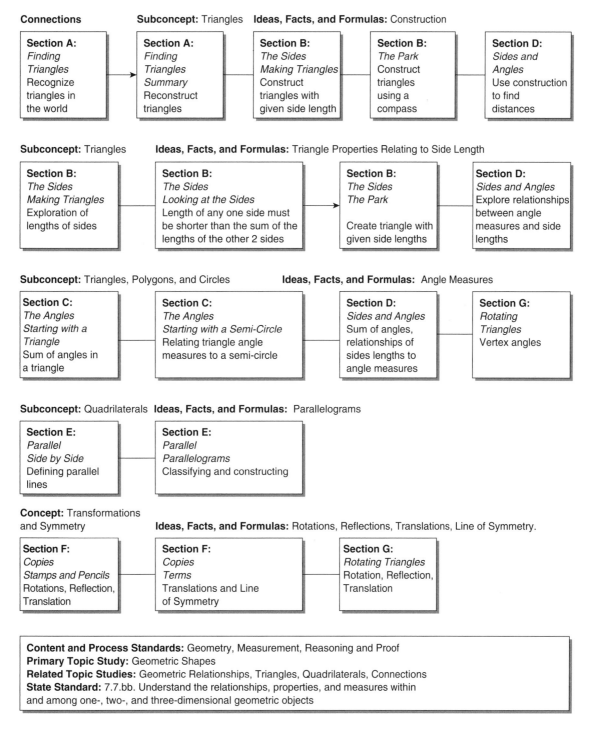

Triangles and Beyond Learning Path Math on Context Unit—Grades 7/8

Connections   **Subconcept:** Triangles   **Ideas, Facts, and Formulas:** Construction

| **Section A:** *Finding Triangles* Recognize triangles in the world | **Section A:** *Finding Triangles Summary* Reconstruct triangles | **Section B:** *The Sides Making Triangles* Construct triangles with given side length | **Section B:** *The Park* Construct triangles using a compass | **Section D:** *Sides and Angles* Use construction to find distances |

Subconcept: Triangles   **Ideas, Facts, and Formulas:** Triangle Properties Relating to Side Length

| **Section B:** *The Sides Making Triangles* Exploration of lengths of sides | **Section B:** *The Sides Looking at the Sides* Length of any one side must be shorter than the sum of the lengths of the other 2 sides | **Section B:** *The Sides The Park* Create triangle with given side lengths | **Section D:** *Sides and Angles* Explore relationships between angle measures and side lengths |

Subconcept: Triangles, Polygons, and Circles   **Ideas, Facts, and Formulas:** Angle Measures

| **Section C:** *The Angles Starting with a Triangle* Sum of angles in a triangle | **Section C:** *The Angles Starting with a Semi-Circle* Relating triangle angle measures to a semi-circle | **Section D:** *Sides and Angles* Sum of angles, relationships of sides lengths to angle measures | **Section G:** *Rotating Triangles* Vertex angles |

Subconcept: Quadrilaterals   **Ideas, Facts, and Formulas:** Parallelograms

| **Section E:** *Parallel Side by Side* Defining parallel lines | **Section E:** *Parallel Parallelograms* Classifying and constructing |

Concept: Transformations and Symmetry   **Ideas, Facts, and Formulas:** Rotations, Reflections, Translations, Line of Symmetry.

| **Section F:** *Copies Stamps and Pencils* Rotations, Reflection, Translation | **Section F:** *Copies Terms* Translations and Line of Symmetry | **Section G:** *Rotating Triangles* Rotation, Reflection, Translation |

> **Content and Process Standards:** Geometry, Measurement, Reasoning and Proof
> **Primary Topic Study:** Geometric Shapes
> **Related Topic Studies:** Geometric Relationships, Triangles, Quadrilaterals, Connections
> **State Standard:** 7.7.bb. Understand the relationships, properties, and measures within and among one-, two-, and three-dimensional geometric objects

example of one curricular sequence a teacher might derive after creating the CTS structure of knowledge summary in Figure 4.14. These learning paths can provide critical support for teachers who are implementing a new curriculum. In addition, the CTS process for development of learning paths can by itself be a powerful professional development experience.

CTS AND INSTRUCTION

CTS can be used to design new lessons, improve instructional delivery of existing lessons, and review and modify lessons to align more closely with standards and research findings. The CTS process supports teachers in improving instruction by helping them do the following:

- Improve their understanding of the content taught
- Focus on important learning goals
- Choose effective strategies and contexts
- Identify developmental issues
- Be aware of potential difficulties and misconceptions their students may have
- Understand how ideas connect and develop over time

Reviewing and Modifying Lessons

Teachers often have lessons that generally work well but could use some improvement. A topic study can provide useful information for improving the lesson's potential to increase student learning. On the other hand, many a lesson simply needs to be "let go," regardless of whether it is a favorite, because it fails to target important ideas or reflect the recommendations of standards and research. How should a teacher judge whether a lesson should be discarded or only needs some modification? Through a study of the topic that matches the lesson, teachers can ask themselves the following questions:

Section I: How well do I understand the content in my lesson or unit? Is there content that may be inaccurate or missing?

Section II: How does this lesson or unit fit into a K–12 perspective? Am I using it in the appropriate context? What are the big ideas?

Section III: Did I miss specific ideas within the learning goals? Are there goals in the national standards that I should be teaching?

Section IV: Is there information in the research that I might need to know to teach the lesson or unit? Is the lesson developmentally appropriate for my students? Are there misconceptions or commonly held ideas students are likely to have?

Section V: How connected are the learning goals in my lesson or unit? What prior knowledge do students need to have? What learning target am I aiming toward? Are there other topics related to this lesson or unit?

Section VI: Does this lesson or unit align with the state standards?

Answers to these questions, based on the CTS results, can be used to analyze, revise, refine, or discard any lesson whether it is a teacher-developed or commercial lesson. By using CTS, teachers can make changes to their instruction that are based on evidence from standards or research.

Developing a Standards- and Research-Based Lesson

Lesson design often starts with interesting activities that are later retrofitted to standards; the CTS lesson design process starts with the specific ideas that are most important for students to learn, then draws on the research base to identify pedagogical strategies and activities that can support students' learning those ideas. Using CTS to design a lesson, teachers can identify:

- The appropriate learning goal(s) for the topic of the lesson
- The research base on common student difficulties and commonly held ideas related to the topic
- Effective instructional strategies to help students learn the concepts and procedures taught in the lesson

> The CTS lesson design process moves instructional design away from starting with an activity to thinking about what an appropriate activity might include based on the concepts and research ideas identified through CTS.

Figure 4.16 describes six steps in developing standards- and research-based lessons using CTS. The CTS Web site provides examples of standards-based and research-based lessons developed by teachers using the CTS lesson design.

CTS and Mathematical Inquiry

Mathematical inquiry, often referred to as investigative mathematics, allows students to examine a problem using various methods, to gather evidence, and, in the process, to develop skills that can be applied to other problems.

> The main purpose of investigative teaching is to make students view mathematics as a way to approach knowledge with a rationally critical attitude and then learn rational thinking through mathematics. The steps include defining a problem, expressing own view about the problem, communicating solution, testing own and others' ideas and hypotheses, and giving own thinking to others for reasonable criticism. This learning theory of mathematics emphasizes that students may make errors during their learning and make progress in the process with errors and rational criticism. (Chen & Lin, 2004, p. 6)

Science for All Americans describes

> using mathematics to express ideas or to solve problems involving at least three phases: (1) representing some aspects of things abstractly, (2) manipulating the abstractions by rules of logic to find new relationships between them, and (3) seeing whether the new relationships say something useful about the original things. (p. 19)

Problem solving, a central feature of learning mathematics, involves using prior knowledge to find a solution without a predetermined strategy or method. The inquiry approach to teaching mathematics requires teachers to have a solid

Figure 4.16   Steps to Developing a CTS Standards- and Research-Based Lesson

CTS Standards and Research-Based Lesson Design

1. IDENTIFY A CORE SET OF LEARNING GOALS

Begin by identifying the important learning goals in your state or local standards. Select a curricular topic or topics these learning goals may be organized around in a unit of instruction. (CTS Section VI)

2. STUDY THE GOALS USING A CTS GUIDE

Carefully study the curricular topic using one or more CTS guides. Keep in mind that some CTS guides can be combined (e.g., combining Algebraic Modeling with Correlation may be useful in designing a lesson on Linear Regression). Take careful notes on specific content knowledge in the learning goals, context, instructional and assessment implications, developmental appropriateness, research-identified difficulties and/or misconceptions, prerequisite student knowledge, and inter-connected and contributing learning goals. (CTS Sections II, III, IV, V)

3. COMPARE RESULTS AND IDENTIFY GAPS AND UNNECESSARY CONTENT

Match the results of your study with your local curriculum guide, existing curriculum materials, and state standards. Modify as needed based on the study results. For example, you might find your curriculum materials contain more content than is necessary or that there are additional important ideas not mentioned in your state standards that provide coherency for the development of a lesson. (CTS Sections III and VI)

4. IDENTIFY THE INSTRUCTIONAL APPROACH

Decide whether you are going to modify an existing lesson or set of lessons or create a new lesson(s). Determine what kinds of experiences or contexts relate to the topic that can be used to develop student understanding. (CTS Sections II, and IV)

5. DESIGN INSTRUCTION USING KNOWLEDGE OF EFFECTIVE TEACHING AND LEARNING

Incorporate pedagogical practices, informed by standards or research, that will help students learn the ideas. No matter how well aligned the content of a lesson is, there is no assurance that students will understand the ideas without appropriate instructional strategies. Be sure to include opportunities to elicit students' existing ideas, including potential difficulties and/or misconceptions, and probe for conceptual understanding throughout the lesson. (CTS Sections II and IV)

6. TRY OUT THE LESSON AND MODIFY AS NEEDED

Try the lesson, making careful notes of where students are having difficulty and also the strengths of the lesson. Record interesting ideas and statements from students for later reference. Collect student work. Make modifications as needed. Have others try the lesson and suggest changes as needed.

7. "PUBLISH" YOUR LESSON

Create a description to go with a write up of your lesson that could be shared with others for the purpose of making teaching practice public. Include findings from the CTS, including the content background, alignment to the learning goals in the topic, your thinking that went into the lesson design, pedagogical strategies, and descriptions of what students would be doing. Include student work if available.

understanding of the base knowledge students need to build new understandings through problem solving. "Teachers also need to know how their own students think about mathematical problems and how most students of similar age and experience are likely to solve problems" (Hiebert, 1997, p. 35). Through this understanding, teachers can define learning targets for their students, choose appropriate problems, and implement appropriate inquiry-based activities to move their students along the described learning continuum.

"Processes can be learned within a content standard, and content can be learned within a process standard," (NCTM, 2000, p. 30). To illuminate the relationship between process and content, CTS includes guides on important process-skill topics that can help teachers understand what skills can and should be embedded within inquiry-based instruction. CTS helps teachers to create rich investigative experiences in which students construct understanding through the use of methods such as, but not limited to, generalization, conjecture, and inference.

> CTS helps move the teaching of mathematics from disconnected process skills and concepts to a richer inquiry experience that empowers students to construct their own mathematical ideas and utilize deep mathematical thinking.

To improve understanding about how important process skills can be used in a lesson, a content-oriented CTS Guide and a process-oriented CTS Guide can be studied together. For example, an intermediate teacher may use the Perimeter, Area, and Volume guide along with the Conjecture, Proof, and Justification guide to design a series of problems in which students collect data, find a pattern, and generalize a formula for finding the area of a rectangle (when given the dimensions). Students learn about indirect measurement while concurrently developing the ability to accept or refute generalizations.

The following general questions can be used to gather information and reflect on the readings from the sections of the CTS Guides that focus on different aspects of process skills, from the CTS category of Problem Solving and Processes, which could be used with any content topic.

Section II: What are the central skills associated with this Problem Solving and Processes topic (i.e., the skills of generalizing, problem solving, modeling, reasoning, etc.)? Why is it important for students to develop these process skills? What are the implications for instruction and assessment? How will my instruction help students see investigation as an important component of learning new content?

Section III: What are the specific process skills students should be proficient in using? How will I include these skills in the design of the lesson?

Section IV: What are the difficulties students might encounter or the developmental implications identified for this process skill? How will I design and monitor their experience to help them work through these difficulties?

Section V: How do these particular process skills build over time? Have my students had previous opportunities to use these skills? What precursor skills do I need to consider as I plan the lesson?

Section VI: What do my state standards identify as important skills related to this Problem Solving and Processes topic? How can I use my CTS findings to design instruction that ensures my students have the opportunity to learn and demonstrate these standards?

Time for Using CTS in Instructional Planning

Initially, the time it takes to do both CTS and lesson planning may appear daunting. In the long run, however, CTS saves time by focusing instruction clearly on learning goals and understandings about how students learn. Designing lessons that fail to meet their target is both frustrating and time consuming. Lessons designed through the CTS process are more likely to be effective because they make effective and explicit use of the guidance and insights in standards and research. Over time, teachers who use CTS describe it as a naturally integrated process for lesson planning, and they remark that it can save them the time and frustration of the backfilling that is needed when instruction fails to reach all students.

CTS AND ASSESSMENT

Teachers, districts, states, and federal agencies use a variety of assessment practices and instruments to probe student learning. Despite differences in assessment policies, programs, and protocols for aligning assessments to standards, one essential step can ensure that assessment is used effectively in mathematics. That essential step is a thorough study of both the content in the learning goal to be assessed and the research on student learning related to that content. If teachers do not thoroughly understand the content, learning goals, and cognitive aspects of the topics they teach, they will usually fail to assess ideas appropriately or use assessment results effectively.

> CTS provides tools and processes to help mathematics teachers better assess student learning and become informed consumers of assessment data.

CTS can be used to think about both formative and summative assessment. The first step in linking CTS to assessment is to define the purpose of the assessment and your stage in the assessment process. The three stages of the assessment process are described below:

Diagnostic Stage: What existing ideas do your students have about the topic? Sections III, IV, and VI in the CTS Guides are used to identify the concepts and specific ideas in the topic and examine research findings on students' conceptions about the topic. Teachers can use this information to investigate their own students' ideas and compare them to the research findings. Diagnostic assessment is formative assessment when the information is used to inform instruction and monitor students' conceptual change.

Formative Stage: How are your students building conceptual understanding or skills? What is their understanding at different points during the instruction? What different paths do you need to direct them toward in order to lead them toward the target? CTS Sections II and IV point out the difficulties students might encounter and alternative ideas that may need to be monitored. Section V indicates steps along the way that may need to be revisited or gaps that should be filled.

Summative Stage: Can students demonstrate their achievement of the learning goals after instruction? Are they able to apply what they learn in new contexts, or is their understanding limited to the context in which they learned the specific ideas? CTS Sections III, V, and VI are used to do the following:

- Clarify the specific knowledge and skills intended by a learning goal
- Design an assessment that is rigorously aligned to a specific idea
- Identify contexts and connections used to demonstrate in-depth understanding in keeping with the integrity of the discipline of mathematics
- Ensure that what an assessment claims to measure is actually measured

Designing Assessment Probes

Mathematics teachers need to use a variety of classroom formative assessments that uncover the student preconceptions that impact their mathematical thinking. CTS refers to this type of assessment instrument as a *probe*, because it probes for students' current understanding about a topic or concept. Probes can also monitor changes in students' thinking through the course of a unit of instruction. Thus, a probe differs from a typical quiz or test item in its purpose—it is intended to uncover student preconceptions or difficulties so that subsequent instruction can address them.

Many resources exist to help educators design assessments to measure student learning. However, there are fewer resources that can help educators design research-based assessments to identify misconceptions and areas of difficulty prior to instruction.

A probe presents students with a problem, then asks them to select a response and explain their reasoning. Analysis of a class set of student responses and explanations provides insight into students' current understanding (or misunderstanding) about the topics or concepts.

Section IV of the CTS Guides provides the research background for developing an assessment probe. This research suggests the kinds of misconceptions or difficulties that students in any particular class may have. The probe is designed so that student responses reveal whether they hold preconceptions or misunderstandings similar to those identified in the research. Ideally, student responses should also reveal any other student preconceptions that have not been identified in the research. Of course, to gather this information, student responses need to be carefully studied and analyzed, not simply marked as right or wrong. With both the analysis of students' responses to the probe and the research as background, a teacher can then design a unit of instruction that builds on students' current ideas and targets their preconceptions in ways that encourage conceptual change and achievement of the learning goal. This process of designing assessment probes is consistent with research on teaching and learning:

> The roles for assessment must be expanded beyond the traditional concept of testing. The use of frequent formative assessment helps make students' thinking visible to themselves, their peers, and their teacher. This provides feedback that can guide modification and refinement in thinking. (Bransford et al., 2000, p. 19)

Seven steps support the design of an effective probe:

Step 1: Identify the CTS Guide(s) that match the topic you plan to teach. You may decide you need to study only a subtopic within a CTS Guide, rather than the entire topic.

Step 2: Examine Sections III, V, and VI from the CTS Guide. Identify and record the mathematical concepts in the topic or subtopic that are related to your instructional unit. Beneath these concepts, list the specific ideas from national, state, or district standards, including any prerequisite knowledge or related learning goals.

Step 3: Examine Section IV and the narrative research notes in Section V. Select the specific concept and ideas you plan to address with the probe you are designing. Identify the relevant research findings.

Step 4: Focus on a concept or a specific idea and the related research findings. Based on the research findings, choose the type of probe format that lends itself to the situation. *Justified selected response* or *justified lists* are good formats for probes that specifically target research-identified areas of difficulty (see Figure 4.18 for an example of a justified selected response).

Step 5: Develop the stem (the prompt), key (correct response), and distracters (incorrect responses derived from research findings) that match the developmental level of your students. Suggestions for selected response stems include contrasting opposing views and asking for a prediction. Justified lists begin with a statement about a mathematical idea followed by several examples; students select the example that represents the idea or matches the statement. Justified lists are useful in determining whether students can transfer ideas to other contexts beyond those in which they learned the ideas.

Step 6: Share your assessment probe(s) with colleagues for constructive feedback, pilot with students, and modify as needed.

Step 7: Administer the assessment probe and analyze student data. What do the responses tell you about correct ideas, misconceptions, or incorrect ideas your students have? What overall patterns do you see across different student responses? What are the implications for your curriculum and instruction? What will you do to address these ideas your students have? What else would you like to know?

Figure 4.17 is an example of an assessment probe that was developed using this process.

Prior to developing this probe, Sections III and IV in the CTS Guide, Probability, were examined. The research in Section IV reveals that many students focus on the absolute size when solving probability problems rather than the relative size of a given outcome. Research points to a continuum of probabilistic thinking including subjective, transitional, informal quantitative, and numerical. Many upper elementary and middle school students, as well as some high school students, have not advanced from the transitional stage. Figure 4.18 summarizes the research and conceptual ideas related to finding the probability of a simple event.

The shaded information was used as the focus in the development of a probe, in the form of a justified selected response. The probe is used to find out whether students apply misconceptions, intuitive ideas, or other faulty reasoning identified in the research or whether they correctly apply the ratio concept.

Figure 4.17 Assessment Probe

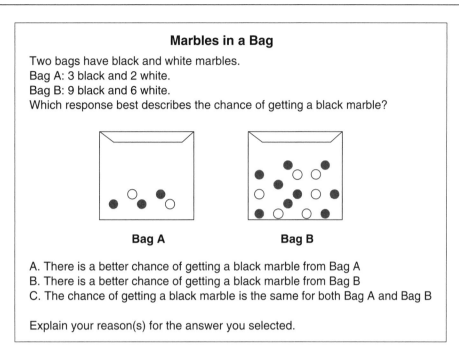

Marbles in a Bag

Two bags have black and white marbles.
Bag A: 3 black and 2 white.
Bag B: 9 black and 6 white.
Which response best describes the chance of getting a black marble?

Bag A   **Bag B**

A. There is a better chance of getting a black marble from Bag A
B. There is a better chance of getting a black marble from Bag B
C. The chance of getting a black marble is the same for both Bag A and Bag B

Explain your reason(s) for the answer you selected.

Developing Culminating Performances

CTS can be used to develop rich, culminating performance tasks. Resources such as *Understanding by Design* (Wiggins & McTighe, 1998) provide guidance to educators on how to design performance tasks that provide evidence of student understanding. CTS complements these resources by providing a front-end process to study the learning goals and research in the topic and to ensure that the performance task aligns with the meaning and intent of the learning goal and takes the relevant research into account.

> Good teacher-designed classroom assessments begin with instructional goals and a consideration of students' opportunities to learn. CTS Sections II and III address each of these critical assessment factors.

The example in Figure 4.19 shows how the CTS Guides, Symbolic Representation and Proof and Justification, were used to develop a classroom performance task, called ""Purchasing CDs," that targets ideas about the relationship between given quantities and ways to represent these relationships using words, symbols, tables, and graphs. The teacher who developed the task did a full topic study prior to development. The teacher's notes, which follow, demonstrate how the results of the study were used to inform the task development and the descriptions of the task and the extent to which it aligns with the learning goals (see Figure 4.20).

Whether teachers are using a culminating classroom performance task or assessments that are part of a school or district program for measuring student achievement and accountability, it is essential that they combine their assessment knowledge with an understanding of the content knowledge and skills to be assessed. CTS can help teachers develop the knowledge they need to ensure that assessments reflect mathematics as a body of knowledge and skills and are substantively aligned to learning goals.

Figure 4.18 Mapping Concepts and Ideas in a Topic to Research Findings, Topic: Probability (Simple Events)

Topic: Probability (Simple Events)	
Concepts and Ideas	**Research Findings**
• Events can be described in terms of being more or less likely, impossible, or certain. (*BSL,* 3–5, page 228) • Probability is the measure of the likelihood of an event and can be represented by a number from 0 to 1. (*PPSM,* 3–5, page 176) • Understand that 0 represents the probability of an impossible event and 1 represents the probability of a certain event. (PSSM, 3–5, page 181) • Probabilities are ratios and can be expressed as fractions, percentages, or odds. (*BSL,* 6–8, page 229) • Methods such as organized lists, tree diagrams, and area models are helpful in finding the number of possible outcomes. (*PSSM,* 6–8, pages 254–255) • The theoretical probability of a simple event can be found using the ratio of the number of favorable outcomes/total possible outcomes (*BSL,* 6–8, page 229) • The probability of an outcome can be tested with simple experiments and simulations. (*PSSM,* 6–8, pages 254–255) • The relative frequency (experimental probability) can be computed using data generated from an experiment or simulation. (*PSSM,* 6–8, pages 254–255) • The experimental and theoretical probability of an event should be compared with discrepancies between predictions and outcomes from a large and representative sample taken seriously. (*PSSM,* 6–8, pages 254–255)	**Understandings of Probability** (*Research Companion,* pages 216–223) • Lack of understanding of ratio leads to difficulties in understanding of chance. • Students tend to focus on absolute rather than relative size • Although young children do not have a complete understanding of ratio, they have some intuitions of chance and randomness • A continuum of probabilistic thinking includes subjective, transitional, informal quantitative and numerical levels. • Third grade (approx.) is an appropriate place to begin systematic instruction. • "Equiprobability" is the notion that all outcomes are equally likely disregarding relative and absolute size • The outcome approach is defined as the misconception of predicting the outcome of an experiment rather than what is likely to occur. Typical responses to questions are "anything can happen" • Intuitive reasoning may lead to incorrect responses. Categories include representativeness and availability • Wording of task may influence reasoning • NAEP results show 4th and 8th graders have difficulty with tasks involving probability as a ratio of "m chances out of n" but not with "1 chance out of n" • Increased understanding of sample space stems from multiple opportunities to determine & discuss possible outcomes and predict and test using simple experiments **Uncertainty** (*BSL,* Chapter 15, page 353) • Upper elementary students can give correct examples for certain, possible, and impossible events, but have difficulties calculating the probability of independent and dependent events. • Upper elementary students create "part to part" rather than "part to whole" relationships.

Note: The shaded information was used as the focus in the development of a probe in the form of a justified selected response.

Figure 4.19 Purchasing CDs Task

Purchasing CDs

You and your friend, Michele, each have a large collection of CDs. You both have decided to add to your collections by joining a CD club. You are trying to figure out which club offers the best deal.

Your Task:

Select two CD clubs to research.

1. Create a single graph that represents the cost of CDs for each club.

2. Look for patterns in the table and graph that would help you to calculate the cost for any number of CDs ordered for each club. Write a rule, using words, that explains how to calculate the total cost for each club for any given number of CDs.

3. Use symbols to write your rule for each club as an equation.

4. Represent your rule in another way. Justify your choice of representation.

5. Is the relationship between the number of CDs ordered and the total cost easier to see in your tables, your equations, or your graph? Explain your reasoning.

Present your findings to a classmate. Justify your selection based on the information from your research. Will the same club always be the cheapest? Explain when this club might not be the best choice for an individual. Refer to your table, graphs, or equations to support your explanations.

CTS AND PRESERVICE AND NOVICE TEACHER SUPPORT

Preservice programs are designed to ensure that teachers have the knowledge and skills they need to be effective when they enter the classroom. Preservice mathematics methods courses often both engage preservice teachers in the process of mathematics as learners and require them to develop sample lessons for teaching mathematics concepts. CTS can enhance these activities by helping preservice teachers learn what content is important to focus on, what is appropriate for students to learn at different grade levels, and what to look for to spot common student misconceptions. Some preservice teachers even have the opportunity to teach their sample lesson to their peers. In these cases, students in the class can use CTS to establish criteria for observing the sample lesson and for making suggestions on how to enhance it. CTS can also help preservice teachers prepare for student teaching by providing them with the knowledge base about the link between national and state standards they will need to address the standards in the particular context in which they are teaching.

> Introducing preservice students to the CTS process will give them a lifeline they can use when they have to teach unfamiliar content or when they want to ensure that they are addressing the key concepts in the curriculum in a developmentally appropriate way.

As beginning teachers enter the workforce, they must face numerous challenges simultaneously. They need to learn how to manage their classroom, figure out how to navigate the policies and procedures in their new school, and get to know the students and their families. As they settle into teaching mathematics, they encounter questions about what to teach, how to reach students who are struggling, and how

Figure 4.20   CTS-Informed Teacher's Notes for "Purchasing CDs" Performance Task

---

Task Summary: This task requires students to explore the relationship between given quantities and represent these relationships using words, symbols, tables, and graphs. Students are asked to research two different clubs and determine which club would be the cheapest to join and if this would always be the best club to join. Students are given the scenario to develop a table, determine the pattern, and represent the pattern using symbolic representation. This task may be used as a culminating assessment, given prior and appropriate instructional opportunities.

Grade Level: Grades 6 to 8

Time Required: Approximately two class periods of 45 to 60 minutes each.

Materials Needed: Graph paper, calculator (graphing calculator is appropriate if students have access), access to Internet or fliers to research CD/DVD clubs; students should also have access to manipulative materials.

CTS Guides Used to Inform Task Development: Symbolic Representation and Conjecture, Proof, and Justification

CTS Section VI: Alignment to State Standards: Grades 5 to 8 Maine *Learning Results Standards G and J*

Patterns, Relations, Functions G1. *Describe and represent relationships with tables, graphs, and equations.* Description of alignment: Students describe a relationship between quantities and represent the identified relationship in a table, graph, and equation.

Mathematical Reasoning J1. *Support reasoning by using models, known facts, properties, and relationships.* Description of alignment: Students support their conclusions using models and relationships and consider other possible conclusions.

CTS Section III: Underlying Concepts, Ideas, and Skills in National Standards:

- The 6-8 NCTM algebra standards state that all students should be able to represent, analyze, and generalize a variety of patterns. Students should be able to represent these patterns in tables, graphs, words, and symbolic rules, if possible. Students should be able to determine the strengths and limitations of each of the representations.
- The 6-8 NCTM representation standards state that all students should become familiar with a range of representations for linear relationships including tables, graphs, and equations. Students should be able to use these representations flexibly and appropriately and be able to move easily from one to another. Students should also be able to recognize equivalent forms including equivalent symbolic expressions that represent the same relationship.
- The 6-8 NCTM reasoning and proof standards state that all students should deepen their evaluations of their assertions and conjectures. Students should be able to develop arguments to support their conclusions as well as consider the limitations of their reasoning.
- The *Benchmarks for Science Literacy* (AAAS, 1993, 9B, Grades 6 to 8) describe the ways graphs can show a variety of relationships. Students determine relationships among quantities and represent them as symbols and simple equations extracted from tables and graphs.
- The *Benchmarks for Science Literacy* (9E, 12E, Grades 6 to 8) states that a general rule may be used to explain how something works by summarizing observations, but there is a tendency to overgeneralize based on a few observations. There may be more than one good way to interpret a set of findings.

CTS Sections II and IV: Instructional Implications and Research on Learning:

- Students have difficulties understanding the many uses of variables. Students tend to use letters as a means of shorthand without an understanding of literal symbols. Students need to practice using symbols to record ideas in many different situations and experiences. Students' understanding moves from variables as a placeholder for a number, to variables represented in equations and mathematical properties, to the use of variables in formulas.
- Students need to have many experiences in translating from a graph to an equation. Moving from one representation (table, graph, equation) to another proves to be difficult for many students. Students need to consider all forms of representation and determine which form will best communicate the ideas in any given situation. Students need many opportunities to compare and contrast different representations.
- Students need to have opportunities to justify their thinking using a variety of evidence, not just a focus on procedures and correct answers. Reasoning should be purposeful and communicate validity to others.

to best assess learning. They realize that all students learn differently, and as a result, they need to develop a repertoire of strategies to reach all learners. Ideally, a mentor will help them design and revise lessons, interpret what is happening in the classroom, and develop their pedagogical content knowledge. But even with effective preservice training and a mentor at their side, this is a challenging time for any teacher.

CTS can play a key role for beginning teachers. CTS can provide just-in-time critical guidance from high-quality professional resources, and new teachers can use the CTS process to fit their decisions into the context of their local and state curriculum framework. Beginning teachers can also use the resources provided by CTS to communicate with their supervisors about their instructional choices. Many beginning teachers rarely get support that is highly focused on teaching mathematics content. Their mentors often have little or no background in mathematics themselves. While such discipline-generic support can help with general teaching skills, beginning teachers are left on their own with regard to content and the appropriate pedagogical strategies specific to that content. In these cases, the beginning teacher and mentor can use CTS to learn more about the content and how to teach it. Of course, teachers also need to communicate with parents about what students are expected to know and how they will be assessed.

> By using CTS, beginning teachers can point to highly respected professional resources as the research-backed rationale for their curricular, instructional, and assessment practices.

CTS AND LEADERSHIP DEVELOPMENT

In our work supporting the development of educational leaders, we have found that principals, teacher leaders, professional developers, and others who are leading reform initiatives in mathematics can benefit from a deeper understanding of the standards and research that inform the many topics taught in K through 12. Even when those leaders have a background in mathematics, they may not know what content is most important for students at different grade levels to know and be able to use. And they may not understand what content and pedagogical strategies are appropriate at different grade levels. Yet, they are often in the positions that demand this kind of background—observing teachers, modeling instruction, leading professional development, selecting curriculum, choosing assessments, and shaping policy.

> Whether leaders are involved in school, regional, or state committee work; advisory roles; staff development; standards setting and review; or other mathematics reform related efforts, they can use CTS as a tool to develop a common core of understanding within the various groups they support.

Section I of the CTS Guides provides important information for school and district leaders. The resources in that section describe what every mathematically literate adult should know by the end of their K–12 experience. Educational leadership must strive to understand these concepts themselves and ensure that their school programs are designed to lead to this vision of mathematical literacy. Furthermore, leaders must understand the "steps along the way" to mathematical literacy that are articulated in the resources used for Sections III and V.

Teachers who have assumed leadership positions—mentors, coaches, curriculum committee leaders, and professional developers—can benefit from using CTS as part of their leadership development. Through CTS, they can become leaders who understand the true implications of the overused phrase "standards- and research-based." In their work, they can engage teachers in looking at the standards and research to inform decisions and choices, rather than simply offering their own opinion or dictums. Through CTS, they learn how to teach others what it means to thoughtfully and knowledgeably apply standards and research to classroom practice.

CTS AND PROFESSIONAL DEVELOPMENT

CTS is both a stand-alone professional development strategy and a valuable addition to most other professional development programs and strategies. As an example of a stand-alone strategy, a group of teachers who teach algebra could use their professional development time to work together using the CTS Guide, Patterns, Relations, and Functions. Their purpose may be to increase their knowledge of when to teach certain concepts, to identify necessary prerequisites and connections to other topics, or to become aware of common student misconceptions.

> CTS fits seamlessly into a variety of professional development strategies. It can ensure that professional development sessions are content driven and make explicit and effective use of standards and research.

Embedding CTS in a Variety of Professional Development Strategies

In our work with teachers, schools, and teacher enhancement and leadership projects, we have used CTS with study groups, case discussions, examination of student work and thinking, lesson study, coaching and mentoring, and demonstration lessons and workshops. For each of these strategies, CTS focused the participants' learning experience on mathematics content, standards, and research. Each professional development strategy is described briefly below.

Study Groups

One purpose of study groups is to examine and solve problems of teaching and learning. Study groups focus on a particular learning need of their students. Often these needs are identified through data, such as state or local assessment results. These needs may relate to difficult concepts in the curriculum or to processes of mathematics with which students commonly struggle. For example, one study group, after analyzing its state test, found their eighth-grade students were having difficulty with ideas in the patterns, relations, and functions cluster. After using CTS to study the topic, they discussed *rate of change* as a big idea that was important across the grade spans and the more specific idea of a *linear rate of change* as important within the Grade 6–8 span. After reviewing the collection of released items from the state test, the group identified items related to this idea and gave them to every seventh- and eighth-grade student so they could analyze trends in student thinking and compare them to findings from the research. With one particular rate problem, the group found that the majority of students were not using a straightedge to draw a trend line but were instead using an extrapolated data point to find the rate, resulting in an incorrect calculation. After identifying this and other areas of concern, the group reviewed CTS findings and discussed instructional implications that members of the study group needed to consider.

Using CTS in a study group context helps teachers grapple with substantive content and issues related to teaching and learning mathematics. The CTS Guide provides a focal point to delve deeply into a topic. "Substantive work challenges and excites teachers. Developing deeper understanding and grappling puts study groups in a context that accelerates learning for teachers and, as a result, accelerates learning for students" (Murphy & Lick, 2001, p. 19). The use of CTS provides a safe, nonjudgmental way in which teachers can have deep conversations about teaching and learning, drawing on a common language and knowledge base. CTS gives teachers a tool to turn to when they inquire into difficult questions that matter to them in the particular context in which they teach.

> CTS helps move the study group conversations from being convivial to making shared meaning through discourse and dialogue.

Case Discussions

There are numerous resources, both text and video, that use mathematical case discussions as a strategy for professional development. In these sessions, teachers read and then discuss the cases—often depicting difficult topics to learn or dilemmas in the classroom. When CTS is used with case studies, teachers read the case or view the video and have a short discussion. They then conduct a topic study on the content in the case, and the results of the study are used to extend and enrich the case discussion, informed by standards and research on the topic.

For example, in preparation for a case discussion, Take One-Third (Barnett, Goldenstein, & Jackson, 1994), we used CTS to ground conversations in research. The "Take One-Third" case focuses on using a representation to show the results of taking one third of one and one third. The participants first worked on the problem individually, read the case, and then discussed only facts about the case. Before engaging the issues related to the case, participants used the CTS Guide on fractions, decimals, and percents, which allowed the group to get insights from the research and standards related to the topic. After the study, discussions about specific issues of the case were resumed, using information gleaned from the study to guide conversations.

By using CTS as a bridge between the case and discussions about the case, participants' increased their content knowledge and their conversations were grounded in effective practices, rather than only the opinions or idiosyncratic practices of the participants.

Curriculum Selection and Implementation

Groups of teachers engaging in curriculum selection and implementation processes present an extensive opportunity to use CTS. Groups selecting curriculum and instructional materials want to choose those materials that align best with both their state or local standards and the research. As committees review materials, CTS can guide them to assess how well the material addresses the learning goals deemed important in the standards. Figures 4.11 and 4.12 show examples of how CTS can be used to inform the selection of curriculum that is informed by standards and research. As the group moves into implementation of the new curriculum, committee members can continue to use CTS; for example, when they encounter areas of student confusion, they can use the process to learn what research on student learning says about students' common misunderstandings about the topic. Professional developers can use existing CTS Guides to develop customized CTS Guides to accompany specific curriculum programs for the purposes of understanding the content and pedagogy during unit implementation (Figure 4.13). CTS-developed learning paths (Figure 4.15) can also be used in supporting curriculum implementation.

> CTS provides the background information and evidence teachers need to embrace and maintain the fidelity of the curriculum they are using.

The goal of curriculum implementation as a professional development strategy is not only for teachers to implement a new mathematics curriculum but also for them to strengthen their knowledge of the mathematics content and pedagogy in the curriculum (Loucks-Horsley et al., 2003). Using the results of CTS as a lens in which to examine the instructional sequence and pedagogical strategies in the material, coupled with furthering an understanding of the content, provides a much richer experience than focusing on the curriculum material alone. In our experience, CTS helps teachers stay true to teaching the material as it is designed rather than picking their favorite sections and omitting others.

Workshops, Courses, Institutes, and Seminars

"Workshops, courses, institutes, and seminars are structured opportunities for educators to learn from facilitators or leaders with specialized expertise as well as from peers" (Loucks-Horsley et al., 2003, p. 118). In these vehicles and structures, especially those focused on increasing teachers' content and pedagogical content knowledge, CTS is used to help teachers see the connection between the new learnings they gain in the workshop, seminar, institute, or course and ways to translate these learnings into actions and knowledge they can use to improve teaching and learning. Whether the workshop is a hands-on experience or learning about a new instructional technique, CTS can provide the specific content focus that is sometimes missing.

Examination of Student Work and Thinking

More and more teachers are engaged in examining student work and thinking as part of their ongoing professional development. But what should teachers look for when examining student work or listening to students' thinking in the classroom?

The CTS Guide's Sections III, Key Concepts and Ideas, and Section IV, Research on Student Learning, are especially helpful in this context. Conversations about stu-

> CTS can alert teachers to the kinds of preconceptions and patterns of thought that they should be aware of when examining student work and thinking.

dent work are much richer when participants have a common understanding of the content in the learning goals and the research related to common student difficulties and misconceptions. After examining their students' work in light of the research, teachers often find their own students have the same common difficulties and misconceptions pointed out in the research. Sometimes teachers find they themselves hold ideas similar to those the research on student learning identifies. When teachers harbor similar misconceptions, it is almost impossible to reliably score student work or use student thinking as the basis for forming instruction. CTS helps teachers identify the ideas that are problematic for both students and themselves and to clarify these ideas before examining student work and thinking.

The process of developing CTS assessment probes (Figure 4.17) can stimulate discussions about student thinking in a particular topic. The use of those probes moves the discussion from the common problems identified in the research to the actual misconceptions and difficulties teachers face with their own students. In a larger sense, these activities also shift the emphasis solely from scoring student work to learning about students' thinking for the purpose of improving teaching and learning.

Lesson Study

Lesson study is a predominant form of professional development in Japan. In the lesson study cycle, teachers come together as a collaborative group, using a structured protocol, to identify goals for student learning; plan and develop a "research lesson" designed to help students reach the identified goals; and observe and discuss the lesson (Lewis, 2002). Lesson study in the United States uses or adapts this Japanese strategy. A key feature of lesson study is studying a lesson that is directly related to the national, state, or local standards that drive student learning goals. As a "research lesson," the lesson is designed to provide insight into student learning. The CTS process provides a way for lesson study teachers to study what standards and research say about the key ideas in the topic of the lesson, including student difficulties and misconceptions to be aware of, and to use this information to develop their lesson.

> CTS grounds lesson study teachers in a common knowledge base and provides a reference point for discussing the impact of the lesson on student learning.

Mentoring, Coaching, and Demonstration Lessons

Mentoring, coaching, and demonstration lessons often involve planning lessons, observing novice or veteran teachers teach the lessons, and then discussing how they can be improved. Using CTS as part of these professional development strategies—especially in the lesson planning and debriefing processes—helps to keep the discussion focused on the standards and the teaching, rather than on the teacher. The CTS tools and strategies help mentors and coaches to assist novice teachers in becoming more intentional about planning instruction that targets explicit learning goals and misconceptions and using formative assessment strategies to monitor students' thinking over the course of an instructional sequence. The CTS tools also help mentors and coaches become more knowledgeable about areas of mathematics that they may be less familiar with so they are better prepared to assist a novice colleague.

> Mentoring and coaching that only address survival skills and general pedagogy do not support teachers in becoming better teachers of mathematics. CTS provides the tools mentors and coaches need to focus deeply on content and pedagogical content knowledge.

Facilitating Professional Development

More and more teachers want learning opportunities that focus directly on their practice—the content they teach and how to best teach it. In addition, professional developers are seeking ways to improve their own knowledge of areas of mathematics they may be less familiar with and to incorporate content-focused tools, like CTS, into their programs. CTS is a powerful tool for making professional development more relevant to teachers' needs. The third book in this series will be designed for professional developers, teacher leaders, and preservice educators who facilitate the use of CTS. The book will contain guiding principles, processes, strategies, tools, and vignettes for using CTS with the 18 professional development strategies described in *Designing Professional Development for Teachers of Science and Mathematics* (Loucks-Horsley et al., 2003); university preservice education courses; and curriculum, instruction, and assessment committee work.

5

Images From Practice

Curriculum Topic Study (CTS) Vignettes

**Vignette 1: A Team of Primary Teachers
Uses CTS to Clarify District Curriculum
Goals for Addition and Subtraction Concepts**

A traditional mathematics program for the primary grades emphasizes numbers and operations, with a significant amount of classroom time devoted to addition and subtraction. Due to the increased focus on student-developed strategies and the use of an exploratory approach, our previous grade level and grade-span meetings were used to discuss our curriculum goals as well as individual units within the math program. These meetings resulted in great discussions that led to many questions, including: What does computational efficiency look like at each grade level? What are the common strategies at each grade level, and how do students show flexibility? Some of us are including the traditional algorithm and some are not. What does the research say about this and how do we make a united decision? Having been introduced to CTS by our district mathematics specialist, we decided to use the CTS process to guide our examination of the national documents for information about relevant and developmentally appropriate addition and subtraction concepts and strategies for Grades K through 2.

We decided to use the "Operations" CTS Guide. We started with readings from Sections II and III. Four group members focused on the *Principles and Standards for School Mathematics* (NCTM, 2000), and two focused on *Benchmarks for Science Literacy* (AAAS, 1993). To guide our reading and discussion, we chose the following questions:

- What are typical examples of strategies demonstrated by students at our grade levels? End of Grade 2? End of Grade 5?
- What are the skills, knowledge, or understandings a student needs to have to use one or more of these strategies successfully?

In our discussion of Sections II and III, the information in *Benchmarks* validated our use of an investigative, student-invented approach to teaching computation. We used the following statement from *Benchmarks* to define computational efficiency in our curriculum guide, "By the end of 2nd grade, students should be able to readily give sums and differences of single digit numbers in familiar contexts . . ." (p. 290).

We identified and discussed statements from the readings that addressed several of the questions generated at our previous meetings. In particular, we were interested in the developmental progression of, first, adding and subtracting by counting concrete objects, then moving to counting on and counting up, then working toward incorporating strategies that emphasize place value (composing and decomposing), and finally developing strategies that could be generalized to other contexts. This progression, revealed through CTS, opened our eyes to why different students choose different strategies—the strategies they chose depended on their developmental readiness. We all agreed this new understanding would help us make better instructional decisions about how to help individual students become more efficient.

Our question of when to introduce an algorithm was also addressed in the Section II and III readings. By the end of Grade 2, the findings revealed that students should have at least two methods that are considered efficient when adding and subtracting two-digit numbers. This computational efficiency centered on the strategies involving composing and decomposing numbers, with the expectation that at the end of Grade 5 students would consolidate and practice a small number of algorithms they could use routinely.

After discussing these findings, we examined the research on teaching and learning in the *Research Companion to Principles and Standards for Mathematics Education* (NCTM, 2003) and in Chapter 15 of *Benchmarks*. We discussed a key finding from the research base on whole numbers in *Benchmarks*, "Students' own meanings for number words to some extent determine their strategies for adding and subtracting and the complexity of the problems they can solve" (p. 358). Another important idea from *Benchmarks* came from the research on operations with whole numbers: "Students should be exposed to a variety of addition and subtraction situations (compare, combine, equalize, change add on, and change taken from)" (p. 358). We began to see that for students to invent a variety of methods and become flexible computers, they must be presented with a variety of types of problems and contexts. We found additional detail in the *Research Companion* to support our understanding of a strategy continuum for computation.

We used Section VI to reflect on the learning goals in our state standards and to explore the difference between two performance indicators: "Use multiple strategies in solving addition and subtraction problems" and "Show understanding of addition and subtraction by using a variety of strategies." Prior to our study and discussion, we found it difficult to distinguish between these two learning goals. We now view the first performance indicator as related to flexibility: Different problems should allow students to choose a strategy that fits the context of the situation being described. The second performance indicator is related to the efficiency portion of our district definition of computational fluency. As students use different methods to demonstrate their understanding of addition and subtraction, they move to more efficient "thinking" methods. This is a necessary step for students to connect their knowledge to more complex numbers, in more sophisticated ways, as they move along in their developmental progression.

At the conclusion of the CTS, our team discussed how we would proceed, based on our findings. First, we want to develop a strategy bank of typical student-invented algorithms and examine the methods for type and computational efficiency. Each member agreed to bring a student example to the monthly staff meeting and to spend 30 minutes after the meeting discussing the student thinking. Second, we would like another half day to work through our number and operations units to review existing problems and situations that are designed to elicit different addition and subtraction strategies and discuss next steps, if gaps are found in the program. In summary, the topic study provided guidance and increased our understanding of how students invent strategies, when students are ready to move to a different strategy or algorithm, and what direction we should take in future examinations of our curriculum units.

Vignette 2: A High School Teacher Uses CTS to Guide Implementation of a Unit on Functions

I signed up for a graduate-level course in mathematics education in the fall of 2004 to complete my certification requirement. The course material, *Dynamic Classroom Assessment: Linking Mathematical Understanding to Instruction,* by George Bright and Jean Joyner (2004), opened my eyes to important components of formative assessment and effective instruction. One particular component, determining conceptual and procedural learning targets, proved difficult for many reasons. The class discussions were extremely valuable, but when I attempted to flesh out the ideas on my own, I had difficulty identifying goals that were not procedural in nature.

Our instructors, noting the difficulty many of us were having, introduced CTS as a process for using the national standards to clarify or identify learning goals for any topic. I started by mapping out my initial ideas, based on the previous times I had taught the functions unit in our textbook (see Figure 5.1). My original thoughts included introducing the formal definition of a function and then "testing" for functionality with multiple representations and strategies, including tables, mapping, equations, and graphs.

After thinking about the learning goals I had previously taught, I began reading the sections from the CTS Guide, Functions. After reading the passages from *Science for All Americans* (AAAS, 1990), I realized that the concept of a function was a part of the bigger idea that "there are many possible kinds of relationships between one variable and another" (p. 133). I realized that this should be my primary learning goal for the unit. I also noted the important idea that relationships can be represented using both symbols and graphs but that graphs are particularly helpful when looking at the relationships between two variables.

Sections II and III were especially helpful in identifying specific learning goals related to the concept of function. My initial focus of tabular, symbolic, and graphic forms was in fact key to understanding functions, but CTS gave me a better sense of

Figure 5.1   Pre-Curriculum Topic Study Concept Map

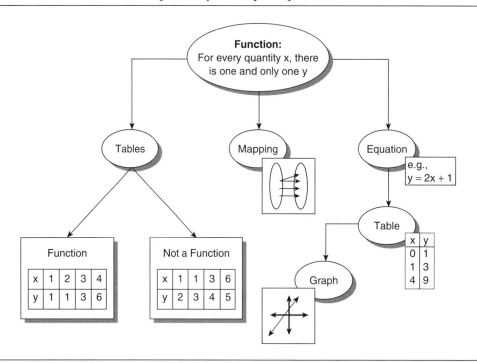

how to make connections between the forms of representation, to identify and use properties of functions, and to provide a context for studying a relationship. In addition to changing my unit implementation to focus on learning about families of functions and their properties, the Section II readings from *Benchmarks for Science Literacy* and the *Principles and Standards for School Mathematics* caused me to revisit the role and use of technological tools. The readings explained that when used appropriately, technology can enhance student understanding of the advantages of the different representations of functions and provide insight to the classes of functions and their defining shapes.

At this point in the CTS process, I refined my original map to include the information from the Section I, II, and III readings (see Figure 5.2).

In reviewing my pre-study ideas, I realize my view of functions was too limited. Through the CTS readings, I expanded and connected my initial ideas of the learning goals to larger ideas about relationships between variables. This process has provided a way to think about and expand on my own preconceived ideas related to teaching a mathematics topic. I no longer have difficulty determining both conceptual and procedural learning targets because CTS provides the resources and information that I need to study most mathematical topics.

Vignette 3: A Department Chair Uses CTS to Help Guide a Discussion on Quadratic Factoring

---

One algebraic concept that has been a main part of our local curriculum is quadratic functions and how to solve them. The process of solving these functions through

Figure 5.2   Post-Curriculum Topic Study Concept Map

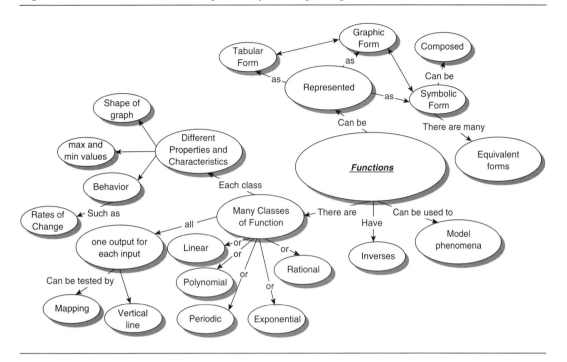

factoring has driven and preoccupied instruction for a minimum of three or four weeks in both Algebra I and Algebra II, a huge commitment considering that each school year is 180 days long and taking into account testing, assemblies, and other educational interferences. From departmental conversations and observations in the classroom, I got the sense that teachers really enjoy factoring in all its forms (perfect square trinomials, difference of two squares, products of sums and differences, etc.). But what are we hoping to achieve when we work with quadratic functions in an average or college prep class? After I was introduced to the CTS, I thought the knowledge, background, and research data that we could gain from the process would help me channel the time and energies of teachers and students into the most advantageous methods of working with quadratic functions.

What exactly should students take away from their study of quadratic functions? Reading *Science for All Americans* in the first section of CTS helped us grapple with the answer. Symbolic representations of relationships are important to us because they allow investigation into the relationship. Examples of these relationships include: the dependence of the displacement of an object on the force of gravity and its velocity at a given point, the point at which maximum profit/minimum cost is reached based on given conditions, or the largest area that can be contained by given linear components, such as a length of fence. The funny thing about most of the textbook problems is that they are designed to mimic real life, but they generally support quadratic equations that have at least rational if not integral solutions, and therefore, they support the process of interminable factoring.

Concepts about symbolic representations of numeric relationships are also addressed in *Beyond Numeracy* (Paulos, 1992), which references the quadratic formula among other mathematical formulas. From these readings, it is evident that quadratic relationships and the ability to recognize them as such are important tools for adults. But we did not find any reference to the process of solving through factoring versus the quadratic formula. The take-away for us is that adults should be able to recognize relationships and apply whatever tools necessary to derive appropriate conclusions from the data based on the function generated, whether it is quadratic, linear, or exponential.

What are the instructional implications for teachers, and what are the concepts and ideas students should know? To factor or not to factor—is there a preference? *Benchmarks for Science Literacy* suggests an approach through symbolic representation and understanding what type of relationship exists. *Benchmarks* encourages us to spend "more time interpreting graphs, exploring the properties of graphs, and determining how these properties relate to the forms of the corresponding equations" (p. 220). The implication was also that students should be doing this "with the help of calculators and computers" (p. 220). The section also referenced the notion that there might be more than one answer to a problem and that the reasonableness of a solution should be considered. So far, factoring has not been a critical component of working with quadratic functions.

The NCTM standards support these findings and indicate that for students to know what types of solutions are appropriate for particular equations, they must understand our number system. Using the factoring method of solving a quadratic equation might lead a student to believe that because the expression cannot be readily factored, there is no solution. The NCTM standards include the use of computer algebra systems (CAS) to explain the effects of changing the coefficients/constants in a quadratic function. Of course, this can be accomplished with pencil and paper, but that method can often be tedious and cause students to lose interest early in the process, therefore missing the intent of the exploration. Exploration, manipulation of the numeric components, and investigation of our number system are pieces that are recommended by the NCTM standards, but no unique process was discussed other than CAS and technology.

Our next question was: What will research on student learning have to say? *Benchmarks* stated that "students have difficulty understanding how symbols are used in algebra" (p. 351). Furthermore, *Benchmarks* added that this problem may persist up to or through postsecondary education. A student's ability to successfully manipulate the variables in a quadratic function into "correct" factored form may be attributable to their dedication to the lock-step process of learning algebra rather than an understanding of the concept. Using graphical interpretations of functions can have similar challenges—students may learn the how-to of graphing and miss the beauty and significance of the graph. Being able to find a solution to an equation without understanding its relevance is also a common occurrence; although not much is known about how to help students "understand what a solution means and why anyone would want it" (*Benchmarks*, p. 352).

Our state standards are currently undergoing close scrutiny and potential revision. Some critics feel that they are too intense for all students and need to be more realistic. Perhaps it is a literal interpretation on their part as the indicators in the state standards closely parallel the concepts identified by the research resources used in the CTS. While the state's performance indicators parallel the national resources, the national documents showed us that the use of quadratic formulas and the interpretation of results are more important than the process of factoring.

Initially, I didn't think I would find what I was looking for in the study of quadratic functions. I really wanted someone or something to boldly state that we should not hold students' feet to the fire for a passing grade in algebra dependent on their ability to perform the ritual of factoring. I like to factor, have all the tricks of the trade, and have indeed forced it on more students than I would like to remember. Many students will never grasp the procedural end of quadratics, but they can and do understand the quadratic phenomena. After the study, I found that CTS validated my predisposition to reduce the emphasis on the procedural value of factoring and to concentrate on the conceptual knowledge students need to gain. But it has also given me a much broader perspective of what we as teachers should be working toward with our students. We need to be aiming for conceptual knowledge, not procedural competence, and that was evident in the reiteration in each section that students should be able to understand and identify reasonable solutions. The process of working with CTS has also given me direction to work with my colleagues on how best to meet student needs with respect to quadratic functions.

Vignette 4: A Multi-Grade Elementary Team Uses CTS to Examine Alignment of Curriculum, Instruction, and Assessment

---

Our state assessment is given each spring to 4th-, 8th-, and 11th-grade students. Because results arrive in early September, our first fall inservice day is devoted, without fail, to item analysis and goal setting. In previous meetings, we used a divide and conquer approach, reviewing results as a K–4 district staff and then working at the Grade 2–4 level to align the released items to our instructional units and devise a plan to use the items for student practice. Because the items were written for the end of Grade 4, the second- and third-grade teachers continuously struggle with how to incorporate them effectively.

This past year, after not seeing a steady increase in our scores, we decided to try a different approach by using the CTS process. As we reviewed the different content strands, we quickly realized a need to focus on one content strand and decided on the measurement performance indicator: "Students will be able to solve and justify solutions to real-life problems involving the measurement of time, length, area, perimeter, weight, temperature, mass, capacity, and volume" (Maine Department of Education, 1997, p. 46). As we reviewed the items aligned to the indicator to get a sense of the target, our conversation quickly turned to instructional strategies and grade-level-appropriate variations of measuring length. The group agreed on the importance of measuring using repeated objects, such as paper clips, before using standard units such as inches. We were unsure, however, of the progression from one to the other. We recorded our ideas on chart paper to compare our initial thinking with the results of our study.

We decided the goal of our study of length would be to create a scope and sequence document describing K–2 and 3–4 content knowledge expectations, related research on student learning, teaching ideas, and alignment to the expectations for Grades 3 and 4. Starting with Section III, we chose to use the *Principles and Standards for School Mathematics* because our state standards used these standards as their foundation. The goals, although more specific than the performance indicator, were similar to those we had generated in our conversation prior to the study. We did, however, discover that measuring with nonstandard units is a K–2 and not a Grade

3–4 expectation, as we had originally thought. Instead of introducing nonstandard units, the Grades 3–5 expectation is familiarity with standard units within the customary and metric systems.

Section II, considering instructional implications, proved to be more enlightening. The statement in the K–2 section, "measurement experiences should include direct comparisons as well as the use of nonstandard and standards units" (*Principles and Standards,* p. 103), confirmed our earlier conversation about the importance of beginning with repeating a nonstandard unit. Other statements that piqued our interest included, "discourse builds students' conceptual and procedural knowledge and gives teachers valuable information" (*Principles and Standards,* p. 103) and "such experiences and discussions can create an awareness of the need for standard units and tools and of the fact that different measuring tools will yield different numerical measurements of the same object" (*Principles and Standards*, p. 105). Both positioning multiple copies of the same item and iterating one unit are important in developing measurement concepts and in moving from nonstandard to standard units of measure. "By emphasizing the question 'what are you counting?' teachers help students focus on the meaning of the measurements they are making" (*Principles and Standards*, p. 106). The Grades 3–5 essay focused instruction on using benchmarks to estimate length, expressing measures in equivalent forms, and understanding measurement as an approximation. These instructional targets, especially the latter two, were beyond what most of us were focusing on in our classrooms.

We came back to another idea highlighted in Section II—paying attention to the zero point—after reading and discussing the related research in Section IV. The measurement chapter in the *Research Companion* states that "only a minority of young children understand that any point on a scale can serve as the starting point, and even a significant minority of older children (e.g., fifth grade) respond to nonzero origins by simply reading off whatever number on a ruler aligns with the end of the object" (p. 182). This was exactly what the group had discussed earlier! How validating to see this as a common misunderstanding. But what could we do about the issue? Studies that showed promising results required students to develop their own measurement tools such as foot strips or paper clip strips. By constructing a tool, two things were accomplished: transitioning from the idea of iterating a single unit and discovering the principles that guide the design of the ruler. As instruction progresses to finer "parts," students have the opportunity to split the units on their tool to include halves, fourths, eighths, and so on, providing them with a deeper conceptual understanding of the marks on a standard ruler.

Additional instructional ideas in the *Research Companion* included providing a variety of measurement objects and watching for students who measure by using objects of various lengths rather than objects of equal length. The Grade 2 teachers admitted that, too often, they would direct students to measure using only one object. They couldn't wait to watch students as they were asked to choose from an assortment of objects. Furthermore, observing what students do when there aren't enough objects to lay end to end can reveal whether a student has a conceptual understanding of measurement.

After reading and discussing Sections II, III, and IV, using the *Principles and Standards* and the *Research Companion,* we reviewed our state grade-level expectations and, as with the Section II learning goals, we felt we had a good understanding of the target. The CTS process provided us an opportunity to extend our understanding of the learning goals to include instructional implications based on standards and research. For the first time, I left our item analysis meeting with a clear picture of how to move students in the right direction. I looked forward to receiving the scope and sequence document in its final form, and I hope other grade-level teams will see the benefit in developing similar documents. The instructional ideas within the document will help teachers develop students' conceptual understanding at the lower grades and provide avenues for remediation at Grades 3 and 4. We now feel ready not only to allow students to practice problems from the released item pool, but also to support a "developmental trajectory for understanding of linear measure in the classroom that promote representation and communication" (*Research Companion*, p. 183).

Vignette 5: A Middle School Teacher Uses CTS to Understand Concepts of Surface Area and Volume

---

Having taught sixth-grade mathematics and science for five years, I was worried about moving to teaching full-time eighth-grade mathematics. My district moved to a standards-based program three years ago, and during the initial implementation, I learned right along with my students and often spent hours working out the student problems prior to each exploration. Although working through the problems was beneficial, I wanted to get a head start prior to reviewing the unit material.

I had participated in CTS through a workshop on planning, designing, and implementing a study group, and I thought the topic study process could help me prepare to teach the eighth-grade mathematics units. Because we start the year with a unit on three-dimensional measurement, I chose the topic study on area and volume and gathered the needed resources.

Before beginning the study, I reflected on what I knew about the topic and what I wanted to find out about the topic. During this reflection, I found myself referring back to the two-dimensional (2-D) geometry unit I taught to my sixth-grade classes. Because much of the sixth-grade unit investigated the relationship between perimeter and area, I began to wonder about the relationship between surface area and volume.

As I read through the sections, my initial reflection provided a lens by which I could sort information and clarify or extend my prior understanding. In reading *Science for All Americans* for adult content knowledge, I found the statement "Changing the size of objects while keeping the same shape can have profound effects owing to the geometry of scaling: Area varies as the square of linear dimensions, and volume varies as the cube" (p. 134). I decided to continue reading to clarify the extent to which eighth graders should understand this relationship. I found the information I was looking for in both *Benchmarks* and *Principles and Standards*. I now understand "surface areas of similar objects are proportional to the squares of the lengths of their corresponding sides but their volumes are proportional to the cubes of those lengths" (*Principles and Standards*, p. 245).

Another statement in *Science for All Americans*, "a spherical container minimizes surface area for any mass or volume" (p. 134), validated my assumption (see Figure 5.3) that there were similar relationships between surface area and volumes as there

Figure 5.3   K-W Elicitation

What I **K**now about the content in the topic:

- 3-D objects have many sides
- Faces and vertices are words used to describe 3-D objects
- Volume is how much room inside a 3-D object
- There is a difference between the dimensions of the object, how many units fill an object, and the amount of material it takes to make or cover the object
- Surface area is found by adding the area of all the faces
- Volume is found by multiplying the base and height

What I **W**ant to learn about the content in the topic:

- What is the relationship between the surface area and the volume of a 3-D figure?
- What is the definition of a net?
- Are there multiple formulas and methods for finding surface area and volume?

are with perimeter and area. Again, I found additional information in *Benchmarks* and *Principles and Standards,* including the following ideas: Volume does not generally determine surface area, and rectangular prisms that are more cubelike have less surface area than other rectangular prisms with the same volume.

Now satisfied with the relationship question I had posed prior to my study (see Figure 5.3), I was ready to move on to another area. The information on nets was tied to my question regarding multiple methods and strategies for finding surface area and volume of three-dimensional (3-D) figures (see Figure 5.3). Two key ideas from the resources I studied can be summarized as follows: Area and volume can be found by breaking an object into known reference shapes, and the surface area of a 3-D object can be determined by finding the area of the object's net (a 2-D representation of a 3-D object). With a conceptual understanding of area and volume of figures such as rectangles, triangles, and rectangular prisms, students will be able to calculate measurements of other types of 3-D objects. By developing their own methods, students will be more likely to understand generalized formulas and therefore to choose and apply the correct formula.

After reading Sections I, II, and III of the Area and Volume topic study, I feel ready to dive into the teacher and student curriculum material. I still plan to work through all student problems, but I now have a foundation to work from when I align the purpose of each of the activities.

Vignette 6: A Team of Middle and High School Teachers Uses CTS to Identify Goals for Learning About Decimals, Fractions, and Percents

---

Because our district does not have a well-articulated K–12 curriculum, teachers use a variety of instructional approaches and emphasize different learning goals, even within the same grade level. Some teachers use a traditional text to deliver content and design instruction, others use a standards-based program, and still others use a mixture of traditional and contemporary programs. The district mathematics leadership team, of which I am a member, is concerned that the lack of a consistent and coherent curriculum might cause gaps in students' learning opportunities. An analysis of the Survey of Enacted Curriculum, an instrument available through the Chief Council of State School Officers (CCSSO), revealed a large amount of instructional time was focused on fractions, decimals, and percents (especially fractions) in both middle and high school. Because fractions are an area of concern, we chose this topic as our first CTS to help us build a curriculum that would foster students' growth of understanding throughout the K–12 learning continuum.

Our topic study on fraction, decimals, and percents was set up as a study group with three groups of five. Each group included a mix of teachers (regular and special education) and administrators for Grades 3–5, 6–8, and 9–12. All participants received their reading assignments several days prior to the meeting. The group then met after school for two hours to discuss the information in the readings.

We broke into small groups to initiate discussion and highlight the main ideas gleaned from members' reading. Small-group conversation led to whole-group discussion focused on a few main ideas that were most important from a district perspective. The main points of discussion and next steps to improve student learning are described below.

The district felt that the current instruction in Grades 3 through 5 was centered more on procedures than on conceptual understanding. CTS brought research to the table that helped us understand appropriate instruction for this grade level. *Principals and Standards* states that in Grades 3 through 5,

> The focus should be on developing students' conceptual understanding of fractions and decimals–what they are, how they are represented, and how they relate to whole numbers–rather than on developing computational fluency with rational numbers. Fluency in rational-number computation will be a major focus of grades 6–8. (p. 152)

The teachers and administrators in our group felt that students were learning procedural techniques before they had a solid foundation of conceptual knowledge. As a result of this conversation, the Grade 3–5 representatives asked the leadership team to plan professional development for all Grade 3–5 teachers that could increase their awareness of the conceptual underpinnings of fractions, decimals, and percents and the instructional implications of this conceptual focus.

Another concern is the amount of class time devoted to fractions, decimals, and percents in Grades 6 through 8. The current curriculum highlights these topics for Grades 6 through 8, but discussions based on the CTS led teachers to realize that students need to have numerous concrete experiences on a regular basis. *Principles and Standards* recommends that Grades 6–8 students deepen their understanding of fractions, decimals, and percents and become proficient in using them to solve problems and have "extensive experience with ratios, rates, and percents, which helps to form a solid foundation for their understanding of, and facility with, proportionality" (p. 215). Because of the nature and depth of these topics, they need to be integrated with other content strands and experienced in as many contexts as possible.

The ninth-grade teachers currently spend a lot of time teaching students procedural knowledge, especially around fractions. The group realized that at ninth grade, students should be working with these concepts in new settings to extend understanding. Discussion brought out the common frustration of not being able to get through grade-level expectations because of so much time being spent on "re-teaching."

Our conversations ended with a look at the current scope and sequence and grade-level expectations. There was unanimous agreement that the district would use a standards-based scope and sequence tool, along with CTS, to begin to create a systematic continuum for student learning. We will also continue to take part in study groups, using CTS to inform instructional practices and to help the district make an educated choice on curriculum selection and implementation. CTS has allowed our leadership team and other educators who participated in the study group to step away from personal pedagogical biases and practices and to focus instead on examining grade-level content and expectations that will move us toward more effective, research-based practices.

Vignette 7: An Intermediate Teacher Uses CTS to Prepare for a Unit on Probability

---

At a professional development session I attended in early fall, I was asked to give a short assessment item, the Marble Problem, to my students and then bring the student work to the workshop. During the workshop, we studied the concept of probability using CTS and then applied our learning by analyzing trends in student thinking. I was fascinated by reviewing student responses across Grades 5 through 9 and seeing the ideas in the research right there in front of us! I wanted to pursue the question—now that I recognize common misunderstandings, what can I do about them?—and couldn't wait for the upcoming unit on probability, from MathTrailblazers, that I would be implementing in a couple of months.

A week before beginning the instructional unit, which I taught for the first time last year, I reviewed my notes from the workshop. While reading Section II on instructional implications, I had highlighted the following from *Principles and Standards*:

> Students should explore probability through experiments that have only a few outcomes, such as using game spinners with certain portions shaded and considering how likely it is that the spinner will land on a particular color. They should come to understand and use 0 to represent the probability of an impossible event and 1 to represent the probability of a certain event, and they should use common fractions to represent the probability of events that are neither certain nor impossible. Through these experiences, students encounter the idea that although they cannot determine an individual outcome, such as which color the spinner will land on next, they can predict the frequency of various outcomes. (p. 181)

This statement encouraged me to look for multiple experiences in generating data and to use that data to make predictions prior to introducing theoretical probability. Because the instructional unit is designed to use probability as a context for comparing equivalent decimals, fractions, and percents, there is limited time devoted to building a solid understanding of these ideas. The unit sections did align nicely to the instructional implications I uncovered through CTS, as the material incorporates two experiments for students to collect data, with the expectation of comparing the results to the calculated probability. The material did not, however, give suggestions for the common areas of misunderstanding pointed out in research studies. I found reference in the *Background Notes* to the following areas of concern, "one of the most commonly held incorrect beliefs about probability relates to the Law of Large Numbers" and "there are other false beliefs about coin flipping" (TIMS Curriculum, 2003, p. 7). Although I found this information to be consistent with the research in *Benchmarks* and the *Research Companion,* the passage implies the misunderstandings will be corrected through the activity. Because most of the misunderstandings pertained to the context of the experiment (coin flipping) rather than to the learning goal itself, which was using experimental data to understand theoretical probability, I decided to ask the question: What do you predict will be the result of your next turn? while observing students in action. The student responses to the question will give me insight into the misconceptions they might have. First, using the idea of equiprobability from the *Research Companion,* students may believe that all outcomes from a probability experiment have the same chance of happening; this belief is characterized by statements such as "anything could happen" (p. 218). This will be especially interesting during the second experiment because the first experiment consists of flipping one coin, which does give an equal chance of outcomes. Another possible response to the question can be referred to as representativeness. "One common misconception is the idea of representativeness, according to which an event is believed to be probable to the extent that it is *typical*" (*Benchmarks*, p. 353). Students with this misconception are likely to look at the past few turns to determine whether heads or tails will come up next. Asking students to predict the outcome of their next turn may uncover some common intuitive ideas that get in the way of understanding probability as a means to predict the frequency of various outcomes.

I found the CTS process especially helpful in preparing for possible stumbling blocks my students may encounter while investigating a difficult to learn topic. I felt much better prepared to address common misunderstandings through specific questions, activities, and class discussions. As I become more familiar with the MathTrailblazers program, I will continue to look for additional areas in which studying the standards and research would be helpful. A few that come to mind are the multiplication of fractions, multidigit division, and the choice of appropriate scales when graphing.

Vignette 8: Teachers Use CTS to Analyze Student Thinking on Area Measurement

At the end of every school year, teachers in Grades 6, 7, and 8 are required to give a summative assessment in mathematics. We call these our end-of-the-year district assessments. During a districtwide middle school math department meeting in September, we learned that only 36% of our students had answered an area problem correctly on the seventh-grade assessment. We were surprised by this and wanted to know why our students were not able to complete the problem correctly.

Figure 5.4   Area of a Parallelogram

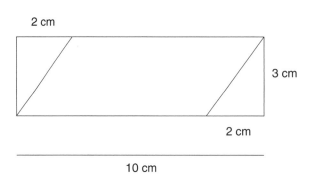

The question required students to find the area of a parallelogram that had been inscribed within a rectangle (see Figure 5.4).

We took the question exactly as it had been written in multiple-choice format and added, "explain your reason(s) for the answer you selected." Our next task was to determine the appropriate grade level(s) to administer the problem. This is the point at which we elected to use the CTS Guide, Area and Volume. We began our reading with Section III: Identifying concepts and specific ideas, and Section IV: Examining research on student learning. Through our reading of *Benchmarks for Science Literacy*, we learned "evidence suggests it is possible for students to understand the abstract properties of geometric figures by 5th grade and can understand the relations that connect the properties of shapes or make simple deductions by 8th or 9th grade" (p. 352). Given this information, we decided to administer the problem to students in Grades 5 through 9.

After collecting almost 800 pieces of student work, six teachers representing Grades 6, 7, and 8 met to analyze the data and to examine student thinking regarding the concept of area. We sorted the information into various trends, including students who made correct calculations but did not make the connection that area is a measurement of square units; students who calculated perimeter; students who used incorrect language; and students who could not communicate effectively. As a group, we brainstormed instructional implications and then turned to Section II of the CTS Guide on area and volume to look for additional implications.

Ideas from the study of Section II that enhanced our discussion included (1) "Concepts of area and volume should first be developed concretely, with procedures for computation following only when the concepts and some of their practical uses are well understood" (*Benchmarks*, p. 223), (2) "In grades six through eight students should draw inferences and make logical deductions from geometric problems" (*Benchmarks*, p. 224), and (3) "Students should investigate and use geometric ideas rather than memorizing definitions and formulas" (*Principles and Standards*, p. 244). The student work we collected showed that many students had memorized formulas but were not necessarily applying them correctly. Through the topic study, we were able to add to our brainstorm instructional implications the notion that "students should become proficient in composing and decomposing two- and three-dimensional shapes in order to find areas of objects. Students should develop formulas and procedures in ways that help them develop an intuitive sense of their reasonableness" (*Principles and Standards*, p. 244). With a focus on not introducing the formula prior to or in conjunction with an investigation, we discussed various activities that would develop our students' conceptual understanding of area.

Through this diagnostic process, we were able to determine that our classroom practices needed to promote the strategy of decomposing and composing shapes to determine area. We needed to develop students' understanding that decomposing a shape and rearranging its parts without overlap does not affect the area of the shape. We also realized that we needed to emphasize the units that are used to measure area.

Personally, my teaching approach with regard to the topic of area changed for the remainder of the school year. I encouraged my students to decompose or compose irregular shapes into shapes they were familiar with to find area. I realized that spatial reasoning and measurement were important for my seventh graders and that this was a developmentally appropriate strategy for most of my students. Through CTS, we were able to include research without having to dedicate a lot of time to the searching and sorting for relevant information. The research provided a common ground for the group, which allowed us to move from diagnosing the problem to finding ways to fix the problem.

Vignette 9: A Teacher Leader Uses CTS to Prepare for a Professional Development Session on Proportionality

I was contracted by the state department of education to be a math consultant for a district identified as "not meeting adequate yearly progress." Part of this consultation required me to provide sessions on various mathematical topics at a week-long content support institute (CSI) for the district leadership team.

For the session focusing on proportionality, my first instinct was to use the CTS Guide on that topic to identify adult content knowledge, consider instructional implications, identify concepts and specific ideas, examine research on student learning, understand coherency, and clarify state standards. Because I understood the research related to these six sections, I was able to focus on specific resources that would help me develop a research-based professional development opportunity for the team.

Initially, I decided to focus on Sections II, III, IV, and VI. For Sections II, III, and IV, I read selected passages from *Benchmarks for Science Literacy, Principles and Standards for School Mathematics,* and *Research Companion to Principles and Standards.* By reading various passages from these resources, I was able to synthesize key points about proportionality and provide focus for the professional development session. Although I knew proportionality was a big idea integrated throughout Grades 6 to 8, the topic study helped me see proportionality as one form of mathematical reasoning. It involves a sense of covariation, multiple comparisons, and the ability to remember and process several pieces of information. The readings also helped me identify the critical component of proportional situations as the multiplicative relationship that exists among the quantities.

In addition to identifying concepts and specific ideas, the study also helped me prepare for common misunderstandings educators may have about proportional reasoning. For example, educators may think that being able to perform mechanical operations with proportions means that the student understands the underlying ideas of proportional thinking. Educators may also underestimate the amount of time and instruction needed to build the idea of proportionality. Proportional reasoning develops slowly over a number of years, not in a single unit. Proportionality is of such great importance that it merits whatever time and effort must be expended to ensure student understanding. Students' understanding of proportionality should grow from problem solving and reasoning and through connections to other mathematical topics (*Principles and Standards*).

I was also able to identify instructional implications based on the research, so that I could give the team a concrete understanding of the continuum of strategies and methods. The standards recommend teaching multiple strategies, including unit rate, factor of change, fractions, and cross-product algorithm. Instruction should begin with more intuitive strategies, which emphasize conceptual knowledge, such as unit rate and factor of change. Having this understanding prior to planning the specific activities of the session gave me a filter for possible materials.

Besides providing professional development on mathematical content, part of my consulting role includes assisting the team in aligning their current K–12 mathematics curriculum to the Grade-Level Expectations (GLEs) for our state. The key ideas clarified through the topic study helped me design an activity that requires participants to use the key research points about proportional reasoning to create a web that connected several GLEs to the theme of proportional reasoning. This activity enabled participants to understand how several GLEs relate to the topic of proportional reasoning.

Without my experience with the general sections of a CTS Guide, I would not have been as efficient or as accurate in locating research relevant to the development of this professional development session. CTS was essential in allowing me to design a research-based session that provided my team with three essential components: (1) a deeper conceptual knowledge of proportional reasoning, (2) ability to align curriculum components to GLEs with understanding, and (3) ability to choose effective series of activities to take back to the classroom.

6

Curriculum Topic Study Guides

ORGANIZATION OF CTS GUIDES

This chapter contains the complete set of mathematics Curriculum Topic Study Guides. The organization and use of these guides are described in Chapter 2. The guides are arranged in seven categories representing major domains in mathematics. Within each category, the individual CTS guides are arranged by alphabetical order. The guides within category reflect a particular focus for the study. It is important to keep in mind that topics are interconnected, just as learning goals are. Two or more topics can be studied together to create a more comprehensive understanding of a general topic.

Topics also come in different grain sizes, ranging from very specific concepts (e.g., "Addition and Subtraction," to much broader topics (e.g., "Properties of Operations"). Broad topics like "Patterns, Relations, and Functions" may subsume multiple CTS topics. It is up to you the user to decide how broad or specific you want your topic study to be. For that reason, a full range of grain sizes is available to the CTS user.

DESCRIPTIONS OF THE CTS CATEGORIES

The following sections describe the seven different categories of CTS guides (see "List of Curriculum Topic Study Guides" at the beginning of this book) and the number of guides in each category. The overview describes the major emphasis of the category in terms of the focus on ideas that are developed by using the different CTS guides in the respective category.

Numbers and Operations

Number of CTS Guides: 23

Overview: The focus of this section is the understanding and use of counting, numbers, arithmetic, and the number system. Ideas such as understanding ways of representing number, relationships among numbers, understanding meanings of operations, and the relationship among operations and estimation are developed through a study of the topics in this section.

- Addition and Subtraction
- Addition and Subtraction of Whole Numbers
- Combinations and Permutations
- Comparing and Ordering Numbers
- Computation and Operations
- Counting
- Decimals
- Exponents
- Factors and Multiples (Elementary Number Theory)
- Facts
- Fractions
- Fractions, Decimals, and Percents
- Integers
- Large and Small Numbers
- Multiplication and Division
- Multiplication and Division of Whole Numbers
- Number Sense
- Numbers and Number Systems
- Percent
- Place Value
- Properties of Operations
- Ratio and Proportion
- Rational Numbers

Standards- and Research-Based Study of a Curricular Topic

ADDITION AND SUBTRACTION

Section and Outcome	Selected Sources and Readings for Study and Reflection Read and examine *related parts* of:
I. Identify Adult Content Knowledge	**IA:** **Science for All Americans** ▶ Chapter 9, *Numbers,* page 131 ▶ Chapter 12, *Computation,* pages 187–190; *Estimation,* pages 190–191 **IB:** **Beyond Numeracy** ▶ *Computation and Rote,* pages 52–55
II. Consider Instructional Implications	**IIA:** **Benchmarks for Science Literacy** ▶ 9A, *Numbers,* grade span essays, pages 211–213 ▶ 12B, *Computation and Estimation* general essay, pages 288–289 **IIB:** **NCTM Principles and Standards for School Mathematics** ▶ Grades PreK–12 Overview Number and Operations general essay, pages 32–33, *Understand Meanings,* page 34, *Compute Fluently,* pages 35–36 ▶ Grades PreK–2 Number and Operations general essay, page 79, *Understand Meanings,* pages 83–84, *Compute Fluently,* pages 84–88 ▶ Grades 3–5 Number and Operations general essay, page 149, *Compute Fluently,* pages 152–153, page 155 ▶ Grades 6–8 Number and Operations, *Understand Meanings,* pages 218–220, *Compute Fluently,* pages 220–221
III. Identify Concepts and Specific Ideas	**IIIA:** **Benchmarks for Science Literacy** ▶ 9A, *Number,* page 213 ▶ 12B, *Computation and Estimation,* pages 290–291 **IIIB:** **NCTM Principles and Standards for School Mathematics** ▶ Grades PreK–2 Number and Operations, page 78 or 392 ▶ Grades 3–5 Number and Operations, page 148 or 392 ▶ Grades 6–8 Number and Operations, page 214 or 393
IV. Examine Research on Student Learning	**IVA:** **Benchmarks for Science Literacy** ▶ 9A, *Whole Numbers,* page 350 ▶ 12B, *Operations With Whole Numbers,* page 358; *Operations With Fractions and Decimals,* pages 358–359; *Calculators,* page 359 **IVB:** **Research Companion** ▶ Chapter 6, *Real World Situations,* pages 68–69, *Types of Real-World Addition,* pages 69–71, *Building Fluency,* pages 71–72, *Single-Digit Computation,* page 72, *Single-Digit Addition and Subtraction,* pages 73–76, *Multidigit Addition and Subtraction,* pages 78–84, *General Issues,* pages 87–91 ▶ Chapter 8, *Facts and Algorithms as Products of Students' Own Mathematical Activity,* pages 114–121
V. Examine Coherency and Articulation	**V:** **Atlas of Science Literacy** ▶ *Mathematical Processes,* page 27 noting the conceptual strand "Computation and Operations" ▶ *Ratio and Proportionality,* page 119 noting the conceptual strand "Computation"
VI. Clarify State Standards and District Curriculum	**VIA:** **State Standards:** Link Sections I–V to learning goals and information from your state standards or frameworks that are informed by the results of the topic study. **VIB:** **District Curriculum Guide:** Link Sections I–V to learning goals and information from your district curriculum guide that are informed by the results of the topic study.
Visit www.curriculumtopicstudy.org for updates or supplementary readings, Web sites, and videos.	

Standards- and Research-Based Study of a Curricular Topic

ADDITION AND SUBTRACTION OF WHOLE NUMBERS

Section and Outcome	Selected Sources and Readings for Study and Reflection Read and examine *related parts* of:
I. Identify Adult Content Knowledge	**IA:** ***Science for All Americans*** ▸ Chapter 9, *Numbers,* pages 130–131 ▸ Chapter 12, *Computation,* pages 187–190 **IB:** ***Beyond Numeracy*** ▸ *Computation and Rote,* pages 52–55
II. Consider Instructional Implications	**IIA:** ***Benchmarks for Science Literacy*** ▸ 9A, *Numbers* grade span essays, page 211, page 213 ▸ 12B, *Computation and Estimation* general essay, pages 288–289 **IIB:** ***NCTM Principles and Standards for School Mathematics*** ▸ Grades PreK–12 Overview Number and Operations *Understand Meanings,* page 34, *Compute Fluently,* pages 35–36 ▸ Grades PreK–2 Number and Operations general essay, page 79, *Understand Meanings,* pages 83–84, *Compute Fluently,* pages 84–88 ▸ Grades 3–5 Number and Operations general essay, page 149, *Compute Fluently,* pages 152–153, page 155 ▸ Grades 6–8 Number and Operations, *Understand Meanings,* page 218
III. Identify Concepts and Specific Ideas	**IIIA:** ***Benchmarks for Science Literacy*** ▸ 9A, *Numbers,* pages 213–214 ▸ 12B, *Computation and Estimation,* page 290 **IIIB:** ***NCTM Principles and Standards for School Mathematics*** ▸ Grades PreK–2 Number and Operations, page 78 or 392 ▸ Grades 3–5 Number and Operations, page 148 or 392 ▸ Grades 6–8 Number and Operations, page 214 or 393
IV. Examine Research on Student Learning	**IVA:** ***Benchmarks for Science Literacy*** ▸ 12B, *Operations With Whole Numbers,* page 358; *Calculators,* page 359 **IVB:** ***Research Companion*** ▸ Chapter 6, *Real World Situations,* pages 68–69, *Types of Real-World Addition,* pages 69–71, *Building Fluency,* pages 71–72, *Single-Digit Computation,* page 72, *Single-Digit Addition and Subtraction,* pages 73–76, *Multidigit Addition and Subtraction,* pages 78–84, *General Issues,* pages 87–91 ▸ Chapter 8, *Facts and Algorithms as Products of Students' Own Mathematical Activity,* pages 114–121
V. Examine Coherency and Articulation	**V:** ***Atlas of Science Literacy*** ▸ *Mathematical Processes,* page 27 noting the conceptual strand "Computation and Operations" ▸ *Ratio and Proportionality,* page 119 noting the conceptual strand "Computation"
VI. Clarify State Standards and District Curriculum	**VIA:** ***State Standards:*** Link Sections I–V to learning goals and information from your state standards or frameworks that are informed by the results of the topic study. **VIB:** ***District Curriculum Guide:*** Link Sections I–V to learning goals and information from your district curriculum guide that are informed by the results of the topic study.
Visit www.curriculumtopicstudy.org for updates or supplementary readings, Web sites, and videos.	

Standards- and Research-Based Study of a Curricular Topic

COMBINATIONS AND PERMUTATIONS

Section and Outcome	Selected Sources and Readings for Study and Reflection Read and examine *related parts* of:
I. Identify Adult Content Knowledge	**IB:** *Beyond Numeracy* ▸ *The Multiplication Principle,* pages 150–153
II. Consider Instructional Implications	**IIB:** *NCTM Principles and Standards for School Mathematics* ▸ 9–12 Number and Operations, *Understand Meanings of Operations,* pages 293–294
III. Identify Concepts and Specific Ideas	**IIIB:** *NCTM Principles and Standards for School Mathematics* ▸ 9–12 Number and Operations, page 290 or 393
IV. Examine Research on Student Learning	**IVA:** *Benchmarks for Science Literacy* ▸ No research available for *Benchmarks.* **IVB:** *Research Companion* ▸ No research available for *Research Companion.*
V. Examine Coherency and Articulation	**V:** *Atlas of Science Literacy* ▸ There are no maps for this topic in Volume I
VI. Clarify State Standards and District Curriculum	**VIA:** *State Standards:* Link Sections I–V to learning goals and information from your state standards or frameworks that are informed by the results of the topic study. **VIB:** *District Curriculum Guide:* Link Sections I–V to learning goals and information from your district curriculum guide that are informed by the results of the topic study.
Visit www.curriculumtopicstudy.org for updates or supplementary readings, Web sites, and videos.	

Standards- and Research-Based Study of a Curricular Topic

COMPARING AND ORDERING NUMBERS

Section and Outcome	Selected Sources and Readings for Study and Reflection Read and examine *related parts* of:
I. Identify Adult Content Knowledge	**IA:** *Science for All Americans* ▶ Chapter 9, *Numbers,* pages 130–132
II. Consider Instructional Implications	**IIA:** *Benchmarks for Science Literacy* ▶ 9A, *Numbers* general essay, page 210; grade span essays, pages 211–214 **IIB:** *NCTM Principles and Standards for School Mathematics* ▶ Grades PreK–12 Overview Number and Operations, *Understand Numbers,* page 33 ▶ Grades PreK–2 Number and Operations, *Understand Numbers,* pages 79–82 ▶ Grades 3–5 Number and Operations general essay, page 149, *Understand Numbers,* pages 149–151 ▶ Grades 6–8 Number and Operations, *Understand Numbers,* pages 216–218 ▶ Grades 9–12 Number and Operations, *Understand Numbers,* page 291
III. Identify Concepts and Specific Ideas	**IIIA:** *Benchmarks for Science Literacy* ▶ 9A, *Numbers,* pages 211–214 ▶ 12B, *Computation,* pages 290–291 **IIIB:** *NCTM Principles and Standards for School Mathematics* ▶ Grades PreK–2 Number and Operations, page 78 or 392 ▶ Grades 3–5 Number and Operations, page 148 or 392 ▶ Grades 6–8 Number and Operations, page 214 or 393 ▶ Grades 9–12 Number and Operations, page 290 or 393
IV. Examine Research on Student Learning	**IVA:** *Benchmarks for Science Literacy* ▶ 9A, *Numbers,* page 350 ▶ 12B, *Computation and Estimation,* page 359
V. Examine Coherency and Articulation	**V:** *Atlas of Science Literacy* ▶ *Mathematical Processes,* page 27 ▶ *Mathematical Models,* page 29
VI. Clarify State Standards and District Curriculum	**VIA:** *State Standards:* Link Sections I–V to learning goals and information from your state standards or frameworks that are informed by the results of the topic study. **VIB:** *District Curriculum Guide:* Link Sections I–V to learning goals and information from your district curriculum guide that are informed by the results of the topic study.
Visit www.curriculumtopicstudy.org for updates or supplementary readings, Web sites, and videos.	

Standards- and Research-Based Study of a Curricular Topic

COMPUTATION AND OPERATIONS

Section and Outcome	Selected Sources and Readings for Study and Reflection Read and examine *related parts* of:	
I. Identify Adult Content Knowledge	**IA:**	***Science for All Americans*** ▸ Chapter 9, *Numbers,* pages 130–131 ▸ Chapter 12, *Computation*, pages 187–190
	IB:	***Beyond Numeracy*** ▸ *Computation and Rote,* pages 52–55
II. Consider Instructional Implications	**IIA:**	***Benchmarks for Science Literacy*** ▸ 9A, *Numbers* grade span essays, pages 211–214 ▸ 12B, *Computation and Estimation* general essay, pages 288–289
	IIB:	***NCTM Principles and Standards for School Mathematics*** ▸ Grades PreK–12 Overview Number and Operations general essay, pages 32–33, *Understanding Meanings,* page 34, *Compute Fluently,* pages 35–36 ▸ Grades PreK–2 Number and Operations general essay, page 79, *Understanding Meanings,* pages 83–84, *Compute Fluently,* pages 84–88 ▸ Grades 3–5 Number and Operations general essay, page 149, *Understanding Meanings,* pages 151– 152, *Compute Fluently,* pages 152–156 ▸ Grades 6–8 Number and Operations general essay, page 215, *Understanding Meanings,* page 218–220, *Compute Fluently,* pages 220–221 ▸ Grades 9–12 Number and Operations general essay, page 291, *Understanding Meanings,* pages 292–294, *Compute Fluently,* page 294
III. Identify Concepts and Specific Ideas	**IIIA:**	***Benchmarks for Science Literacy*** ▸ 9A, *Numbers,* pages 213–214 ▸ 12B, *Computation and Estimation,* pages 290–291
	IIIB:	***NCTM Principles and Standards for School Mathematics*** ▸ Grades PreK–2 Number and Operations, page 78 or 392 ▸ Grades 3–5 Number and Operations, page 148 or 392 ▸ Grades 6–8 Number and Operations, page 214 or 393 ▸ Grades 9–12 Number and Operations, page 290 or 393
IV. Examine Research on Student Learning	**IVA:**	***Benchmarks for Science Literacy*** ▸ 12B, *Operations With Whole Numbers,* page 358; *Operations With Fractions and Decimals,* pages 358–359; *Calculators,* page 359
	IVB:	***Research Companion*** ▸ Chapter 6, Developing Mathematical Power in Whole Number Operations, pages 68–91 ▸ Chapter 8, Facts and Algorithms as Products of Students' Own Mathematical Activity, pages 114–121
V. Examine Coherency and Articulation	**V:**	***Atlas of Science Literacy*** ▸ *Mathematical Processes,* page 27 noting the conceptual strand "Computation and Operations" ▸ *Ratio and Proportionality,* page 119 noting the conceptual strand "Computation"
VI. Clarify State Standards and District Curriculum	**VIA:**	***State Standards:*** Link Sections I–V to learning goals and information from your state standards or frameworks that are informed by the results of the topic study.
	VIB:	***District Curriculum Guide:*** Link Sections I–V to learning goals and information from your district curriculum guide that are informed by the results of the topic study.

Visit www.curriculumtopicstudy.org for updates or supplementary readings, Web sites, and videos.

Standards- and Research-Based Study of a Curricular Topic

COUNTING

Section and Outcome	Selected Sources and Readings for Study and Reflection Read and examine *related parts* of:
I. Identify Adult Content Knowledge	**IA:** *Science for All Americans* ▸ Chapter 9, *Numbers,* page 130, page 132
II. Consider Instructional Implications	**IIA:** *Benchmarks for Science Literacy* ▸ 9A, *Numbers* general essay, page 210; grade span essays, pages 211–212 **IIB:** *NCTM Principles and Standards for School Mathematics* ▸ Grades PreK–12 Overview Number and Operations general essay, page 32, *Understand Numbers,* page 33 ▸ Grades PreK–2 Number and Operations general essay, page 79, *Understand Numbers,* pages 79–80, page 82; Connections, *What Should Connections Look Like,* page 133, Vignette, pages 133–134 ▸ Grades 3–5 Number and Operations, *Understand Numbers,* page 149
III. Identify Concepts and Specific Ideas	**IIIA:** *Benchmarks for Science Literacy* ▸ 9A, *Numbers,* pages 211–212 ▸ 12B, *Computation,* page 290 **IIIB:** *NCTM Principles and Standards for School Mathematics* ▸ Grades PreK–2 Number and Operations, page 78 or 392
IV. Examine Research on Student Learning	**IVA:** *Benchmarks for Science Literacy* ▸ 9A, *Whole Numbers,* page 350; *Number Symbols,* page 350 **IVB:** *NCTM Research Companion* ▸ Chapter 3, *A Framework for Mathematical Reasoning,* pages 31–32 ▸ Chapter 6, *Building Fluency,* page 71, *Single Digit,* pages 73–76 ▸ Chapter 8, *Number Sense,* pages 115–116 ▸ Chapter 20, *Cardinality,* page 290, *Ordinality,* page 291
V. Examine Coherency and Articulation	**V.** *Atlas of Science Literacy* ▸ *Mathematical Processes,* page 27 ▸ *Mathematical Models,* page 29
VI. Clarify State Standards and District Curriculum	**VIA:** *State Standards:* Link Sections I–V to learning goals and information from your state standards or frameworks that are informed by the results of the topic study. **VIB:** *District Curriculum Guide:* Link Sections I–V to learning goals and information from your district curriculum guide that are informed by the results of the topic study.
Visit www.curriculumtopicstudy.org for updates or supplementary readings, Web sites, and videos.	

Standards- and Research-Based Study of a Curricular Topic

DECIMALS

Section and Outcome	Selected Sources and Readings for Study and Reflection Read and examine *related parts* of:
I. Identify Adult Content Knowledge	**IA:** *Science for All Americans* ▸ Chapter 9, *Numbers,* pages 130–131 ▸ Chapter 12, *Computation,* pages 187–190 **IB:** *Beyond Numeracy* ▸ *Computation and Rote,* pages 52–55 ▸ *Rational and Irrational Numbers,* pages 205–208
II. Consider Instructional Implications	**IIA:** *Benchmarks for Science Literacy* ▸ 9A, *Numbers* general essay, page 210; grade span essays, pages 212–214 ▸ 12B, *Computation and Estimation* general essay, pages 288–289 **IIB:** *NCTM Principles and Standards for School Mathematics* ▸ Grades PreK–12 Overview Number and Operations, *Understand Numbers,* page 33, *Understand Meanings,* page 34, *Compute Fluently,* page 35 ▸ Grades 3–5 Number and Operations general essay, page 149, *Understand Numbers,* pages 149–151, *Compute Fluently,* page 152, pages 155–156 ▸ Grades 6–8 Number and Operations general essay, page 215, *Understand Numbers,* pages 215–217, *Understand Meanings,* pages 218–219, *Compute Fluently,* pages 220–221 ▸ Grades 9–12 Number and Operations general essay, page 291, *Understand Numbers,* pages 291–292, *Compute Fluently,* page 294
III. Identify Concepts and Specific Ideas	**IIIA:** *Benchmarks for Science Literacy* ▸ 9A, *Numbers,* page 211, pages 212–214 ▸ 12B, *Computation and Estimation,* pages 290–291 **IIIB:** *NCTM Principles and Standards for School Mathematics* ▸ Grades 3–5 Number and Operations, page 148 or 392 ▸ Grades 6–8 Number and Operations, page 214 or 393 ▸ Grades 9–12 Number and Operations, page 290 or 393
IV. Examine Research on Student Learning	**IVA:** *Benchmarks for Science Literacy* ▸ 9A, *Rational Numbers,* page 350 ▸ 12B, *Operations With Fractions and Decimals,* pages 358–359; *Converting Between Fractions and Decimals,* page 359; *Number Comparison,* page 359
V. Examine Coherency and Articulation	**V:** *Atlas of Science Literacy* ▸ *Mathematical Processes,* page 27 noting the conceptual strand "computation and operations" ▸ *Ratios and Proportionality,* page 119 noting the conceptual strand "computation"
VI. Clarify State Standards and District Curriculum	**VIA:** *State Standards:* Link Sections I–V to learning goals and information from your state standards or frameworks that are informed by the results of the topic study. **VIB:** *District Curriculum Guide:* Link Sections I–V to learning goals and information from your district curriculum guide that are informed by the results of the topic study.
Visit www.curriculumtopicstudy.org for updates or supplementary readings, Web sites, and videos.	

Standards- and Research-Based Study of a Curricular Topic

EXPONENTS

Section and Outcome	Selected Sources and Readings for Study and Reflection Read and examine *related parts* of:
I. Identify Adult Content Knowledge	**IA:** ***Science for All Americans*** ▸ Chapter 11, *Scale,* page 179 ▸ Chapter 12, *Computation,* pages 187–188, *Estimation,* pages 190–191 **IB:** ***Beyond Numeracy*** ▸ *Exponential Growth,* pages 71–74 ▸ *Scientific Notation,* pages 218–220
II. Consider Instructional Implications	**IIA:** ***Benchmarks for Science Literacy*** ▸ 11D, *Scale* general essay, page 276; grade span essays, pages 278–279 **IIB:** ***NCTM Principles and Standards for School Mathematics*** ▸ Grades 3–5 Number and Operations, *Understand Numbers,* page 149 ▸ Grades 6–8 Number and Operations, *Understand Numbers,* page 217 ▸ Grades 9–12 Number and Operations, *Understand Numbers,* page 291
III. Identify Concepts and Specific Ideas	**IIIA:** ***Benchmarks for Science Literacy*** ▸ 9A, *Numbers,* page 214 ▸ 11D, *Scale,* page 279 ▸ 12B, *Computation,* page 291 **IIIB:** ***NCTM Principles and Standards for School Mathematics*** ▸ Grades 3–5 Number and Operations, page 148 or 392 ▸ Grades 6–8 Number and Operations, page 214 or 393 ▸ Grades 9–12 Number and Operations, page 290 or 393
IV. Examine Research on Student Learning	**IV:** No research available for *Benchmarks* or *Research Companion*
V. Examine Coherency and Articulation	**V:** ***Atlas of Science Literacy:*** There are no maps for this topic in Volume 1.
VI. Clarify State Standards and District Curriculum	**VIA:** ***State Standards:*** Link Sections I–V to learning goals and information from your state standards or frameworks that are informed by the results of the topic study. **VIB:** ***District Curriculum Guide:*** Link Sections I–V to learning goals and information from your district curriculum guide that are informed by the results of the topic study.
Visit www.curriculumtopicstudy.org for updates or supplementary readings, Web sites, and videos.	

Standards- and Research-Based Study of a Curricular Topic

FACTORS AND MULTIPLES (Elementary Number Theory)

Section and Outcome	Selected Sources and Readings for Study and Reflection Read and examine *related parts* of:
I. Identify Adult Content Knowledge	**IB:** *Beyond Numeracy* ▸ *Prime Numbers,* pages 184–186
II. Consider Instructional Implications	**IIA:** *Benchmarks for Science Literacy* ▸ 9A, *Numbers* general essay, page 210; grade span essays, pages 212–213 **IIB:** *NCTM Principles and Standards for School Mathematics* ▸ Grades PreK–12 Overview Number and Operations general essay, pages 32–33 ▸ Grades 3–5 Number and Operations, *Understand Numbers,* page 151, *Understand Meanings,* page 152 ▸ Grades 6–8 Number and Operations, *Understand Numbers,* page 217
III. Identify Concepts and Specific Ideas	**IIIA:** *Benchmarks for Science Literacy* ▸ 9A, *Numbers,* page 213 **IIIB:** *NCTM Principles and Standards for School Mathematics* ▸ Grades 3–5 Number and Operations, page 148 or 392 ▸ Grades 6–8 Number and Operations, page 214 or 393
IV. Examine Research on Student Learning	**IV:** No research findings available in *Benchmarks* or *Research Companion*
V. Examine Coherency and Articulation	**V:** *Atlas of Science Literacy:* There are no maps for this topic in Volume 1.
VI. Clarify State Standards and District Curriculum	**VIA:** *State Standards:* Link Sections I–V to learning goals and information from your state standards or frameworks that are informed by the results of the topic study. **VIB:** *District Curriculum Guide:* Link Sections I–V to learning goals and information from your district curriculum guide that are informed by the results of the topic study.
Visit www.curriculumtopicstudy.org for updates or supplementary readings, Web sites, and videos.	

Standards- and Research-Based Study of a Curricular Topic

FACTS

Section and Outcome	Selected Sources and Readings for Study and Reflection Read and examine *related parts* of:
I. Identify Adult Content Knowledge	**IA:** ***Science for All Americans*** ▸ Chapter 9, *Numbers,* page 131 ▸ Chapter 12, *Computation*, pages 187– 188 **IB:** ***Beyond Numeracy*** ▸ *Computation and Rote,* pages 52–55
II. Consider Instructional Implications	**IIA:** ***Benchmarks for Science Literacy*** ▸ 9A, *Numbers* general essay, page 210; grade span essays, pages 211–212 ▸ 12B, *Computation and Estimation* general essay, pages 288–289 **IIB:** ***NCTM Principles and Standards for School Mathematics*** ▸ Grades PreK–12 Overview Number and Operations general essay, page 32, *Understand Meanings,* page 34 ▸ Grades PreK–2 Number and Operations general essay, page 79, *Understand Meanings,* pages 83–84, *Compute Fluently,* pages 84–85, page 87 ▸ Grades 3–5 Number and Operations general essay, page 149, *Understand Meanings,* pages 151–152, *Compute Fluently,* pages 152–153
III. Identify Concepts and Specific Ideas	**IIIA:** ***Benchmarks for Science Literacy*** ▸ 12B, *Computation and Estimation,* page 290 **IIIB:** ***NCTM Principles and Standards for School Mathematics*** ▸ Grades PreK–2 Number and Operations, page 78 or 392 ▸ Grades 3–5 Number and Operations, page 148 or 392
IV. Examine Research on Student Learning	**IVA:** ***Benchmarks for Science Literacy*** ▸ 12B, *Operations With Whole Numbers,* page 358; *Calculators,* page 359 **IVB:** ***Research Companion*** ▸ Chapter 6, *Single–Digit Computation,* pages 72, *Single–Digit Addition and Subtraction,* pages 73–76, *Single–Digit Multiplication and Division,* pages 76–78 ▸ Chapter 8, *Facts and Algorithms as Products of Students' Own Mathematical Activity Overview,* pages 114–115, *Number Sense as a Basis,* pages 115–117
V. Examine Coherency and Articulation	**V:** ***Atlas of Science Literacy*** ▸ *Mathematical Processes,* page 27 noting the conceptual strand "Computation and Operations" ▸ *Ratio and Proportionality,* page 119 noting the conceptual strand "Computation"
VI. Clarify State Standards and District Curriculum	**VIA:** ***State Standards:*** Link Sections I–V to learning goals and information from your state standards or frameworks that are informed by the results of the topic study. **VIB:** ***District Curriculum Guide:*** Link Sections I–V to learning goals and information from your district curriculum guide that are informed by the results of the topic study.
Visit www.curriculumtopicstudy.org for updates or supplementary readings, Web sites, and videos.	

Standards- and Research-Based Study of a Curricular Topic

FRACTIONS

Section and Outcome	Selected Sources and Readings for Study and Reflection Read and examine *related parts* of:
I. Identify Adult Content Knowledge	**IA:** *Science for All Americans* ▸ Chapter 9, *Numbers,* pages 130–131 ▸ Chapter 12, *Computation,* pages 187–191 **IB:** *Beyond Numeracy* ▸ *Computation and Rote,* pages 52–55 ▸ *Rational and Irrational Numbers,* pages 205–208
II. Consider Instructional Implications	**IIA:** *Benchmarks for Science Literacy* ▸ 9A, *Numbers* general essay, page 210; grade span essays, pages 211–214 ▸ 12B, *Computation and Estimation* general essay, pages 288–289 **IIB:** *NCTM Principles and Standards for School Mathematics* ▸ Grades PreK–12 Overview Number and Operations general essay, pages 32–33, *Understand Numbers,* pages 33–34, *Understand Meanings,* page 34, *Compute Fluently,* pages 35–36 ▸ Grades PreK–2 Number and Operations, *Understand Numbers,* pages 82–83 ▸ Grades 3–5 Number and Operations general essay, page 149, *Understand Numbers,* pages 150–151, *Understand Meanings,* page 152, *Compute Fluently,* page 152, pages 155–156 ▸ Grades 6–8 Number and Operations general essay, page 215, *Understand Numbers,* pages 215–217, *Understand Meanings,* pages 218–220, *Compute Fluently,* page 220–221 ▸ Grades 9–12 Number and Operations general essay, page 291, *Understand Numbers,* pages 291–292, *Understand Meanings,* pages 292–293, *Compute Fluently,* page 294
III. Identify Concepts and Specific Ideas	**IIIA:** *Benchmarks for Science Literacy* ▸ 9A, *Numbers,* pages 211–213 ▸ 12B, *Computation and Estimation,* pages 290–291 **IIIB:** *NCTM Principles and Standards for School Mathematics* ▸ Grades PreK–2 Number and Operations, page 78 or 392 ▸ Grades 3–5 Number and Operations, page 148 or 392 ▸ Grades 6–8 Number and Operations, page 214 or 393 ▸ Grades 9–12 Number and Operations, page 290 or 393
IV. Examine Research on Student Learning	**IVA:** *Benchmarks for Science Literacy* ▸ 9A, *Rational Numbers,* page 350 ▸ 12B, *Operations With Fractions and Decimals,* pages 358–359; *Converting Between Fractions and Decimals,* page 359; *Number Comparison,* page 359 **IVB:** *NCTM Research Companion* ▸ Chapter 7, Fractions and Multiplicative Reasoning, pages 95–110
V. Examine Coherency and Articulation	**V:** *Atlas of Science Literacy* ▸ *Mathematical Processes,* page 27 noting the conceptual strand "Computation and operations." ▸ *Ratios and Proportionality,* page 119
VI. Clarify State Standards and District Curriculum	**VIA:** *State Standards:* Link Sections I–V to learning goals and information from your state standards or frameworks that are informed by the results of the topic study. **VIB:** *District Curriculum Guide:* Link Sections I–V to learning goals and information from your district curriculum guide that are informed by the results of the topic study.
Visit www.curriculumtopicstudy.org for updates or supplementary readings, Web sites, and videos.	

Standards- and Research-Based Study of a Curricular Topic

FRACTIONS, DECIMALS, AND PERCENTS

Section and Outcome	Selected Sources and Readings for Study and Reflection Read and examine *related parts* of:
I. Identify Adult Content Knowledge	**IA:** ***Science for All Americans*** ▸ Chapter 9, *Numbers*, pages 130–131 ▸ Chapter 12, *Computation*, pages 187–190 **IB:** ***Beyond Numeracy*** ▸ *Computation and Rote*, pages 52–55 ▸ *Rational and Irrational Numbers*, pages 205–208
II. Consider Instructional Implications	**IIA:** ***Benchmarks for Science Literacy*** ▸ 9A, *Numbers* general essay, page 210; grade span essays, pages 211–214 ▸ 12B, *Computation and Estimation* general essay, pages 288–289 **IIB:** ***NCTM Principles and Standards for School Mathematics*** ▸ Grades PreK–12 Overview Number and Operations general essay, pages 32–33, *Understand Numbers*, pages 33–34, *Understand Meanings*, page 34, *Compute Fluently*, pages 35–36 ▸ Grades PreK–2 Number and Operations, *Understand Numbers*, pages 82–83 ▸ Grades 3–5 Number and Operations general essay, page 149, *Understand Numbers*, pages 150–151, *Understand Meanings*, page 152, *Compute Fluently*, page 152, pages 155–156 ▸ Grades 6–8 Number and Operations general essay, page 215, *Understand Numbers*, pages 215–217, *Understand Meanings*, pages 218–220, *Compute Fluently*, pages 220–221 ▸ Grades 9–12 Number and Operations general essay, page 291, *Understand Numbers*, pages 291–292, *Understand Meanings*, pages 292–293, *Compute Fluently*, page 294
III. Identify Concepts and Specific Ideas	**IIIA:** ***Benchmarks for Science Literacy*** ▸ 9A, *Numbers*, pages 211–213 ▸ 12B, *Computation and Estimation*, pages 290–291 **IIIB:** ***NCTM Principles and Standards for School Mathematics*** ▸ Grades PreK–2 Number and Operations, page 78 or 392 ▸ Grades 3–5 Number and Operations, page 148 or 392 ▸ Grades 6–8 Number and Operations, page 214 or 393 ▸ Grades 9–12 Number and Operations, page 290 or 393
IV. Examine Research on Student Learning	**IVA:** ***Benchmarks for Science Literacy*** ▸ 9A, *Rational Numbers*, page 350 ▸ 12B, *Operations With Fractions and Decimals*, pages 358–359; *Converting Between Fractions and Decimals*, page 359; *Number Comparison*, page 359 **IVB:** ***Research Companion*** ▸ Chapter 7, Fractions and Multiplicative Reasoning, pages 95–110
V. Examine Coherency and Articulation	**V:** ***Atlas of Science Literacy*** ▸ *Mathematical Processes*, page 27 noting the conceptual strand "computation and operations." ▸ *Ratios and Proportionality*, page 119
VI. Clarify State Standards and District Curriculum	**VIA:** ***State Standards:*** Link Sections I–V to learning goals and information from your state standards or frameworks that are informed by the results of the topic study. **VIB:** ***District Curriculum Guide:*** Link Sections I–V to learning goals and information from your district curriculum guide that are informed by the results of the topic study.
	Visit www.curriculumtopicstudy.org for updates or supplementary readings, Web sites, and videos.

Standards- and Research-Based Study of a Curricular Topic

INTEGERS

Section and Outcome	Selected Sources and Readings for Study and Reflection Read and examine *related parts* of:
I. Identify Adult Content Knowledge	**IA:** *Science for All Americans* ▶ Chapter 9 *Numbers,* page 131, *Computation,* pages 187–191 **IB:** *Beyond Numeracy* ▶ *Imaginary and Negative Numbers,* pages 115–116
II. Consider Instructional Implications	**IIA:** *Benchmarks for Science Literacy* ▶ 9A, *Numbers* general essay, page 210, grade span essays, pages 211–214 ▶ 12B, *Computation and Estimation* general essay, pages 288–289, grade span essays, pages 290–291 **IIB:** *NCTM Principles and Standards for School Mathematics* ▶ Grades K–12 overview Number and Operations, pages 33–34 ▶ Grades 3–5 Number and Operations, pages 149,151 ▶ Grades 6–8 Number and Operations, pages 215, 217–218, 219–220 ▶ Grades 9–12 Number and Operations, pages 291–293
III. Identify Concepts and Specific Ideas	**IIIA:** *Benchmarks for Science Literacy* ▶ 9A *Numbers,* pages 211–214 ▶ 12B *Computation and Estimation,* pages 290–291 **IIIB:** *NCTM Principles and Standards for School Mathematics* ▶ Grades 3–5 Number and Operations, pages 148–392 ▶ Grades 6–8 Number and Operations, pages 214–393 ▶ Grades 9–12 Number and Operations, pages 290–393
IV. Examine Research on Student Learning	**IVA:** *Benchmarks for Science Literacy* ▶ No research available for *Benchmarks.* **IVB:** *Research Companion* ▶ No research available for *Research Companions.*
V. Examine Coherency and Articulation	**V:** *Atlas of Science Literacy* ▶ *Ratios and Proportionality,* pages 118–119 noting the conceptual strand "computation"
VI. Clarify State Standards and District Curriculum	**VIA:** *State Standards:* Link Sections I–V to learning goals and information from your state standards or frameworks that are informed by the results of the topic study. **VIB:** *District Curriculum Guide:* Link Sections I–V to learning goals and information from your district curriculum guide that are informed by the results of the topic study.
Visit www.curriculumtopicstudy.org for updates or supplementary readings, Web sites, and videos.	

Standards- and Research-Based Study of a Curricular Topic

LARGE AND SMALL NUMBERS

Section and Outcome	Selected Sources and Readings for Study and Reflection Read and examine *related parts* of:
I. Identify Adult Content Knowledge	**IA:** ***Science for All Americans*** ▸ Chapter 11, *Scale*, page 179 ▸ Chapter 12, *Basic Number Skills*, pages 187–188 **IB:** ***Beyond Numeracy*** ▸ *Exponential Growth*, pages 71–74 ▸ *Scientific Notation*, pages 218–220
II. Consider Instructional Implications	**IIA:** ***Benchmarks for Science Literacy*** ▸ 9A, *Numbers* general essay, page 210 ▸ 11D, *Scale* general essay, page 276, grade span essays, pages 277–279 **IIB:** ***NCTM Principles and Standards for School Mathematics*** ▸ Grades 3–5 Number and Operations general essay, page 149, *Understand Numbers,* page 149 ▸ Grades 6–8 Number and Operations, *Understand Numbers,* page 217 ▸ Grades 9–12 Number and Operations, *Understand Numbers,* page 291
III. Identify Concepts and Specific Ideas	**IIIA:** ***Benchmarks for Science Literacy*** ▸ 9A, *Numbers*, page 214 ▸ 11D, *Scale*, page 279 ▸ 12B, *Computation*, page 291 **IIIB:** ***NCTM Principles and Standards for School Mathematics*** ▸ Grades 3–5 Number and Operations, page 148 or 392 ▸ Grades 6–8 Number and Operations, page 214 or 393 ▸ Grades 9–12 Number and Operations, page 290 or 393
IV. Examine Research on Student Learning	**IVA:** ***Benchmarks for Science Literacy*** ▸ 9A, *Numbers,* page 350
V. Examine Coherency and Articulation	**V.** ***Atlas of Science Literacy:*** There are no maps for this topic in Volume 1.
VI. Clarify State Standards and District Curriculum	**VIA:** ***State Standards:*** Link Sections I–V to learning goals and information from your state standards or frameworks that are informed by the results of the topic study. **VIB:** ***District Curriculum Guide:*** Link Sections I–V to learning goals and information from your district curriculum guide that are informed by the results of the topic study.
Visit www.curriculumtopicstudy.org for updates or supplementary readings, Web sites, and videos.	

Standards- and Research-Based Study of a Curricular Topic

MULTIPLICATION AND DIVISION

Section and Outcome	Selected Sources and Readings for Study and Reflection Read and examine *related parts* of:
I. Identify Adult Content Knowledge	**IA:** *Science for All Americans* ▸ Chapter 9, *Numbers,* page 131 ▸ Chapter 12, *Computation,* pages 187–191 **IB:** *Beyond Numeracy* ▸ *Computation and Rote,* pages 52–55
II. Consider Instructional Implications	**IIA:** *Benchmarks for Science Literacy* ▸ 9A, *Numbers,* grade span essays, pages 212–213 ▸ 12B, *Computation and Estimation,* general essay, pages 288–289 **IIB:** *NCTM Principles and Standards for School Mathematics* ▸ Grades K–12 Overview Number and Operations, page 32, *Understand Meanings,* page 34, *Compute Fluently,* pages 35–36 ▸ Grades PreK–2 Number and Operations, *Understand Meanings,* page 84, *Compute Fluently,* page 87 ▸ Grades 3–5 Number and Operations, page 149; *Understand Meanings,* pages 151–152, *Compute Fluently,* pages 152–156 ▸ Grades 6–8 Number and Operations, *Understand Meanings,* pages 218–220, *Compute Fluently,* pages 220–221
III. Identify Concepts and Specific Ideas	**IIIA:** *Benchmarks for Science Literacy* ▸ 9A, *Numbers,* pages 212–213 ▸ 12B, *Computation and Estimation,* pages 290–291 **IIIB:** *NCTM Principles and Standards for School Mathematics* ▸ Grades PreK–2 Number and Operations, page 78 or 392 ▸ Grades 3–5 Number and Operations, page 148 or 392 ▸ Grades 6–8 Number and Operations, page 214 or 393 ▸ Grades 9–12 Number and Operations, page 290 or 393
IV. Examine Research on Student Learning	**IVA:** *Benchmarks for Science Literacy* ▸ 12B, *Operations With Whole Numbers,* page 358, *Operations With Fractions and Decimals,* pages 358–359, *Calculators,* page 359 **IVB:** *Research Companion* ▸ Chapter 6, *Types of Real–World Situations,* page 69, *Building Fluency,* pages 71–72, *Multidigit Multiplication and Division,* pages 84–87, *General Issues,* pages 87–90 ▸ Chapter 7, *Pedagogical Contexts,* page 96, *Understanding Fractions,* pages 99–100, *Multiplication Schemes,* pages 103–105, *Division Schemes,* pages 105–107, *Fraction Schemes,* pages 107–109, *Conclusion,* pages 109–110 ▸ Chapter 8, *Semi–informal Algorithms,* page 120; *Conclusions,* pages 120–121
V. Examine Coherency and Articulation	**V:** *Atlas of Science Literacy* ▸ *Mathematical Processes,* page 27 noting the conceptual strand "Computation and Operations" ▸ *Ratio and Proportionality,* page 119 noting the conceptual strand "Computation"
VI. Clarify State Standards and District Curriculum	**VIA:** *State Standards:* Link Sections I–V to learning goals and information from your state standards or frameworks that are informed by the results of the topic study. **VIB:** *District Curriculum Guide:* Link Sections I–V to learning goals and information from your district curriculum guide that are informed by the results of the topic study.
	Visit www.curriculumtopicstudy.org for updates or supplementary readings, Web sites, and videos.

Standards- and Research-Based Study of a Curricular Topic

MULTIPLICATION AND DIVISION OF WHOLE NUMBERS

Section and Outcome	Selected Sources and Readings for Study and Reflection Read and examine *related parts* of:	
I. Identify Adult Content Knowledge	**IA:**	***Science for All Americans*** ▸ Chapter 9, *Numbers,* page 131 ▸ Chapter 12, *Computation,* pages 187–191
	IB:	***Beyond Numeracy*** ▸ *Computation and Rote,* pages 52–55
II. Consider Instructional Implications	**IIA:**	***Benchmarks for Science Literacy*** ▸ 9A, *Numbers,* grade span essay, page 212 ▸ 12B, *Computation and Estimation,* general essay pages 288–289
	IIB:	***NCTM Principles and Standards for School Mathematics*** ▸ Grades K–12 Overview Number and Operations, pages 32–33, *Understand Meanings,* page 34, *Compute Fluently,* pages 35–36 ▸ Grades PreK–2 Number and Operations, *Understand Meanings,* page 84, *Compute Fluently,* page 87 ▸ Grades 3–5 Number and Operations, page 149, *Understand Meanings,* pages 151–152, *Compute Fluently,* pages 152–156 ▸ Grades 6–8 Number and Operations, *Understand Meanings,* pages 218–219
III. Identify Concepts and Specific Ideas	**IIIA:**	***Benchmarks for Science Literacy*** ▸ 9A, *Numbers,* page 213 ▸ 12B, *Computation and Estimation,* page 290
	IIIB:	***NCTM Principles and Standards for School Mathematics*** ▸ Grades PreK–2 Number and Operations, page 78 or 392 ▸ Grades 3–5 Number and Operations, page 148 or 392 ▸ Grades 6–8 Number and Operations, page 214 or 393 ▸ Grades 9–12 Number and Operations, page 290 or 393
IV. Examine Research on Student Learning	**IVA:**	***Benchmarks for Science Literacy*** ▸ 12B, *Operations With Whole Numbers,* page 358, *Calculators,* page 359
	IVB:	***Research Companion*** ▸ Chapter 6, *Types of Real–World Situations,* page 69, *Building Fluency,* pages 71–72, *Multidigit Multiplication and Division,* pages 84–87 ▸ Chapter 8, pages 114–115, *Guided Reinvention,* page 117, *Conclusion,* pages 120–121
V. Examine Coherency and Articulation	**V:**	***Atlas of Science Literacy*** ▸ *Mathematical Processes,* page 27 noting the conceptual strand "Computation and Operations" ▸ *Ratio and Proportionality,* page 119 noting the conceptual strand "Computation"
VI. Clarify State Standards and District Curriculum	**VIA:**	***State Standards:*** Link Sections I–V to learning goals and information from your state standards or frameworks that are informed by the results of the topic study.
	VIB:	***District Curriculum Guide:*** Link Sections I–V to learning goals and information from your district curriculum guide that are informed by the results of the topic study.
Visit www.curriculumtopicstudy.org for updates or supplementary readings, Web sites, and videos.		

Standards- and Research-Based Study of a Curricular Topic

NUMBER SENSE

Section and Outcome	Selected Sources and Readings for Study and Reflection Read and examine *related parts* of:
I. Identify Adult Content Knowledge	**IA:** ***Science for All Americans*** ▸ Chapter 9, *Numbers,* pages 130–132 ▸ Chapter 12, *Computation and Estimation,* pages 187–191 **IB:** ***Beyond Numeracy*** ▸ *Computation and Rote,* pages 52–55
II. Consider Instructional Implications	**IIA:** ***Benchmarks for Science Literacy*** ▸ 9A, *Numbers* general essay, page 210; grade span essays, pages 211–214 ▸ 12B, *Computation and Estimation* general essay, pages 288–289 **IIB:** ***NCTM Principles and Standards for School Mathematics*** ▸ Grades PreK–12 Overview Number and Operations general essay, pages 32–33, *Understand Numbers,* pages 33–34, *Compute Fluently,* pages 35–36 ▸ Grades PreK–2 Number and Operations general essay, page 79, *Understand Numbers,* pages 79–82, *Compute Fluently,* pages 84–85 ▸ Grades 3–5 Number and Operations general essay, page 149, *Understand Numbers,* pages 149–151, *Compute Fluently,* pages 152–153 ▸ Grades 6–8 Number and Operations general essay, page 215, *Understand Numbers,* pages 215–218, *Compute Fluently,* pages 220–221 ▸ Grades 9–12 Number and Operations general essay, page 291, *Understand Numbers,* pages 291–292, *Compute Fluently,* page 294
III. Identify Concepts and Specific Ideas	**IIIA:** ***Benchmarks for Science Literacy*** ▸ 9A, *Numbers,* pages 211–214 ▸ 12B, *Computation and Estimation,* pages 290–291 **IIIB:** ***NCTM Principles and Standards for School Mathematics*** ▸ Grades PreK–2 Number and Operations, page 78 or 392 ▸ Grades 3–5 Number and Operations, page 148 or 392 ▸ Grades 6–8 Number and Operations, page 214 or 393 ▸ Grades 9–12 Number and Operations, page 290 or 393
IV. Examine Research on Student Learning	**IVA:** ***Benchmarks for Science Literacy*** ▸ 9A, *Numbers,* page 350 ▸ 12B, *Calculators,* page 359, *Number Comparisons,* page 359, *Estimation Skills,* page 360 **IVB:** ***Research Companion*** ▸ Chapter 8, *Number Sense as a Basis,* pages 115–117
V. Examine Coherency and Articulation	**V:** ***Atlas of Science Literacy*** ▸ *Mathematical Processes,* page 27
VI. Clarify State Standards and District Curriculum	**VIA:** ***State Standards:*** Link Sections I–V to learning goals and information from your state standards or frameworks that are informed by the results of the topic study. **VIB:** ***District Curriculum Guide:*** Link Sections I–V to learning goals and information from your district curriculum guide that are informed by the results of the topic study.
Visit www.curriculumtopicstudy.org for updates or supplementary readings, Web sites, and videos.	

Standards- and Research-Based Study of a Curricular Topic

NUMBERS AND NUMBER SYSTEMS

Section and Outcome	Selected Sources and Readings for Study and Reflection Read and examine *related parts* of:
I. Identify Adult Content Knowledge	**IA:** *Science for All Americans* ▸ Chapter 9, *Numbers*, pages 130–132 **IB:** *Beyond Numeracy* ▸ *Arabic Numerals*, pages 15–17 ▸ *Imaginary and Negative Numbers*, pages 115–117 ▸ *Notation*, pages 163–165 ▸ *Rational and Irrational Numbers*, pages 205–208 ▸ *Scientific Notation*, pages 218–220 ▸ *Time, Space, and Immensity*, pages 241–245
II. Consider Instructional Implications	**IIA:** *Benchmarks for Science Literacy* ▸ 9A, *Numbers*, general essay, page 210, grade span essays, pages 211–214 **IIB:** *NCTM Principles and Standards for School Mathematics* ▸ Grades K–12 Overview Number and Operations, pages 32–33, *Understand Numbers*, pages 33–34 ▸ Grades PreK–2 Number and Operations, page 79, *Understand Numbers*, pages 79–82 ▸ Grades 3–5 Number and Operations, page 149, *Understand Numbers*, pages 149–151 ▸ Grades 6–8 Number and Operations, page 215, *Understand Numbers*, pages 215–218 ▸ Grades 9–12 Number and Operations, page 291, *Understand Numbers*, pages 291–292
III. Identify Concepts and Specific Ideas	**IIIA:** *Benchmarks for Science Literacy* ▸ 9A, *Numbers*, pages 211–214 **IIIB:** *NCTM Principles and Standards for School Mathematics* ▸ Grades PreK–2 Number and Operations, page 78 or 392 ▸ Grades 3–5 Number and Operations, page 148 or 392 ▸ Grades 6–8 Number and Operations, page 214 or 393 ▸ Grades 9–12 Number and Operations, page 290 or 393
IV. Examine Research on Student Learning	**IVA:** *Benchmarks for Science Literacy* ▸ 9A, *Numbers*, page 350 **IVB:** *Research Companion* ▸ Chapter 8, *Facts and Algorithms as Products of Students' Own Mathematical Activity*, pages 114–121
V. Examine Coherency and Articulation	**V:** *Atlas of Science Literacy* ▸ *Mathematical Processes*, page 27
VI. Clarify State Standards and District Curriculum	**VIA:** *State Standards:* Link Sections I–V to learning goals and information from your state standards or frameworks that are informed by the results of the topic study. **VIB:** *District Curriculum Guide:* Link Sections I–V to learning goals and information from your district curriculum guide that are informed by the results of the topic study.
Visit www.curriculumtopicstudy.org for updates or supplementary readings, Web sites, and videos.	

Standards- and Research-Based Study of a Curricular Topic

PERCENT

Section and Outcome	Selected Sources and Readings for Study and Reflection Read and examine *related parts* of:
I. Identify Adult Content Knowledge	**IA:** ***Science for All Americans*** ▸ Chapter 9, *Uncertainty,* pages 135–137 ▸ Chapter 12, *Computation,* pages 187–189, *Estimation,* pages 190–191 **IB:** ***Beyond Numeracy*** ▸ *Computation and Rote,* pages 52–53
II. Consider Instructional Implications	**IIA:** ***Benchmarks for Science Literacy*** ▸ 9A, *Numbers,* grade span essay, page 213 **IIB:** ***NCTM Principles and Standards for School Mathematics*** ▸ Grades PreK–12 Overview Number and Operations, *Understand Numbers,* page 33 ▸ Grades 3–5 Number and Operations, page 149, *Understand Numbers,* pages 150–151 ▸ Grades 6–8 Number and Operations, page 215, *Understand Numbers,* pages 215–217
III. Identify Concepts and Specific Ideas	**IIIA:** ***Benchmarks for Science Literacy*** ▸ 9A, *Numbers,* page 213 ▸ 12B, *Computation and Estimation,* page 291 **IIIB:** ***NCTM Principles and Standards for School Mathematics*** ▸ Grades 3–5 Number and Operations, page 148 or 392 ▸ Grades 6–8 Number and Operations, page 214 or 393
IV. Examine Research on Student Learning	**IVA:** ***Benchmarks for Science Literacy***: No research available in *Benchmarks.* **IVB:** ***Research Companion***: No research available in *Research Companion.*
V. Examine Coherency and Articulation	**V:** ***Atlas of Science Literacy*** ▸ *Mathematical Processes,* page 27 noting the conceptual strand "Computation and Operations" ▸ *Ratios and Proportionality,* page 119
VI. Clarify State Standards and District Curriculum	**VIA:** ***State Standards:*** Link Sections I–V to learning goals and information from your state standards or frameworks that are informed by the results of the topic study. **VIB:** ***District Curriculum Guide:*** Link Sections I–V to learning goals and information from your district curriculum guide that are informed by the results of the topic study.
Visit www.curriculumtopicstudy.org for updates or supplementary readings, Web sites, and videos. (after publication in 2005)	

Standards- and Research-Based Study of a Curricular Topic

PLACE VALUE

Section and Outcome	Selected Sources and Readings for Study and Reflection Read and examine *related parts* of:
I. Identify Adult Content Knowledge	**IA:** ***Science for All Americans*** ▸ Chapter 9, *Numbers,* page 130 **IB:** ***Beyond Numeracy*** ▸ *Arabic Numerals,* pages 15–17 ▸ *Binary Numbers,* pages 24–25
II. Consider Instructional Implications	**IIA:** ***Benchmarks for Science Literacy*** ▸ 9A, *Numbers,* general essay, page 210, grade span essays, pages 212–213 **IIB:** ***NCTM Principles and Standards for School Mathematics*** ▸ Grades PreK–12 Overview Number and Operations, page 32, *Understand Numbers,* page 33 ▸ Grades PreK–2 Number and Operations, page 79, *Understand Numbers* pages 80–82 ▸ Grades 3–5 Number and Operations, *Understand Numbers,* pages 149–150 ▸ Grades 6–8 Number and Operations, *Understand Numbers,* page 216
III. Identify Concepts and Specific Ideas	**IIIA:** ***Benchmarks for Science Literacy*** ▸ 9A, *Numbers,* pages 212–214 **IIIB:** ***NCTM Principles and Standards for School Mathematics*** ▸ Grades PreK–2 Number and Operations, page 78 or 392 ▸ Grades 3–5 Number and Operations, page 148 or 392 ▸ Grades 6–8 Number and Operations, page 214 or 393
IV. Examine Research on Student Learning	**IVA:** ***Benchmarks for Science Literacy*** ▸ 9A, *Whole Numbers,* page 350, *Rational Numbers* page 350 **IVB:** ***Research Companion*** ▸ Chapter 6, *Multidigit Addition and Subtraction,* pages 78–84
V. Examine Coherency and Articulation	**V:** ***Atlas of Science Literacy:*** There are no maps for this topic in Volume 1.
VI. Clarify State Standards and District Curriculum	**VIA:** ***State Standards:*** Link Sections I–V to learning goals and information from your state standards or frameworks that are informed by the results of the topic study. **VIB:** ***District Curriculum Guide:*** Link Sections I–V to learning goals and information from your district curriculum guide that are informed by the results of the topic study.
Visit www.curriculumtopicstudy.org for updates or supplementary readings, Web sites, and videos.	

Standards- and Research-Based Study of a Curricular Topic

PROPERTIES OF OPERATIONS

Section and Outcome	Selected Sources and Readings for Study and Reflection Read and examine *related parts* of:
I. Identify Adult Content Knowledge	**IA:** *Science for All Americans* ▸ Chapter 12, *Computation*, pages 187–188 **IB:** *Beyond Numeracy* ▸ *Arabic Numerals,* pages 15–17 ▸ *Groups and Abstract Algebra,* pages 102–106
II. Consider Instructional Implications	**IIA:** *Benchmarks for Science Literacy* ▸ 9A, *Numbers,* general essay, page 210, grade span essays, pages 212–214 **IIB:** *NCTM Principles and Standards for School Mathematics* ▸ Grades PreK–12 Overview Number and Operations, page 32, *Understand Meanings,* page 34; Algebra, *Represent and Analyze,* pages 38–39 ▸ Grades PreK–2 Number and Operations, *Understand Meanings,* pages 83–84; Algebra, *Represent and Analyze,* pages 93–94 ▸ Grades 3–5 Number and Operations, *Understand Meanings,* pages 151–152; Algebra, *Represent and Analyze,* pages 160–161 ▸ Grades 6–8 Number and Operations, *Understand Meanings,* pages 218–220; Algebra, *Represent and Analyze,* pages 226–227 ▸ Grades 9–12 Number and Operations, *Understand Meanings,* pages 292–294; Algebra, *Represent and Analyze,* pages 300–303
III. Identify Concepts and Specific Ideas	**IIIA:** *Benchmarks for Science Literacy* ▸ 9A, *Numbers,* pages 212–214 **IIIB:** *NCTM Principles and Standards for School Mathematics* ▸ Grades PreK–2 Number and Operations, page 78 or 392; Algebra, page 90 or 394 ▸ Grades 3–5 Number and Operations, page 148 or 392; Algebra, page 158 or 394 ▸ Grades 6–8 Number and Operations, page 214 or 393; Algebra, page 222 or 395 ▸ Grades 9–12 Number and Operations, page 290 or 393; Algebra, page 296 or 395
IV. Examine Research on Student Learning	**IVA:** *Benchmarks for Science Literacy* ▸ 9A, *Algebraic Equations,* pages 351–352 **IVB:** *Research Companion* ▸ Chapter 6, *Developing Mathematical Power in Whole Number Operations,* pages 68–91 ▸ Chapter 8, *Facts and Algorithms as Products of Students' Own Mathematical Activity,* pages 114–121
V. Examine Coherency and Articulation	**V:** *Atlas of Science Literacy* ▸ *Mathematical Processes,* page 27 noting the conceptual strand "Computation and Operations"
VI. Clarify State Standards and District Curriculum	**VIA:** *State Standards:* Link Sections I–V to learning goals and information from your state standards or frameworks that are informed by the results of the topic study. **VIB:** *District Curriculum Guide:* Link Sections I–V to learning goals and information from your district curriculum guide that are informed by the results of the topic study.
Visit www.curriculumtopicstudy.org for updates or supplementary readings, Web sites, and videos.	

Standards- and Research-Based Study of a Curricular Topic

RATIO AND PROPORTION

Section and Outcome	Selected Sources and Readings for Study and Reflection Read and examine *related parts* of:
I. Identify Adult Content Knowledge	**IA:** ***Science for All Americans*** ▸ Chapter 9, *Numbers,* pages 130–132, *Probability,* page 137 **IB:** ***Beyond Numeracy*** ▸ *Trigonometry,* pages 251–253
II. Consider Instructional Implications	**IIA:** ***Benchmarks for Science Literacy*** ▸ 9A, *Numbers,* general essay, page 210, grade span essays, pages 211–214 ▸ 11D, *Scale,* general essay, page 276, grade span essays, pages 277–279 **IIB:** ***NCTM Principles and Standards for School Mathematics*** ▸ Grades K–12 Overview Number and Operations, page 32, *Understand Numbers,* pages 33–34, *Understand Meanings,* page 34; Connections, *Recognize and Use,* pages 64–65, *Understand How Mathematical,* page 65 ▸ Grades PreK–2 Number and Operations, *Understand Numbers,* pages 79–82 ▸ Grades 3–5 Number and Operations, *Understand Numbers,* pages 150–151 ▸ Grades 6–8 Number and Operations, page 215, *Understand Numbers,* pages 215–218; Geometry, *Analyze Characteristics,* pages 234–235; Measurement, *Apply Appropriate Techniques,* pages 245–246; Connections, page 277 ▸ Grades 9–12 Number and Operations, pages 291–292
III. Identify Concepts and Specific Ideas	**IIIA:** ***Benchmarks for Science Literacy*** ▸ 9A, *Numbers,* pages 211–214 ▸ 12B, *Computation,* pages 290–291 **IIIB:** ***NCTM Principles and Standards for School Mathematics*** ▸ Grades K–12 Overview Number and Operations, *Understand Numbers,* page 33, *Understand Meanings,* page 34 ▸ Grades PreK–2 Number and Operations, page 78 or 392 ▸ Grades 3–5 Number and Operations, page 148 or 392 ▸ Grades 6–8 Number and Operations, page 214 or 393; Measurement, page 240 or 399 ▸ Grades 9–12 Number and Operations, page 290 or 393
IV. Examine Research on Student Learning	**IVA:** ***Benchmarks for Science Literacy*** ▸ 9A, *Numbers,* page 350 ▸ 12B, *Proportional Reasoning,* page 360 **IVB:** ***Research Companion*** ▸ Chapter 7, *Measurement Schemes,* pages 100–101, *Proportionality and Measurement,* pages 102–103 ▸ Chapter 11, *Shape, Congruence, and Similarity,* pages 160–161 ▸ Chapter 14, *The Ratio Concept,* page 217
V. Examine Coherency and Articulation	**V:** ***Atlas of Science Literacy*** ▸ *Ratios and Proportionality,* page 119
VI. Clarify State Standards and District Curriculum	**VIA:** ***State Standards:*** Link Sections I–V to learning goals and information from your state standards or frameworks that are informed by the results of the topic study. **VIB:** ***District Curriculum Guide:*** Link Sections I–V to learning goals and information from your district curriculum guide that are informed by the results of the topic study.
Visit www.curriculumtopicstudy.org for updates or supplementary readings, Web sites, and videos.	

Standards- and Research-Based Study of a Curricular Topic

RATIONAL NUMBERS

Section and Outcome	Selected Sources and Readings for Study and Reflection Read and examine *related parts* of:
I. Identify Adult Content Knowledge	**IA:** ***Science for All Americans*** ▸ Chapter 9, *Numbers,* pages 130–132 **IB:** ***Beyond Numeracy*** ▸ *Golden Rectangle,* pages 98–101 ▸ *Rational and Irrational Numbers,* pages 205–208
II. Consider Instructional Implications	**IIA:** ***Benchmarks for Science Literacy*** ▸ 9A, *Numbers,* grade span essay, pages 213 **IIB:** ***NCTM Principles and Standards for School Mathematics*** ▸ Grades PreK–12 Overview Number and Operations, *Understand Numbers,* pages 33–34, *Compute Fluently,* page 35 ▸ Grades PreK–2 Number and Operations, *Understand Numbers,* page 82 ▸ Grades 3–5 Number and Operations, *Understand Numbers,* pages 149–151, *Compute Fluently,* page 152 ▸ Grades 6–8 Number and Operations, pages 215–221 ▸ Grades 9–12 Number and Operations, *Understand Numbers,* pages 291–292
III. Identify Concepts and Specific Ideas	**IIIA:** ***Benchmarks for Science Literacy*** ▸ 9A, *Numbers,* page 213 ▸ 12B, *Computation,* pages 290–291 **IIIB:** ***NCTM Principles and Standards for School Mathematics*** ▸ Grades PreK–2 Number and Operations, page 78 or 392 ▸ Grades 3–5 Number and Operations, page 148 or 392 ▸ Grades 6–8 Number and Operations, page 214 or 393 ▸ Grades 9–12 Number and Operations, page 290 or 393
IV. Examine Research on Student Learning	**IVA:** ***Benchmarks for Science Literacy*** ▸ 9A, *Numbers,* page 350 ▸ 12B, *Computation and Estimation,* pages 358–359 **IVB:** ***Research Companion*** ▸ Chapter 7, *Distinction Between Fractions,* page 98
V. Examine Coherency and Articulation	**V:** ***Atlas of Science Literacy*** ▸ *Ratios and Proportionality,* page 119
VI. Clarify State Standards and District Curriculum	**VIA:** ***State Standards:*** Link Sections I–V to learning goals and information from your state standards or frameworks that are informed by the results of the topic study. **VIB:** ***District Curriculum Guide:*** Link Sections I–V to learning goals and information from your district curriculum guide that are informed by the results of the topic study.
Visit www.curriculumtopicstudy.org for updates or supplementary readings, Web sites, and videos.	

Algebra

Number of CTS Guides: 12

Overview: The primary focus of this section is on the relationship among quantities, representing mathematical relationships, and the analysis of change. Ideas such as understanding patterns, relations and functions, representing situations and structures using symbolic notation, algebraic modeling, and rate of change are developed through a study of the topics in this section.

- Algebraic Modeling
- Expressions and Equations
- Formulas
- Functions
- Linear Relationships
- Nonlinear Relationships
- Numeric Patterns
- Patterns, Relations, and Functions
- Quadratics
- Rates of Change
- Symbolic Representation
- Variables

Standards- and Research-Based Study of a Curricular Topic

ALGEBRAIC MODELING

Section and Outcome	Selected Sources and Readings for Study and Reflection Read and examine *related parts* of:
I. Identify Adult Content Knowledge	**IA:** ***Science for All Americans*** ▸ Chapter 2, *Mathematical Inquiry,* pages 19–22 ▸ Chapter 11, *Models,* pages 168; *Mathematical Models,* pages 171–172 **IB:** ***Beyond Numeracy*** ▸ *Functions,* pages 87–90
II. Consider Instructional Implications	**IIA:** ***Benchmarks for Science Literacy*** ▸ 2C, *Mathematical Inquiry* general essay, pages 34–35; grade span essays, pages 36–38 ▸ 9B, *Symbolic Relationships* general essay, pages 215–216; grade span essays, pages 217–220 ▸ 11B, *Models,* general essay, page 267; grade span essays, pages 268–270 **IIB:** ***NCTM Principles and Standards for School Mathematics*** ▸ Grades PreK–12 Overview Algebra, *Using Mathematical Models,* pages 39–40; Representations, *Use representations,* pages 70–71 ▸ Grades PreK–2 Algebra general essay, page 91, *Using Mathematical Models,* page 95; Representations, pages 136–141 ▸ Grades 3–5 Algebra, *Using Mathematical Models,* pages 162–163; Representations, *What Should Representation Look Like,* pages 206–208 41 ▸ Grades 6–8 Algebra, *Using Mathematical Models,* pages 227–229; Representations, *What Should Representation Look Like,* pages 280–284 41 ▸ Grades 9–12 Algebra general essay, page 297, *Using Mathematical Models,* pages 303–305; Representations, *What Should Representation Look Like,* pages 360–362
III. Identify Concepts and Specific Ideas	**IIIA:** ***Benchmarks for Science Literacy*** ▸ 2C, *Mathematical Inquiry,* pages 36–38 ▸ 9B, *Symbolic Relationships,* pages 217–221 ▸ 9D, *Uncertainty,* page 230 ▸ 11B, *Models,* pages 268–270 **IIIB:** ***NCTM Principles and Standards for School Mathematics*** ▸ Grades PreK–2 Algebra, page 90 or 394 ▸ Grades 3–5 Algebra, page 158 or 394 ▸ Grades 6–8 Algebra, page 222 or 395 ▸ Grades 9–12 Algebra, page 296 or 395
IV. Examine Research on Student Learning	**IVA:** ***Benchmarks for Science Literacy*** ▸ 11B, *Models,* page 357 **IVB:** ***Research Companion*** ▸ Chapter 10, *Algebra,* pages 138–141, *Discussion,* pages 148–149 ▸ Chapter 18, *Definitions of Representations,* pages 264–266
V. Examine Coherency and Articulation	**V:** ***Atlas of Science Literacy*** ▸ *Mathematical Models,* page 29
VI. Clarify State Standards and District Curriculum	**VIA:** ***State Standards:*** Link Sections I–V to learning goals and information from your state standards or frameworks that are informed by the results of the topic study. **VIB:** ***District Curriculum Guide:*** Link Sections I–V to learning goals and information from your district curriculum guide that are informed by the results of the topic study.
	Visit www.curriculumtopicstudy.org for updates or supplementary readings, Web sites, and videos.

Standards- and Research-Based Study of a Curricular Topic

EXPRESSIONS AND EQUATIONS

Section and Outcome	Selected Sources and Readings for Study and Reflection Read and examine *related parts* of:
I. Identify Adult Content Knowledge	**IA:** ***Science for All Americans*** ▸ Chapter 9, *Symbolic Relationships,* pages 132–134 **IB:** ***Beyond Numeracy*** ▸ *Algebra—Some Basic Principles,* pages 7–9
II. Consider Instructional Implications	**IIA:** ***Benchmarks for Science Literacy*** ▸ 9B, *Symbolic Relationships,* general essay pages 215–216; grade span essays, pages 217–220 **IIB:** ***NCTM Principles and Standards for School Mathematics*** ▸ Grades PreK–12 Overview Algebra, pages 37–38, *Represent and Analyze,* pages 38–39 ▸ Grades PreK–2 Algebra, *Represent and Analyze,* pages 93–94 ▸ Grades 3–5 Algebra general essay, page 159, *Represent and Analyze,* pages 160–162 ▸ Grades 6–8 Algebra general essay, page 223, *Represent and Analyze,* pages 225–227 ▸ Grades 9–12 Algebra general essay, page 297, *Represent and Analyze,* pages 300–303
III. Identify Concepts and Specific Ideas	**IIIA:** ***Benchmarks for Science Literacy*** ▸ 9B, *Symbolic Relationships,* pages 217–221 **IIIB:** ***NCTM Principles and Standards for School Mathematics*** ▸ Grades PreK–2 Algebra, page 90 or 394 ▸ Grades 3–5 Algebra, page 158 or 394 ▸ Grades 6–8 Algebra, page 222 or 395 ▸ Grades 9–12 Algebra, page 296 or 395
IV. Examine Research on Student Learning	**IVA:** ***Benchmarks for Science Literacy*** ▸ 9B, *Algebraic Equations,* pages 351–352 **IVB:** ***Research Companion*** ▸ Chapter 9, On Appreciating the Cognitive Complexity of School Algebra: Research on Algebra Learning and Directions of Curricular Change, pages 123–133 ▸ Chapter 10, *Algebra,* pages 138–141, *Functions,* pages 141–142, *Stasis and Change,* pages 142–148, *Discussion,* pages 148–149
V. Examine Coherency and Articulation	**V:** ***Atlas of Science Literacy*** ▸ *Symbolic Representation,* page 117, noting the conceptual strands "Symbols and Equations" and "Working with Equations"
VI. Clarify State Standards and District Curriculum	**VIA:** ***State Standards:*** Link Sections I–V to learning goals and information from your state standards or frameworks that are informed by the results of the topic study. **VIB:** ***District Curriculum Guide:*** Link Sections I–V to learning goals and information from your district curriculum guide that are informed by the results of the topic study.
	Visit www.curriculumtopicstudy.org for updates or supplementary readings, Web sites, and videos.

Standards- and Research-Based Study of a Curricular Topic

FORMULAS

Section and Outcome	Selected Sources and Readings for Study and Reflection Read and examine *related parts* of:
I. Identify Adult Content Knowledge	**IA:** ***Science for All Americans*** ▶ Chapter 2, *Manipulating Mathematical Statements*, page 20 ▶ Chapter 9, *Symbolic Relationships*, pages 132–134 **IB:** ***Beyond Numeracy*** ▶ *Areas and Volumes*, pages 18–23 ▶ *Functions*, pages 87–90 ▶ *Quadratic and Other Formulas*, pages 198–201
II. Consider Instructional Implications	**IIA:** ***Benchmarks for Science Literacy*** ▶ 9B, *Symbolic Relationships*, general essay, pages 215–216; grade span essays, pages 217–220 ▶ 9C, *Shapes*, grade span essay, page 224 **IIB:** ***NCTM Principles and Standards for School Mathematics*** ▶ Grades PreK–12 Overview Algebra, *Understand Patterns, Relations, and Functions*, pages 37–38 ▶ Grades 3–5 Measurement, *Apply Appropriate Techniques, Tools and Formulas*, pages 174–175 ▶ Grades 6–8 Measurement, *Apply Appropriate Techniques, Tools and Formulas*, pages 244–245; Algebra, general essay page 223, *Understand Patterns, Relations, and Functions*, pages 223–224, *Represent and Analyze*, pages 225–226 ▶ Grades 9–12 Measurement, *Apply Appropriate Techniques, Tools and Formulas*, pages 322–323; Algebra, *Represent and Analyze*, pages 301–302
III. Identify Concepts and Specific Ideas	**IIIA:** ***Benchmarks for Science Literacy*** ▶ 9B, *Symbolic Relationships*, pages 219–221 ▶ 9C, *Shapes*, page 225 ▶ 12B, *Computation and Estimation*, page 291 **IIIB:** ***NCTM Principles and Standards for School Mathematics*** ▶ Grades 3–5 Measurement, page 170 or 398 ▶ Grades 6–8 Measurement, page 240 or 399; Algebra, page 222 or 395 ▶ Grades 9–12 Measurement, page 320 or 399; Algebra, page 296 or 395
IV. Examine Research on Student Learning	**IVA:** ***Benchmarks for Science Literacy*** ▶ 9B, *Symbolic Relationships*, pages 350–352 **IVB:** ***Research Companion*** ▶ Chapter 9, *Getting a Feel for the Symbols*, page 125 ▶ Chapter 10, *Algebra*, page 138
V. Examine Coherency and Articulation	**V:** ***Atlas of Science Literacy*** ▶ *Symbolic Representation*, page 117
VI. Clarify State Standards and District Curriculum	**VIA:** ***State Standards:*** Link Sections I–V to learning goals and information from your state standards or frameworks that are informed by the results of the topic study. **VIB:** ***District Curriculum Guide:*** Link Sections I–V to learning goals and information from your district curriculum guide that are informed by the results of the topic study.
	Visit www.curriculumtopicstudy.org for updates or supplementary readings, Web sites, and videos.

Standards- and Research-Based Study of a Curricular Topic

FUNCTIONS

Section and Outcome	Selected Sources and Readings for Study and Reflection Read and examine *related parts* of:
I. Identify Adult Content Knowledge	**IA:** *Science for All Americans* ▶ Chapter 9, *Symbolic Relationships,* pages 132–134 **IB:** *Beyond Numeracy* ▶ *Functions,* pages 87–90
II. Consider Instructional Implications	**IIA:** *Benchmarks for Science Literacy* ▶ 9B, *Symbolic Relationships* general essay, pages 215–216; grade span essays, pages 217–220 **IIB:** *NCTM Principles and Standards for School Mathematics* ▶ Grades PreK–12 Overview Algebra general essay, pages 37–38, *Understand Patterns, Relations, and Functions,* page 38, *Analyze Change in Various Contexts,* page 40 ▶ Grades 3–5 Algebra, *Understand Patterns, Relations, and Functions,* pages 159–160 ▶ Grades 6–8 Algebra general essay, page 223, *Understand Patterns, Relations, and Functions,* pages 223–225, *Represent and Analyze,* pages 225–227, *Use Mathematical Models,* pages 227–229 ▶ Grades 9–12 Algebra, pages 297–306, vignette page 302; *Problem Solving* vignette, pages 338–340
III. Identify Concepts and Specific Ideas	**IIIA:** *Benchmarks for Science Literacy* ▶ 9B, *Symbolic Relationships,* pages 218–221 **IIIB:** *NCTM Principles and Standards for School Mathematics* ▶ Grades 3–5 Algebra, page 158 or 394 ▶ Grades 6–8 Algebra, page 222 or 395 ▶ Grades 9–12 Algebra, page 296 or 395
IV. Examine Research on Student Learning	**IVA:** *Benchmarks for Science Literacy* ▶ 2A, *Patterns and Relationships,* page 334 ▶ 9B, *Symbolic Relationships,* page 351 **IVB:** *Research Companion* ▶ Chapter 9, *Functions–Based Approaches to Algebra,* pages 132–133 ▶ Chapter 10, *Functions,* pages 141–142, *Stasis and Change,* pages 142–149
V. Examine Coherency and Articulation	**V:** *Atlas of Science Literacy* ▶ *Symbolic Representation,* page 117
VI. Clarify State Standards and District Curriculum	**VIA:** *State Standards:* Link Sections I–V to learning goals and information from your state standards or frameworks that are informed by the results of the topic study. **VIB:** *District Curriculum Guide:* Link Sections I–V to learning goals and information from your district curriculum guide that are informed by the results of the topic study.
	Visit www.curriculumtopicstudy.org for updates or supplementary readings, Web sites, and videos.

Standards- and Research-Based Study of a Curricular Topic

LINEAR RELATIONSHIPS

Section and Outcome	Selected Sources and Readings for Study and Reflection Read and examine *related parts* of:
I. Identify Adult Content Knowledge	**IA:** ***Science for All Americans*** ▸ Chapter 2, *The Nature of Mathematics,* pages 19–20 ▸ Chapter 9, *Symbolic Relationships,* pages 132–133; *Shapes,* page 135 ▸ Chapter 11, *Mathematical Models,* pages 171–172 **IB:** ***Beyond Numeracy*** ▸ *Algebra–Some Basic Principles,* pages 7–9 ▸ *Variables and Pronouns,* pages 260–261
II. Consider Instructional Implications	**IIA:** ***Benchmarks for Science Literacy*** ▸ 9B, *Symbolic Relationships* general essay, pages 215–216; grade span essays, pages 217–220 ▸ 9C *Shapes* grade span essay, page 224 ▸ 11C *Constancy and Change* general essay, pages 271–272; grade span essays, pages 272–275 **IIB:** ***NCTM Principles and Standards for School Mathematics*** ▸ Grades PreK–12 Overview Algebra, *Analyze Change,* page 40 ▸ Grades PreK–2 Algebra, *Analyze Change,* page 95 ▸ Grades 3–5 Algebra general essay, page 159, *Use Mathematical Models,* page 162, *Analyze Change,* page 163 ▸ Grades 6–8 Algebra, pages 223–230; Measurement, *Apply Appropriate Techniques,* page 247 ▸ Grades 9–12 Algebra general essay, page 297, *Understand Patterns,* pages 297–299, *Use Mathematical Models,* page 303, *Analyze Change,* page 305
III. Identify Concepts and Specific Ideas	**IIIA:** ***Benchmarks for Science Literacy*** ▸ 9B, *Symbolic Relationships,* pages 217–221 ▸ 9C, *Shapes,* page 224 ▸ 11C, *Constancy and Change,* pages 272–275 **IIIB:** ***NCTM Principles and Standards for School Mathematics*** ▸ Grades PreK–2 Algebra, page 90 or 394 ▸ Grades 3–5 Algebra, page 158 or 394 ▸ Grades 6–8 Algebra, page 222 or 395; Measurement, page 240 or 399 ▸ Grades 9–12 Algebra, page 296 or 395
IV. Examine Research on Student Learning	**IVA:** ***Benchmarks for Science Literacy*** ▸ 9B, *Symbolic Relationships,* pages 350–352 ▸ 11C, *Constancy and Change,* pages 357–358 **IVB:** ***Research Companion*** ▸ Chapter 9, *The Power of Symbols,* pages 126–128 ▸ Chapter 10, *Patterns, Functions, and Algebra,* pages 145–148
V. Examine Coherency and Articulation	**V:** ***Atlas of Science Literacy*** ▸ *Describing Change,* page 121 ▸ *Symbolic Representation,* page 117
VI. Clarify State Standards and District Curriculum	**VIA:** *State Standards:* Link Sections I–V to learning goals and information from your state standards or frameworks that are informed by the results of the topic study. **VIB** *District Curriculum Guide:* Link Sections I–V to learning goals and information from your district curriculum guide that are informed by the results of the topic study.
	Visit www.curriculumtopicstudy.org for updates or supplementary readings, Web sites, and videos.

Standards- and Research-Based Study of a Curricular Topic

NONLINEAR RELATIONSHIPS

Section and Outcome	Selected Sources and Readings for Study and Reflection Read and examine *related parts* of:
I. Identify Adult Content Knowledge	**IA:** *Science for All Americans* ▶ Chapter 9, *Symbolic Relationships*, pages 132–134 **IB:** *Beyond Numeracy* ▶ *Exponential Growth,* pages 71–74 ▶ *Functions,* pages 87–90 ▶ *The Quadratic and Other Formulas,* pages 198–201 ▶ *Trigonometry,* pages 251–254
II. Consider Instructional Implications	**IIA:** *Benchmarks for Science Literacy* ▶ 2A, *Patterns and Relationships* general essay, page 25–26 ▶ 9B, *Symbolic Relationships* general essay, pages 215–216; grade span essays, pages 218–220 **IIB:** *NCTM Principles and Standards for School Mathematics* ▶ Grades 6–8 Algebra general essay, page 223, *Understand Patterns,* page 225, *Use mathematical models,* pages 227–229, *Analyze change,* pages 229–230 ▶ Grades 9–12 Algebra general essay, page 297, *Understand Patterns,* pages 297–300, *Represent and Analyze,* pages 301–302, *Use Mathematical Models,* pages 303–305; Problem Solving vignette, pages 338–340
III. Identify Concepts and Specific Ideas	**IIIA:** *Benchmarks for Science Literacy* ▶ 9B, *Symbolic Relationships*, pages 218–221 **IIIB:** *NCTM Principles and Standards for School Mathematics* ▶ 6–8 Algebra, page 222 or 395 ▶ 9–12 Algebra, page 296 or 395
IV. Examine Research on Student Learning	**IVA:** *Benchmarks for Science Literacy* ▶ 2A, *Patterns and Relationships,* page 334 ▶ 9B, *Symbolic Relationships,* page 351 **IVB:** *Research Companion* ▶ Chapter 9, *Getting a Feel for the Symbols,* pages 125, *Solving Systems,* pages 128–130, *Adding Representations,* pages 130–131
V. Examine Coherency and Articulation	**V:** *Atlas of Science Literacy* ▶ *Symbolic Representation,* page 117
VI. Clarify State Standards and District Curriculum	**VIA:** *State Standards:* Link Sections I–V to learning goals and information from your state standards or frameworks that are informed by the results of the topic study. **VIB:** *District Curriculum Guide:* Link Sections I–V to learning goals and information from your district curriculum guide that are informed by the results of the topic study.
Visit www.curriculumtopicstudy.org for updates or supplementary readings, Web sites, and videos.	

Standards- and Research-Based Study of a Curricular Topic

NUMERIC PATTERNS

Section and Outcome	Selected Sources and Readings for Study and Reflection Read and examine *related parts* of:
I. Identify Adult Content Knowledge	**IA:** **Science for All Americans** ▸ Chapter 2, *Patterns and Relationships*, pages 16–17 **IB:** **Beyond Numeracy** ▸ *Computation and Rote*, pages 52–55 ▸ *Fractals*, pages 82–86 ▸ *Golden Rectangle, Fibonacci Sequence*, pages 98–101 ▸ *Pascal's Triangle,* page 171–174
II. Consider Instructional Implications	**IIA:** **Benchmarks for Science Literacy** ▸ 2A, *Patterns and Relationships* general essay, pages 25–26; grade span essays, page 27, page 29 **IIB:** **NCTM Principles and Standards for School Mathematics** ▸ Grades PreK–12 Overview Algebra, *Understand Patterns*, page 38 ▸ Grades PreK–2 Algebra general essay, page 91, *Understand Patterns*, pages 91–92; Reasoning and Proof, pages 122–125 ▸ Grades 3–5 Algebra general essay, page 159, *Understand Patterns*, pages 159–160 ▸ Grades 6–8 Algebra general essay, page 223; Reasoning and Proof, pages 262–265, Vignette, pages 262–264 ▸ Grades 9–12 Representation, pages 360–362
III. Identify Concepts and Specific Ideas	**IIIA:** **Benchmarks for Science Literacy** ▸ 2A, *Patterns and Relationships*, page 27, page 29 **IIIB:** **NCTM Principles and Standards for School Mathematics** ▸ Grades PreK–2 Algebra, page 90 or 394 ▸ Grades 3–5 Algebra, page 158 or 394 ▸ Grades 6–8 Algebra, page 222 or 395
IV. Examine Research on Student Learning	**IVA:** **Benchmarks for Science Literacy** ▸ 2A, *Patterns and Relationships*, page 334 **IVB:** **Research Companion** ▸ Chapter 10, *Patterns*, pages 137–138, *Stasis and Change*, pages 142–143
V. Examine Coherency and Articulation	**V:** **Atlas of Science Literacy** ▸ *Mathematical Processes*, page 27
VI. Clarify State Standards and District Curriculum	**VIA:** *State Standards:* Link Sections I–V to learning goals and information from your state standards or frameworks that are informed by the results of the topic study. **VIB:** *District Curriculum Guide:* Link Sections I–V to learning goals and information from your district curriculum guide that are informed by the results of the topic study.
Visit www.curriculumtopicstudy.org for updates or supplementary readings, Web sites, and videos.	

Standards- and Research-Based Study of a Curricular Topic

PATTERNS, RELATIONS, AND FUNCTIONS

Section and Outcome	Selected Sources and Readings for Study and Reflection Read and examine *related parts* of:
I. Identify Adult Content Knowledge	**IA:** *Science for All Americans* ▸ Chapter 2, *Patterns and Relationships*, pages 16–17 ▸ Chapter 9, *Symbolic Relationships*, pages 132–134 **IB:** *Beyond Numeracy* ▸ *Exponential Growth*, pages 71–74 ▸ *Functions*, pages 87–90 ▸ *Recursion–From Definition to Life*, pages 209–213 ▸ *Trigonometry*, pages 251–256
II. Consider Instructional Implications	**IIA:** *Benchmarks for Science Literacy* ▸ 2A, *Patterns and Relationships* general essay, pages 25–26; grade span essays, pages 26–29 ▸ 9B, *Symbolic Relationships* general essay, pages 215–216; grade span essays, pages 217–221 **IIB:** *NCTM Principles and Standards for School Mathematics* ▸ Grades PreK–12 Overview Algebra, page 37, *Understand Patterns*, pages 38–39, *Use Mathematical Models*, page 39, *Analyze Change*, page 40 ▸ Grades K–2 Algebra general essay, page 91, *Understand Patterns*, pages 91–92 ▸ Grades 3–5 Algebra general essay, page 159, *Understand Patterns*, pages 159–160, *Use Mathematical Models*, page 162, *Analyze Change*, page 163 ▸ Grades 6–8 Algebra general essay, page 223, *Understand Patterns*, pages 223–225, *Use Mathematical Models*, pages 227–229, *Analyze Change*, pages 229–230 ▸ Grades 9–12 Algebra general essay, page 297, *Understand Patterns*, pages 297–300, *Represent and Analyze*, pages 302–303, Vignette, page 302; *Use Mathematical Models*, pages 303–305, *Analyze Change*, pages 305–306; Problem Solving Vignette, pages 338–340
III. Identify Concepts and Specific Ideas	**IIIA:** *Benchmarks for Science Literacy* ▸ 2A, *Patterns and Relationships*, pages 26–29 ▸ 9B, *Symbolic Relationships*, pages 218–221 **IIIB:** *NCTM Principles and Standards for School Mathematics* ▸ Grades PreK–2 Algebra, page 90 or 394 ▸ Grades 3–5 Algebra, page 158 or 394 ▸ Grades 6–8 Algebra, page 222 or 395 ▸ Grades 9–12 Algebra, page 296 or 395
IV. Examine Research on Student Learning	**IVA:** *Benchmarks for Science Literacy* ▸ 2A, *Patterns and Relationships*, page 334 ▸ 9B, *Symbolic Relationships*, page 351 **IVB:** *Research Companion* ▸ Chapter 9, *The Power of Symbols*, pages 126–130, *Adding Representations*, pages 130–132, *Functions–Based Approaches to Algebra*, page 132, *Conclusion*, pages 132–133 ▸ Chapter 10, *Stasis and Change: Integrating Patterns, Functions, and Algebra*, pages 136–149
V. Examine Coherency and Articulation	**V:** *Atlas of Science Literacy* ▸ *Mathematical Processes*, page 27 ▸ *Symbolic Representation*, page 117 ▸ *Describing Change*, page 121
VI. Clarify State Standards and District Curriculum	**VIA:** *State Standards:* Link Sections I–V to learning goals and information from your state standards or frameworks that are informed by the results of the topic study. **VIB:** *District Curriculum Guide:* Link Sections I–V to learning goals and information from your district curriculum guide that are informed by the results of the topic study.
Visit www.curriculumtopicstudy.org for updates or supplementary readings, Web sites, and videos.	

Standards- and Research-Based Study of a Curricular Topic

QUADRATICS

Section and Outcome	Selected Sources and Readings for Study and Reflection Read and examine *related parts* of:
I. Identify Adult Content Knowledge	**IA:** *Science for All Americans* ▸ Chapter 9, *Symbolic Relationships,* pages 132–134 **IB:** *Beyond Numeracy* ▸ *The Quadratic and Other Formulas,* pages 198–201
II. Consider Instructional Implications	**IIA:** *Benchmarks for Science Literacy* ▸ 9B, *Symbolic Relationships* grade span essays, pages 218–220 **IIB:** *NCTM Principles and Standards for School Mathematics* ▸ Grades 6–8 Algebra general essay, page 223, *Understand Patterns,* pages 223–225, *Use Mathematical Models,* pages 227–229 ▸ Grades 9–12 Number and Operations general essay, page 291, *Understand Numbers,* page 291; Algebra general essay, page 297, *Understand Patterns,* pages 297–300; Problem Solving vignette, pages 338–340
III. Identify Concepts and Specific Ideas	**IIIA:** *Benchmarks for Science Literacy* ▸ 9B, *Symbolic Relationships,* pages 219–221 **IIIB:** *NCTM Principles and Standards for School Mathematics* ▸ Grades PreK–2 Algebra, page 90 or 394 ▸ Grades 3–5 Algebra, page 158 or 394 ▸ Grades 6–8 Algebra, page 222 or 395 ▸ Grades 9–12 Number and Operations, page 290 or 393; Algebra, page 296 or 395
IV. Examine Research on Student Learning	**IVA:** *Benchmarks for Science Literacy* ▸ 9B, *Symbolic Relationships,* page 351 **IVB:** *Research Companion* ▸ Chapter 9 *Solving Systems,* pages 128–130, *Adding Representations,* pages 130–131
V. Examine Coherency and Articulation	**V:** *Atlas of Science Literacy* ▸ *Symbolic Representation,* page 117
VI. Clarify State Standards and District Curriculum	**VIA:** *State Standards:* Link Sections I–V to learning goals and information from your state standards or frameworks that are informed by the results of the topic study. **VIB:** *District Curriculum Guide:* Link Sections I–V to learning goals and information from your district curriculum guide that are informed by the results of the topic study.
Visit www.curriculumtopicstudy.org for updates or supplementary readings, Web sites, and videos.	

Standards- and Research-Based Study of a Curricular Topic

RATES OF CHANGE

Section and Outcome	Selected Sources and Readings for Study and Reflection Read and examine *related parts* of:
I. Identify Adult Content Knowledge	**IA:** **Science for All Americans** ▶ Chapter 9, *Symbolic Relationships,* pages 132–134; *Shapes,* page 135 ▶ Chapter 11, *Patterns of Change,* pages 174–176 **IB:** **Beyond Numeracy** ▶ *Analytic Geometry,* pages 10–14 ▶ *Calculus,* pages 27–31
II. Consider Instructional Implications	**IIA:** **Benchmarks for Science Literacy** ▶ 9B, *Symbolic Relationships* general essay, pages 215–216; grade span essays, pages 217–220 ▶ 9C, *Shapes* general essay, page 222; grade span essay, page 224 ▶ 11C, *Constancy and Change* general essay, pages 271–272; grade span essays, pages 272–275 **IIB:** **NCTM Principles and Standards for School Mathematics** ▶ Grades PreK–12 Overview Algebra, *Analyze Change,* page 40 ▶ Grades PreK–2 Algebra, *Analyze Change,* page 95 ▶ Grades 3–5 Algebra general essay, page 159, *Analyze Change,* page 163 ▶ Grades 6–8 Algebra general essay, page 223, *Analyze Change,* pages 229–231 ▶ Grades 9–12 Algebra general essay, page 297, *Analyze Change,* pages 305–306
III. Identify Concepts and Specific Ideas	**IIIA:** **Benchmarks for Science Literacy** ▶ 9B, *Symbolic Relationships,* pages 217–221 ▶ 9C, *Shapes,* page 224 ▶ 11C, *Constancy and Change,* pages 272–275 **IIIB:** **NCTM Principles and Standards for School Mathematics** ▶ Grades PreK–2 Algebra, page 90 or 394 ▶ Grades 3–5 Algebra, page 158 or 394 ▶ Grades 6–8 Algebra, page 222 or 395 ▶ Grades 9–12 Algebra, page 296 or 395
IV. Examine Research on Student Learning	**IVA:** **Benchmarks for Science Literacy** ▶ 9B, *Symbolic Relationships–Graphs,* page 351 ▶ 11C, *Constancy and Change,* pages 357–358 **IVB:** **Research Companion** ▶ Chapter 10, Stasis and Change: Integrating Patterns, Function and Algebra Throughout the K–12 Curriculum, pages 136–148 ▶ Chapter 17, *Ways of Making Meaning With a Graph,* pages 252–256. *Graphs–The Visual Medium,* pages 256–258, *Graphs and Related Representations,* pages 258–260
V. Examine Coherency and Articulation	**V:** **Atlas of Science Literacy** ▶ *Graphic Representation,* page 115 ▶ *Symbolic Representation,* page 117 ▶ *Describing Change,* page 121 ▶ *Correlation,* page 125 noting the conceptual strand "related changes"
VI. Clarify State Standards and District Curriculum	**VIA:** **State Standards:** Link Sections I–V to learning goals and information from your state standards or frameworks that are informed by the results of the topic study. **VIB:** **District Curriculum Guide:** Link Sections I–V to learning goals and information from your district curriculum guide that are informed by the results of the topic study.
Visit www.curriculumtopicstudy.org for updates or supplementary readings, Web sites, and videos.	

Standards- and Research-Based Study of a Curricular Topic

SYMBOLIC REPRESENTATION

Section and Outcome	Selected Sources and Readings for Study and Reflection Read and examine *related parts* of:
I. Identify Adult Content Knowledge	**IA:** *Science for All Americans* ▸ Chapter 2, *Mathematical Inquiry*, page 19 ▸ Chapter 9, *Symbolic Relationships*, pages 132–134 **IB:** *Beyond Numeracy* ▸ *Variables and Pronouns*, pages 260–261 ▸ *Notation*, pages 163–165 ▸ *Arabic Numerals*, pages 15–17
II. Consider Instructional Implications	**IIA:** *Benchmarks for Science Literacy* ▸ 9B, *Symbolic Relationships* general essay, pages 215–216; grade span essays, pages 217–220 **IIB:** *NCTM Principles and Standards for School Mathematics* ▸ Grades PreK–12 Overview Algebra, pages 37–40; Representation, pages 67–71 ▸ Grades PreK–2 Algebra general essay, page 91, *Represent and Analyze*, pages 93–94; Representation, page 141 ▸ Grades 3–5 Algebra general essay, page 159, *Represent and Analyze*, pages 159–163; Representation, pages 207–208 ▸ Grades 6–8 Algebra general essay, page 223, *Represent and Analyze*, pages 223–231; Representation, pages 281–285 ▸ Grades 9–12 Algebra general essay, page 297, *Represent and Analyze*, pages 297–306; Representation, pages 361–364
III. Identify Concepts and Specific Ideas	**IIIA:** *Benchmarks for Science Literacy* ▸ 9B, *Symbolic Relationships*, pages 217–221 **IIIB:** *NCTM Principles and Standards for School Mathematics* ▸ Grades PreK–2 Algebra, page 90 or 394; Representation, page 136 or 394 ▸ Grades 3–5 Algebra, page 158 or 394; Representation, page 206 or 394 ▸ Grades 6–8 Algebra, page 222 or 395; Representation, page 280 or 395 ▸ Grades 9–12 Algebra, page 296 or 395; Representation, page 360 or 395
IV. Examine Research on Student Learning	**IVA:** *Benchmarks for Science Literacy* ▸ 9B, *Symbolic Relationships*, pages 350–352 **IVB:** *Research Companion* ▸ Chapter 9, *Getting a Feel for the Symbols*, pages 125–126, *The Power of Symbols*, pages 126–130
V. Examine Coherency and Articulation	**V:** *Atlas of Science Literacy* ▸ *Symbolic Representation*, page 117
VI. Clarify State Standards and District Curriculum	**VIA:** *State Standards:* Link Sections I–V to learning goals and information from your state standards or frameworks that are informed by the results of the topic study. **VIB:** *District Curriculum Guide:* Link Sections I–V to learning goals and information from your district curriculum guide that are informed by the results of the topic study.
Visit www.curriculumtopicstudy.org for updates or supplementary readings, Web sites, and videos.

Standards- and Research-Based Study of a Curricular Topic

VARIABLES

Section and Outcome	Selected Sources and Readings for Study and Reflection Read and examine *related parts* of:	
I. Identify Adult Content Knowledge	**IA:**	***Science for All Americans*** ▸ Chapter 9, *Symbolic Relationships*, pages 132–134
	IB:	***Beyond Numeracy*** ▸ *Variables and Pronoun*, pages 260–261
II. Consider Instructional Implications	**IIA:**	***Benchmarks for Science Literacy*** ▸ 9B, *Symbolic Relationships* general essay, pages 215–216; grade span essays, pages 217–220
	IIB:	***NCTM Principles and Standards for School Mathematics*** ▸ Pre K–12 Overview Algebra, pages 37–40 ▸ K–2 Algebra general essay, page 91, *Represent and Analyze*, pages 93–94 ▸ Grades 3–5 Algebra general essay, page 159, *Represent and Analyze*, pages 160–162 ▸ Grades 6–8 Algebra general essay, page 223, *Represent and Analyze*, pages 225–227 ▸ Grades 9–12 Algebra general essay, page 297, *Represent and Analyze*, pages 300–303
III. Identify Concepts and Specific Ideas	**IIIA:**	***Benchmarks for Science Literacy*** ▸ 9B, *Symbolic Relationship*, pages 217–221
	IIIB:	***NCTM Principles and Standards for School Mathematics*** ▸ Grades PreK–2 Algebra, page 90 or 394 ▸ Grades 3–5 Algebra, page 158 or 394 ▸ Grades 6–8 Algebra, page 222 or 395 ▸ Grades 9–12 Algebra, page 296 or 395
IV. Examine Research on Student Learning	**IVA:**	***Benchmarks for Science Literacy*** ▸ 9B, *Symbolic Relationships – Variables*, page 351
	IVB:	***Research Companion*** ▸ Chapter 9, On Appreciating the Cognitive Complexity of School Algebra; Research on Algebra Learning and Directions of Curricular Change, pages 123–133 ▸ Chapter 10, Stasis and Change: Integrating Patterns, Functions, and Algebra Throughout the K–12 Curriculum, pages 136–149
V. Examine Coherency and Articulation	**V:**	***Atlas of Science Literacy*** ▸ *Symbolic Representation*, page 117
VI. Clarify State Standards and District Curriculum	**VIA:**	***State Standards:*** Link Sections I–V to learning goals and information from your state standards or frameworks that are informed by the results of the topic study.
	VIB:	***District Curriculum Guide:*** Link Sections I–V to learning goals and information from your district curriculum guide that are informed by the results of the topic study.
Visit www.curriculumtopicstudy.org for updates or supplementary readings, Web sites, and videos.		

Geometry

Number of CTS Guides: 19

Overview: The primary focus of this section is on the study of geometric shapes, spatial visualization, and geometric modeling. Ideas such as characteristics and properties of geometric figures, coordinate geometry and spatial relationships, transformations and symmetry, and use of modeling to solve problems are developed through a study of the topics in this section.

- Three-Dimensional Geometry
- Two-Dimensional Geometry
- Two- and Three-Dimensional Geometry
- Circles
- Congruence and Similarity
- Coordinate Geometry
- Geometric Modeling
- Geometric Patterns
- Geometric Proof
- Geometric Relationships
- Geometric Shapes
- Geometric Theorems
- Networks
- Quadrilaterals
- Sorting and Classifying
- Spatial Visualization
- Transformations and Symmetry
- Triangles
- Trigonometry

Standards- and Research-Based Study of a Curricular Topic

THREE–DIMENSIONAL GEOMETRY

Section and Outcome	Selected Sources and Readings for Study and Reflection Read and examine *related parts* of:
I. Identify Adult Content Knowledge	**IA:** ***Science for All Americans*** ▸ Chapter 9, *Shapes*, pages 134–135 **IB:** ***Beyond Numeracy*** ▸ *Areas and Volumes*, pages 18–23 ▸ *Platonic Solids*, pages 181–183
II. Consider Instructional Implications	**IIA:** ***Benchmarks for Science Literacy*** ▸ 9C, *Shapes*, general essay, page 222; grade span essays, pages 223–225 **IIB:** ***NCTM Principles and Standards for School Mathematics*** ▸ Grades PreK–12 Overview Geometry, pages 41–43; Measurement, pages 44–47 ▸ Grades PreK–2 Geometry general essay, page 97, *Analyze Characteristics*, pages 97–98 ▸ Grades 3–5 Geometry general essay, page 165, *Analyze Characteristics*, pages 165–166, *Use Visualization*, pages 168–169 ▸ Grades 6–8 Geometry general essay, page 233, *Analyze Characteristics*, pages 233–235, *Use Visualization*, page 237; Measurement page 241, *Understand Measurable*, pages 242–243, *Apply Appropriate Techniques*, pages 244–245 ▸ Grades 9–12 Geometry general essay, page 309, *Analyze Characteristics*, pages 310–311, *Use Visualization*, pages 315–316, Measurement general essay, page 321, *Apply Appropriate Techniques*, pages 322–323
III. Identify Concepts and Specific Ideas	**IIIA:** ***Benchmarks for Science Literacy*** ▸ 9C, *Shapes,* pages 223–225 **IIIB:** ***NCTM Principles and Standards for School Mathematics*** ▸ Grades PreK–2 Geometry, page 96 or 396 ▸ Grades 3–5 Geometry, page 164 or 396 ▸ Grades 6–8 Geometry, page 232 or 397; Measurement, page 240 or 397 ▸ Grades 9–12 Geometry, page 308 or 397; Measurement, page 320 or 397
IV. Examine Research on Student Learning	**IVA:** ***Benchmarks for Science Literacy*** ▸ 9C, *Shapes*, pages 352–353 **IVB:** ***NCTM Research Companion*** ▸ Chapter 11, *Theories of Geometric Thinking*, pages 152–155, *Selected Geometric Topics*, pages 161–162, page 166 ▸ Chapter 12, *Volume Measure*, pages 186–187
V. Examine Coherency and Articulation	**V.** ***Atlas of Science Literacy***: There are no maps for this topic in Volume 1.
VI. Clarify State Standards and District Curriculum	**VIA:** ***State Standards:*** Link Sections I–V to learning goals and information from your state standards or frameworks that are informed by the results of the topic study. **VIB:** ***District Curriculum Guide:*** Link Sections I–V to learning goals and information from your district curriculum guide that are informed by the results of the topic study.
Visit www.curriculumtopicstudy.org for updates or supplementary readings, Web sites, and videos.	

Standards- and Research-Based Study of a Curricular Topic

TWO-DIMENSIONAL GEOMETRY

Section and Outcome	Selected Sources and Readings for Study and Reflection Read and examine *related parts* of:
I. Identify Adult Content Knowledge	**IA:** *Science for All Americans* ▸ Chapter 9, *Shapes,* pages 134–135 **IB:** *Beyond Numeracy* ▸ *Areas and Volumes,* pages 18–23
II. Consider Instructional Implications	**IIA:** *Benchmarks for Science Literacy* ▸ 9C, *Shapes,* general essay, page 222; grade span essays, pages 223–225 ▸ 2A, *Patterns and Relationships,* general essay, pages 25–27; grade span essays, pages 26–27 ▸ 2C, *Mathematical Inquiry,* grade span essays, page 36 **IIB:** *NCTM Principles and Standards for School Mathematics* ▸ Grades PreK–12 Overview Geometry, pages 41–43; Measurement, pages 44–47 ▸ Grades PreK–2 Geometry general essay, page 97, *Analyze Characteristics,* pages 97–98 ▸ Grades 3–5 Geometry general essay, page 165, *Analyze Characteristics,* pages 165–166, *Use Visualization,* pages 168–169 ▸ Grades 6–8 Geometry general essay, page 233, *Analyze Characteristics,* pages 233–235, *Use Visualization,* pages 237–239; Measurement general essay, page 241, *Understand Measurable Attributes,* pages 241–243, *Apply Appropriate Techniques,* pages 243–245 ▸ Grades 9–12 Geometry general essay, pages 309–310, *Analyze Characteristics,* pages 310–311, Vignette, pages 311–312
III. Identify Concepts and Specific Ideas	**IIIA:** *Benchmarks for Science Literacy* ▸ 9C, *Shapes,* pages 223–225 ▸ 2A, *Patterns and Relationships,* page 26 ▸ 2C, *Mathematical Inquiry,* page 36 ▸ 12B, *Computation and Estimation,* pages 290–291 **IIIB:** *NCTM Principles and Standards for School Mathematics* ▸ Grades PreK–2 Geometry, page 96 or 396 ▸ Grades 3–5 Geometry, page 164 or 396 ▸ Grades 6–8 Geometry, page 232 or 397; Measurement, page 240 or 397 ▸ Grades 9–12 Geometry, page 308 or 397; Measurement, page 320 or 397
IV. Examine Research on Student Learning	**IVA:** *Benchmarks for Science Literacy* ▸ 9C, *Shapes,* pages 352–353 **IVB:** *NCTM Research Companion* ▸ Chapter 11, Teaching and Learning Geometry, pages 151–171 ▸ Chapter 12, *Area Measure,* pages 184–186
V. Examine Coherency and Articulation	**V.** *Atlas of Science Literacy* ▸ *Graphic Representation,* page 115 ▸ *Mathematical Models,* page 27
VI. Clarify State Standards and District Curriculum	**VIA:** *State Standards:* Link Sections I–V to learning goals and information from your state standards or frameworks that are informed by the results of the topic study. **VIB:** *District Curriculum Guide:* Link Sections I–V to learning goals and information from your district curriculum guide that are informed by the results of the topic study.
Visit www.curriculumtopicstudy.org for updates or supplementary readings, Web sites, and videos.	

Standards- and Research-Based Study of a Curricular Topic

TW0- AND THREE-DIMENSIONAL GEOMETRY

Section and Outcome	Selected Sources and Readings for Study and Reflection Read and examine *related parts* of:
I. Identify Adult Content Knowledge	**IA:** ***Science for All Americans*** ▸ Chapter 9, *Shapes,* pages 134–135 **IB:** ***Beyond Numeracy*** ▸ *Areas and Volumes,* pages 18–23 ▸ *Platonic Solids,* pages 181–183
II. Consider Instructional Implications	**IIA:** ***Benchmarks for Science Literacy*** ▸ 9C, *Shapes,* general essay, page 222; grade span essays, pages 223–225 ▸ 2A, *Patterns and Relationships,* general essay, pages 25–27; grade span essays, pages 26 –27 ▸ 2C, *Mathematical Inquiry,* grade span essays, page 36 **IIB:** ***NCTM Principles and Standards for School Mathematics*** ▸ Grades PreK–12 Overview Geometry, pages 41–43; Measurement, pages 44–47 ▸ Grades PreK–2 Geometry general essay, page 97, *Analyze Characteristics,* pages 97–98 ▸ Grades 3–5 Geometry general essay, page 165, *Analyze Characteristics,* pages 165–166, *Use Visualization,* pages 168–169 ▸ Grades 6–8 Geometry general essay, page 233, *Analyze Characteristics,* pages 233–235, *Use Visualization,* pages 237–239; Measurement general essay, pages 241–243, *Understand Measurable Attributes,* pages 241–243, *Apply Appropriate Techniques,* pages 243–245 ▸ Grades 9–12 Geometry general essay, pages 309–310, *Analyze Characteristics,* pages 310–311, Vignette, pages 311–312, *Use Visualization,* pages 315–316; Measurement general essay, page 21; *Apply Appropriate Techniques,* pages 322–323
III. Identify Concepts and Specific Ideas	**IIIA:** ***Benchmarks for Science Literacy*** ▸ 9C, *Shapes,* pages 223–225 ▸ 2A, *Patterns and Relationships,* page 26 ▸ 2C, *Mathematical Inquiry,* page 36 ▸ 12B, *Computation and Estimation,* pages 290–291 **IIIB:** ***NCTM Principles and Standards for School Mathematics*** ▸ Grades PreK–2 Geometry, page 96 or 396 ▸ Grades 3–5 Geometry, page 164 or 396 ▸ Grades 6–8 Geometry, page 232 or 397; Measurement, page 240 or 397 ▸ Grades 9–12 Geometry, page 308 or 397; Measurement, page 320 or 397
IV. Examine Research on Student Learning	**IVA:** ***Benchmarks for Science Literacy*** ▸ 9C, *Shapes,* pages 352–353 **IVB:** ***NCTM Research Companion*** ▸ Chapter 11, Teaching and Learning Geometry, pages 151–171; *Selected Geometric Topics,* pages 161–162, page 166 ▸ Chapter 12, *Area Measure,* pages 184–186; *Volume Measure,* pages 186–187
V. Examine Coherency and Articulation	**V:** ***Atlas of Science Literacy*** ▸ *Graphic Representation,* page 115 ▸ *Mathematical Models,* page 27
VI. Clarify State Standards and District Curriculum	**VIA:** ***State Standards:*** Link Sections I–V to learning goals and information from your state standards or frameworks that are informed by the results of the topic study. **VIB:** ***District Curriculum Guide:*** Link Sections I–V to learning goals and information from your district curriculum guide that are informed by the results of the topic study.
Visit www.curriculumtopicstudy.org for updates or supplementary readings, Web sites, and videos.	

Standards- and Research-Based Study of a Curricular Topic

CIRCLES

Section and Outcome	Selected Sources and Readings for Study and Reflection Read and examine *related parts* of:
I. Identify Adult Content Knowledge	**IA:** ***Science for All Americans*** ▸ Chapter 9, *Shapes,* pages 134–135 ▸ Chapter 12, *Calculator Skills,* page 189 **IB:** ***Beyond Numeracy*** ▸ *Analytic Geometry,* pages 10–14 ▸ *Area and Volume,* pages 18–23 ▸ *Pi,* pages 178–180
II. Consider Instructional Implications	**IIA:** ***Benchmarks for Science Literacy*** ▸ 9C, *Shapes,* general essay, page 222; grade span essays, pages 223–225 **IIB:** ***NCTM Principles and Standards for School Mathematics*** ▸ Grades PreK–2 Geometry general essay, page 97, *Analyze Characteristics,* pages 97–98, *Use Visualization,* pages 100–101 ▸ Grades 3–5 Geometry general essay, page 165, *Analyze Characteristics,* page 165–166, *Use Visualization,* pages 168–169, Measurement, *Apply Appropriate Techniques,* page 173 ▸ Grades 6–8 Geometry general essay, page 233, *Analyze Characteristics,* pages 233–235; Measurement, *Apply Appropriate Techniques,* pages 243–245 ▸ Grades 9–12 Geometry general essay, pages 309–310, *Analyze Characteristics,* page 310; Measurement, *Understand Measurable Attributes,* page 321
III. Identify Concepts and Specific Ideas	**IIIA:** ***Benchmarks for Science Literacy*** ▸ 9C, *Shapes,* pages 223–225 **IIIB:** ***NCTM Principles and Standards for School Mathematics*** ▸ Grades PreK–2 Geometry, page 96 or 396 ▸ Grades 3–5 Geometry, page 164 or 396; Measurement, page 170 or 398 ▸ Grades 6–8 Geometry, page 232 or 397; Measurement, page 240 or 399 ▸ Grades 9–12 Geometry, page 308 or 397; Measurement, page 320 or 399
IV. Examine Research on Student Learning	**IVA:** ***Benchmarks for Science Literacy*** ▸ 9C, *Shapes,* pages 352–353 **IVB:** ***Research Companion*** ▸ Chapter 11, *Theories of Geometric Thinking,* pages 152–155
V. Examine Coherency and Articulation	**V:** ***Atlas of Science Literacy*:** There are no maps for this topic in Volume 1.
VI. Clarify State Standards and District Curriculum	**VIA:** ***State Standards:*** Link Sections I–V to learning goals and information from your state standards or frameworks that are informed by the results of the topic study. **VIB:** ***District Curriculum Guide:*** Link Sections I–V to learning goals and information from your district curriculum guide that are informed by the results of the topic study.
Visit www.curriculumtopicstudy.org for updates or supplementary readings, Web sites, and videos.	

Standards- and Research-Based Study of a Curricular Topic

CONGRUENCE AND SIMILARITY

Section and Outcome	Selected Sources and Readings for Study and Reflection Read and examine *related parts* of:
I. Identify Adult Content Knowledge	**IA:** ***Science for All Americans*** ▸ Chapter 9, *Shapes*, pages 134–135 **IB:** ***Beyond Numeracy*** ▸ *Trigonometry*, pages 251–256
II. Consider Instructional Implications	**IIA:** ***Benchmarks for Science Literacy*** ▸ 9C, *Shapes*, general essay page 222; grade span essays, pages 223–224 **IIB:** ***NCTM Principles and Standards for School Mathematics*** ▸ Grades PreK–12 Overview Geometry, *Analyze Characteristics*, page 42, *Use Visualization*, page 43 ▸ Grades 3–5 Geometry general essay, page 165, *Analyze Characteristics*, pages 165–166, *Apply Transformation*, pages 167–168 ▸ Grades 6–8 Geometry, *Analyze Characteristics*, pages 234–235, *Apply Transformation*, pages 235–236 ▸ Grades 9–12 Geometry general essay, page 309–310, *Analyze Characteristics*, pages 310–311, page 313, *Vignette*, page 312
III. Identify Concepts and Specific Ideas	**IIIA:** ***Benchmarks for Science Literacy*** ▸ 9C, *Shapes*, pages 223 ▸ 12D, *Communication Skills*, page 297 **IIIB:** ***NCTM Principles and Standards for School Mathematics*** ▸ Grades 3–5 Geometry, page 164 or 396 ▸ Grades 6–8 Geometry, page 232 or 397 ▸ Grades 9–12 Geometry, page 308 or 397
IV. Examine Research on Student Learning	**IVA:** ***Benchmarks for Science Literacy*** ▸ 9C, *Development of geometrical thinking*, page 352 ▸ 12B, *Proportional Reasoning*, page 360 **IVB:** ***Research Companion*** Chapter 11, *Theories of Geometric Thinking*, pages 152–155; *Selected Geometric Topics*, pages 160–162
V. Examine Coherency and Articulation	**V:** ***Atlas of Science Literacy*** ▸ *Ratios and Proportionality*, page 119
VI. Clarify State Standards and District Curriculum	**VIA:** *State Standards:* Link Sections I–V to learning goals and information from your state standards or frameworks that are informed by the results of the topic study. **VIB:** *District Curriculum Guide:* Link Sections I–V to learning goals and information from your district curriculum guide that are informed by the results of the topic study.
Visit www.curriculumtopicstudy.org for updates or supplementary readings, Web sites, and videos.	

Standards- and Research-Based Study of a Curricular Topic

COORDINATE GEOMETRY

Section and Outcome	Selected Sources and Readings for Study and Reflection Read and examine *related parts* of:
I. Identify Adult Content Knowledge	**IA:** ***Science for All Americans*** ▸ Chapter 2, *Patterns and Relationships,* page 16 ▸ Chapter 9, *Shapes,* pages 134–135 ▸ Chapter 12, *Communication,* pages 192–193 **IB:** ***Beyond Numeracy*** ▸ *Analytic Geometry,* pages 10–14 ▸ *Linear Programming,* pages 133–135 ▸ *Matrices and Vectors,* pages 136–140
II. Consider Instructional Implications	**IIA:** ***Benchmarks for Science Literacy*** ▸ 9C, *Shapes,* general essay, page 222; grade span essays, pages 223–225 **IIB:** ***NCTM Principles and Standards for School Mathematics*** ▸ Grades PreK–12 Overview Geometry general essay, page 41, *Specify Locations,* pages 42–43 ▸ Grades PreK–2 Geometry general essay, page 97, *Specify Locations,* pages 98–99 ▸ Grades 3–5 Geometry general essay, page 165, *Specify Locations,* page 167 ▸ Grades 6–8 Geometry general essay, page 233, *Specify Locations,* page 235 ▸ Grades 9–12 Geometry general essay, page 309–310, *Specify locations,* pages 313–314
III. Identify Concepts and Specific Ideas	**IIIA:** ***Benchmarks for Science Literacy*** ▸ 9C, *Shapes,* pages 223–225 ▸ 12D, *Communication,* page 297 **IIIB:** ***NCTM Principles and Standards for School Mathematics*** ▸ Grades PreK–2 Geometry, page 96 or 396 ▸ Grades 3–5 Geometry, page 164 or 396 ▸ Grades 6–8 Geometry, page 232 or 397 ▸ Grades 9–12 Geometry, page 308 or 397
IV. Examine Research on Student Learning	**IVA:** ***Benchmarks for Science Literacy*** ▸ 9B, *Graphs,* page 351 **IVB:** ***Research Companion*** ▸ Chapter 11, *Navigation, Coordinates and Structuring Two–Dimensional Space,* pages 164–167
V. Examine Coherency and Articulation	**V:** ***Atlas of Science Literacy*** ▸ *Graphic Representation,* page 115
VI. Clarify State Standards and District Curriculum	**VIA:** ***State Standards:*** Link Sections I–V to learning goals and information from your state standards or frameworks that are informed by the results of the topic study. **VIB:** ***District Curriculum Guide:*** Link Sections I–V to learning goals and information from your district curriculum guide that are informed by the results of the topic study.
	Visit www.curriculumtopicstudy.org for updates or supplementary readings, Web sites, and videos.

Standards- and Research-Based Study of a Curricular Topic

GEOMETRIC MODELING

Section and Outcome	Selected Sources and Readings for Study and Reflection Read and examine *related parts* of:
I. Identify Adult Content Knowledge	**IA:** **Science for All Americans** ▸ Chapter 2, *Mathematical Inquiry,* page 19 ▸ Chapter 9, *Shapes,* pages 134–135 ▸ Chapter 11, *Models,* page 168; *Mathematical Models,* pages 171–172 **IB:** **Beyond Numeracy** ▸ *Non–Euclidean Geometry,* pages 158–162 ▸ *Topology,* pages 246–250 ▸ *Combinatorics, Graphs, and Maps,* pages 42–46
II. Consider Instructional Implications	**IIA:** **Benchmarks for Science Literacy** ▸ 2C, *Mathematical Inquiry* general essay, pages 34–35; grade span essays, pages 36–38 ▸ 11B, *Models* general essay, page 267; grade span essays, pages 268–270 **IIB:** **NCTM Principles and Standards for School Mathematics** ▸ Grades PreK–12 Overview Geometry general essay, page 41, *Use Visualization,* page 43; Representations, pages 67–71 ▸ Grades PreK–2 Geometry general essay, page 97, *Use Visualization,* pages 100–101; Representations, page 136–141 ▸ Grades 3–5 Geometry general essay, page 165, *Use Visualization,* pages 168–169; Representations, pages 206–209 ▸ Grades 6–8 Geometry, *Use Visualization,* pages 237–239; Representations, pages 280–285 ▸ Grades 9–12 Geometry general essay, pages 309–310, *Use Visualization,* pages 315–318; Representations, pages 360–364
III. Identify Concepts and Specific Ideas	**IIIA:** **Benchmarks for Science Literacy** ▸ 2C, *Mathematical Inquiry,* pages 36–38 ▸ 11B, *Models,* pages 268–270 **IIIB:** **NCTM Principles and Standards for School Mathematics** ▸ Grades PreK–2 Geometry, page 96 or 396 ▸ Grades 3–5 Geometry, page 164 or 396 ▸ Grades 6–8 Geometry, page 232 or 397 ▸ Grades 9–12 Geometry, page 308 or 397
IV. Examine Research on Student Learning	**IVA:** **Benchmarks for Science Literacy** ▸ 11B, *Models,* page 357 **IVB:** **Research Companion** ▸ Chapter 11, *Instructional Tools,* pages 155–160, *Shape, Congruence, and Similarity,* pages 160–162, *Symmetry and Geometric Motions,* page 162, *Navigation, Coordinates,* pages 164–166 ▸ Chapter 18, *Definitions of Representation,* pages 264–266
V. Examine Coherency and Articulation	**V:** **Atlas of Science Literacy** ▸ *Mathematical Processes,* page 27 ▸ *Mathematical Models,* page 29
VI. Clarify State Standards and District Curriculum	**VIA:** **State Standards:** Link Sections I–V to learning goals and information from your state standards or frameworks that are informed by the results of the topic study. **VIB:** **District Curriculum Guide:** Link Sections I–V to learning goals and information from your district curriculum guide that are informed by the results of the topic study.
Visit www.curriculumtopicstudy.org for updates or supplementary readings, Web sites, and videos.	

Standards- and Research-Based Study of a Curricular Topic

GEOMETRIC PATTERNS

Section and Outcome	Selected Sources and Readings for Study and Reflection Read and examine *related parts* of:
I. Identify Adult Content Knowledge	**IA:** ***Science for All Americans*** ▸ Chapter 2, *Patterns and Relationships*, page 16 ▸ Chapter 9, *Shapes*, pages 134–135 **IB:** ***Beyond Numeracy*** ▸ *Recursion–From Definition to Life,* pages 211–213 ▸ *Analytical Geometry,* pages 10–14 ▸ *Fractals,* pages 82–86
II. Consider Instructional Implications	**IIA:** ***Benchmarks for Science Literacy*** ▸ 2A, *Patterns and Relationships* general essay, pages 25–26; grade span essays, pages 26–29 **IIB:** ***NCTM Principles and Standards for School Mathematics*** ▸ Grades PreK–2 Algebra general essay, page 91, *Understand Patterns,* pages 91–92; Reasoning and Proof, pages 122–123; Connections, page 133 ▸ Grades 3–5 Algebra general essay, page 159, *Understand Patterns,* pages 159–160, *Use Mathematical Models,* page 162 ▸ Grades 6–8 Algebra, *Use Mathematical Models,* pages, 227–229; Geometry, *Use Visualization,* page 239; Reasoning and Proof, pages 262–264; Vignettes, pages 262–264, pages 266–267
III. Identify Concepts and Specific Ideas	**IIIA:** ***Benchmarks for Science Literacy*** ▸ 2A, *Patterns and Relationships,* pages 26–27, page 29 **IIIB:** ***NCTM Principles and Standards for School Mathematics*** ▸ Grades PreK–2 *Algebra,* page 90 or 394 ▸ Grades 3–5 *Algebra,* page 158 or 394 ▸ Grades 6–8 *Algebra,* page 222 or 395 ▸ Grades 9–12 *Algebra,* page 296 or 395
IV. Examine Research on Student Learning	**IVA:** ***Benchmarks for Science Literacy*** ▸ 2A, *Patterns and Relationships,* page 334 **IVB:** ***Research Companion*** ▸ Chapter 10, *Patterns,* pages 137–138, *Stasis and Change,* pages 142–145
V. Examine Coherency and Articulation	**V:** ***Atlas of Science Literacy*** ▸ *Mathematical Processes,* page 27
VI. Clarify State Standards and District Curriculum	**VIA:** ***State Standards:*** Link Sections I–V to learning goals and information from your state standards or frameworks that are informed by the results of the topic study. **VIB:** ***District Curriculum Guide:*** Link Sections I–V to learning goals and information from your district curriculum guide that are informed by the results of the topic study.
	Visit www.curriculumtopicstudy.org for updates or supplementary readings, Web sites, and videos.

Standards- and Research-Based Study of a Curricular Topic

GEOMETRIC PROOF

Section and Outcome	Selected Sources and Readings for Study and Reflection Read and examine *related parts* of:
I. Identify Adult Content Knowledge	**IA:** *Science for All Americans* ▶ Chapter 9, *Reasoning,* pages 140–143 ▶ Chapter 12, *Communication,* pages 192–193 **IB:** *Beyond Numeracy* ▶ *QED, Proofs, and Theorems,* pages 195–197
II. Consider Instructional Implications	**IIA:** *Benchmarks for Science Literacy* ▶ 9C, *Shapes,* grade span essays, page 224–225 ▶ 9E, *Reasoning,* general essay, page 231; grade span essays, pages 232–234 **IIB:** *NCTM Principles and Standards for School Mathematics* ▶ Grades PreK–12 Overview Geometry, page 41, *Analyze Characteristics,* pages 41–42; Reasoning and Proof, page 56, *Recognize Reasoning,* pages 56–57, *Develop and Evaluate,* pages 58–59 ▶ Grades PreK–2 Reasoning and Proof, pages 122–126 ▶ Grades 3–5 Geometry general essay, page 165, *Analyze Characteristics,* pages 165–166; Reasoning and Proof, pages 188–192 ▶ Grades 6–8 Geometry general essay, page 233, *Analyze Characteristics,* pages 234–235; Reasoning and Proof, pages 262–267 ▶ Grades 9–12 Geometry general essay, page 309–310, *Analyze Characteristics,* pages 310–311, page 313, Vignette, page 311–312; Reasoning and Proof, pages 342–346
III. Identify Concepts and Specific Ideas	**IIIA:** *Benchmarks for Science Literacy* ▶ 9E, *Reasoning,* pages 232–234 **IIB:** *NCTM Principles and Standards for School Mathematics* ▶ Grades 3–5 Geometry, page 164 or 396 ▶ Grades 6–8 Geometry, page 232 or 397 ▶ Grades 9–12 Geometry, page 308 or 397
IV. Examine Research on Student Learning	**IVA:** *Benchmarks for Science Literacy* ▶ 2C, *Mathematical Inquiry,* page 334 ▶ 9C, *Shapes,* pages 352–353 **IVB:** *Research Companion* ▶ Chapter 11, *Instructional Tools,* page 156, *The van Hieles,* pages 152–155, *Proof,* pages 167–169 ▶ Chapter 15, *Reasoning, Explaining, and Justifying,* page 231, *Proof and the Activity of Proving,* pages 231–233
V. Examine Coherency and Articulation	**V:** *Atlas of Science Literacy*: There are no maps for this topic in Volume 1.
VI. Clarify State Standards and District Curriculum	**VIA:** *State Standards:* Link Sections I–V to learning goals and information from your state standards or frameworks that are informed by the results of the topic study. **VIB:** *District Curriculum Guide:* Link Sections I–V to learning goals and information from your district curriculum guide that are informed by the results of the topic study.
Visit www.curriculumtopicstudy.org for updates or supplementary readings, Web sites, and videos.	

Standards- and Research-Based Study of a Curricular Topic

GEOMETRIC RELATIONSHIPS

Section and Outcome	Selected Sources and Readings for Study and Reflection Read and examine *related parts* of:
I. Identify Adult Content Knowledge	**IA:** *Science for All Americans* ▸ Chapter 2, *Patterns and Relationships,* page 16; *Mathematical Inquiry,* page 19 ▸ Chapter 9, *Shapes,* pages 134–135 ▸ Chapter 12, *Communication,* pages 192–193
II. Consider Instructional Implications	**IIA:** *Benchmarks for Science Literacy* ▸ 2A, *Patterns and Relationships,* general essay, pages 25–26; grade span essays, pages 26–29 ▸ 9C, *Shapes,* general essay, page 222; grade span essays, pages 223–225 **IIB:** *NCTM Principles and Standards for School Mathematics* ▸ Grades PreK–12 Overview Geometry general essay, page 41, *Analyze Characteristics and Properties,* pages 41–42, *Specify Locations,* page 42 ▸ Grades PreK–2 Algebra, *Understand Patterns,* page 91; Geometry general essay, page 97, *Analyze Characteristics and Properties,* pages 97–98, *Specify Locations,* pages 98–99, *Use Visualization,* page 100 ▸ Grades 3–5 Algebra, *Understand Patterns,* pages 159–160; Geometry general essay, page 165, *Analyze Characteristics and Properties,* 165–166, *Specify Locations,* pages 167, *Use Visualization,* pages 168–169 ▸ Grades 6–8 Geometry general essay, page 233, *Analyze Characteristics and Properties,* pages 233–235, *Specify Locations,* page 235, *Apply Transformations,* pages 235–237, *Use Visualization,* pages 237–238 ▸ Grades 9–12 Geometry general essay, pages 309–310, *Analyze Characteristics and Properties,* pages 310–313, *Specify Locations,* pages 313–314, *Use Visualization,* pages 315–316
III. Identify Concepts and Specific Ideas	**IIIA:** *Benchmarks for Science Literacy* ▸ 2A, *Patterns and Relationships,* page 29 ▸ 9C, *Shapes,* pages 223–225 **IIIB:** *NCTM Principles and Standards for School Mathematics* ▸ Grades PreK–2 Algebra, page 90 or 394; Geometry, page 96 or 396 ▸ Grades 3–5 Geometry, page 164 or 396 ▸ Grades 6–8 Geometry, page 232 or 397 ▸ Grades 9–12 Geometry, page 308 or 397
IV. Examine Research on Student Learning	**IVA:** *Benchmarks for Science Literacy* ▸ 9C, *Development of Geometric Thinking,* page 352 **IVB:** *Research Companion* ▸ Chapter 11, *Theories of Geometric Thinking,* pages 152–155, *Shape, Congruence,* page 160–162, *Angle, Parallelism,* pages 162–164, *Navigation, Coordinates,* pages 164–167
V. Examine Coherency and Articulation	**V:** *Atlas of Science Literacy* ▸ *Mathematical Processes,* page 27 ▸ *Graphic Representation,* page 115
VI. Clarify State Standards and District Curriculum	**VIA:** *State Standards:* Link Sections I–V to learning goals and information from your state standards or frameworks that are informed by the results of the topic study. **VIB:** *District Curriculum Guide:* Link Sections I–V to learning goals and information from your district curriculum guide that are informed by the results of the topic study.
Visit www.curriculumtopicstudy.org for updates or supplementary readings, Web sites, and videos.	

Standards- and Research-Based Study of a Curricular Topic

GEOMETRIC SHAPES

Section and Outcome	Selected Sources and Readings for Study and Reflection Read and examine *related parts* of:
I. Identify Adult Content Knowledge	**IA:** *Science for All Americans* ▸ Chapter 9, *Shapes,* pages 134–135
II. Consider Instructional Implications	**IIA:** *Benchmarks for Science Literacy* ▸ 9C, *Shapes,* general essay, page 222; grade span essays, pages 223–225 **IIB:** *NCTM Principles and Standards for School Mathematics* ▸ Grades PreK–12 Overview Geometry general essay, page 41, *Analyze Characteristics,* pages 41–42; Measurement, *Understand Measurable,* pages 44–45 ▸ Grades PreK–2 Geometry general essay, page 97, *Analyze Characteristics,* pages 97–98 ▸ Grades 3–5 Geometry general essay, page 165, *Analyze Characteristics,* pages 165–166 ▸ Grades 6–8 Geometry general essay, page 233, *Analyze Characteristics,* pages 233–235 ▸ Grades 9–12 Geometry general essay, pages 309–310, *Analyze Characteristics,* pages 310–311, page 312, Vignette, page 312
III. Identify Concepts and Specific Ideas	**IIIA:** *Benchmarks for Science Literacy* ▸ 9C, *Shapes,* pages 223–225 **IIIB:** *NCTM Principles and Standards for School Mathematics* ▸ Grades PreK–2 Geometry, page 96 or 396 ▸ Grades 3–5 Geometry, page 164 or 396 ▸ Grades 6–8 Geometry, page 232 or 397 ▸ Grades 9–12 Geometry, page 308 or 397
IV. Examine Research on Student Learning	**IVA:** *Benchmarks for Science Literacy* ▸ 9C, *Shapes,* pages 352–353 **IVB:** *Research Companion* ▸ Chapter 11, *Theories of Geometric Thinking,* pages 152–155, *Instructional Tools,* pages 155–160, *Selected Geometric Topics,* pages 160–162
V. Examine Coherency and Articulation	**V:** *Atlas of Science Literacy* ▸ *Graphic Representation,* page 115 ▸ *Symbolic Representation,* page 117
VI. Clarify State Standards and District Curriculum	**VIA:** *State Standards:* Link Sections I–V to learning goals and information from your state standards or frameworks that are informed by the results of the topic study. **VIB:** *District Curriculum Guide:* Link Sections I–V to learning goals and information from your district curriculum guide that are informed by the results of the topic study.
Visit www.curriculumtopicstudy.org for updates or supplementary readings, Web sites, and videos.	

Standards- and Research-Based Study of a Curricular Topic

GEOMETRIC THEOREMS

Section and Outcome	Selected Sources and Readings for Study and Reflection Read and examine *related parts* of:

I. Identify Adult Content Knowledge	**IA:** ***Science for All Americans***
	  ▸ Chapter 2, *Patterns and Relationships*, pages 16–17; *Manipulating Mathematical Statements*, page 20
	
	IB: ***Beyond Numeracy***
	  ▸ *Non–Euclidean Geometry*, pages 158–162
	  ▸ *QED, Proofs, and Theorems*, pages 195–197
	  ▸ *Symmetry and Invariance*, pages 234–236
	  ▸ *The Pythagorean Theorem*, pages 192–194

II. Consider Instructional Implications	**IIA:** ***Benchmarks for Science Literacy***
	  ▸ 2A, *Patterns and Relationships*, grade span essay, page 29
	
	IIB: ***NCTM Principles and Standards for School Mathematics***
	  ▸ Grades PreK–12 Overview Geometry general essay, page 41, *Analyze Characteristics and Properties*, pages 41–42
	  ▸ Grades PreK–2 Geometry, *Analyze Characteristics and Properties*, pages 97–98
	  ▸ Grades 3–5 Geometry, *Analyze Characteristics and Properties*, pages 165–166
	  ▸ Grades 6–8 Geometry, *Analyze Characteristics and Properties*, pages 233–235
	  ▸ Grades 9–12 Geometry, general essay pages 309–310, *Analyze Characteristics and Properties*, pages 310–311, page 313, Vignette, page 311–312, *Specify Locations*, pages 313–314

III. Identify Concepts and Specific Ideas	**IIIA:** ***Benchmarks for Science Literacy***
	  ▸ 2A, *Patterns and Relationships*, page 29
	
	IIIB: ***NCTM Principles and Standards for School Mathematics***
	  ▸ Grades PreK–2 Geometry, page 96 or 396
	  ▸ Grades 3–5 Geometry, page 164 or 396
	  ▸ Grades 6–8 Geometry, page 232 or 397
	  ▸ Grades 9–12 Geometry, page 308 or 397

IV. Examine Research on Student Learning	**IVB:** ***Research Companion***
	  ▸ Chapter 11, *Theories of Geometric Thinking*, pages 152–155, *Proof*, pages 167–169
	  ▸ Chapter 15, *Proof and the Activity*, page 231

V. Examine Coherency and Articulation	**V:** ***Atlas of Science Literacy***: There are no maps for this topic in Volume 1.
VI. Clarify State Standards and District Curriculum	**VIA:** ***State Standards:*** Link Sections I–V to learning goals and information from your state standards or frameworks that are informed by the results of the topic study. **VIB:** ***District Curriculum Guide:*** Link Sections I–V to learning goals and information from your district curriculum guide that are informed by the results of the topic study.
Visit www.curriculumtopicstudy.org for updates or supplementary readings, Web sites, and videos.	

Standards- and Research-Based Study of a Curricular Topic

NETWORKS

Section and Outcome	Selected Sources and Readings for Study and Reflection Read and examine *related parts* of:
I. Identify Adult Content Knowledge	**IA:** **Science for All Americans** ▸ Chapter 2, *Patterns and Relationships*, page 17 ▸ Chapter 9, *Shapes*, page 135 **IB:** **Beyond Numeracy** ▸ *Combinatorics, Graphs, and Maps*, pages 42–46
II. Consider Instructional Implications	**IIB:** **NCTM Principles and Standards for School Mathematics** ▸ Grades PreK–12 Overview Geometry general essay, page 41, *Specify Locations*, pages 42–43 ▸ Grades PreK–2 Geometry general essay, page 97, *Specify Locations*, pages 98–99 ▸ Grades 3–5 Geometry general essay, page 165, *Specify Locations*, page 167 ▸ Grades 6–8 Geometry general essay, page 233, *Use Visualization*, pages 237–239 ▸ Grades 9–12 Geometry general essay, pages 309–310, *Use Visualization*, pages 317–318
III. Identify Concepts and Specific Ideas	**IIIB:** **NCTM Principles and Standards for School Mathematics** ▸ Grades PreK–2 Geometry, page 96 or 396 ▸ Grades 3–5 Geometry, page 164 or 396 ▸ Grades 6–8 Geometry, page 232 or 397 ▸ Grades 9–12 Geometry, page 308 or 397
IV. Examine Research on Student Learning	**IVB:** **Research Companion** ▸ Chapter 11, *Navigation, Coordinates*, pages 164–167
V. Examine Coherency and Articulation	**V:** **Atlas of Science Literacy**: There are no maps for this topic available in Volume 1.
VI. Clarify State Standards and District Curriculum	**VIA:** **State Standards:** Link Sections I–V to learning goals and information from your state standards or frameworks that are informed by the results of the topic study. **VIB:** **District Curriculum Guide:** Link Sections I–V to learning goals and information from your district curriculum guide that are informed by the results of the topic study.
Visit www.curriculumtopicstudy.org for updates or supplementary readings, Web sites, and videos.	

Standards- and Research-Based Study of a Curricular Topic

QUADRILATERALS

Section and Outcome	Selected Sources and Readings for Study and Reflection Read and examine *related parts* of:
I. Identify Adult Content Knowledge	**IA:** *Science for All Americans* ▸ Chapter 9, *Shapes,* pages 134–135 ▸ Chapter 12, *Calculator Skills,* page 189 **IB:** *Beyond Numeracy* ▸ *Areas and Volumes,* pages 18–23
II. Consider Instructional Implications	**IIA:** *Benchmarks for Science Literacy* ▸ 9C, *Shapes* general essay, page 222; grade span essays, pages 223–225 **IIB:** *NCTM Principles and Standards for School Mathematics* ▸ Grades PreK–12 Overview Geometry general essay, page 41, *Analyze Characteristics,* pages 41–42; Measurement general essay, page 44, *Understand Measurable,* page 44, *Apply Appropriate Techniques,* page 46 ▸ Grades PreK–2 Geometry general essay, page 97, *Analyze Characteristics,* pages 97–98 ▸ Grades 3–5 Geometry general essay, page 165, *Analyze Characteristics,* pages 165–166, *Use Visualization,* page 168; Measurement, *Apply Appropriate Techniques,* pages 174–175 ▸ Grades 6–8 Geometry general essay, page 233, *Analyze Characteristics,* pages 233–235, *Use Visualization,* page 237, pages 238–239; Measurement general essay, page 241, *Understand Measurable,* pages 241–242, *Apply Appropriate Techniques,* page 243, pages 244–245 ▸ Grades 9–12 Geometry general essay, page 309, *Analyze Characteristics,* pages 310–311
III. Identify Concepts and Specific Ideas	**IIIA:** *Benchmarks for Science Literacy* ▸ 9C, *Shapes,* pages 223–225 ▸ 12B, *Computation and Estimation,* pages 290–291 **IIIB:** *NCTM Principles and Standards for School Mathematics* ▸ Grades PreK–2 Geometry, page 96 or 396 ▸ Grades 3–5 Geometry, page 164 or 396; Measurement, page 170 or 398 ▸ Grades 6–8 Geometry, page 232 or 397; Measurement, page 240 or 399 ▸ Grades 9–12 Geometry, page 308 or 397
IV. Examine Research on Student Learning	**IVA:** *Benchmarks for Science Literacy* ▸ 9C, *Shapes,* pages 352–353 **IVB:** *Research Companion* ▸ Chapter 11, *Theories of Geometric Thinking,* pages 152–155, *Shape, Congruence, and Similarity,* page 160, *Angle, Parallelism, and Perpendicularity,* pages 162–164 ▸ Chapter 12, *Area Measure,* pages 184–185, page 187
V. Examine Coherency and Articulation	**V:** *Atlas of Science Literacy:* There are no maps for this topic in Volume 1.
VI. Clarify State Standards and District Curriculum	**VIA:** *State Standards:* Link Sections I–V to learning goals and information from your state standards or frameworks that are informed by the results of the topic study. **VIB:** *District Curriculum Guide:* Link Sections I–V to learning goals and information from your district curriculum guide that are informed by the results of the topic study.
Visit www.curriculumtopicstudy.org for updates or supplementary readings, Web sites, and videos.	

Standards- and Research-Based Study of a Curricular Topic

SORTING AND CLASSIFYING

Section and Outcome	Selected Sources and Readings for Study and Reflection Read and examine *related parts* of:
I. Identify Adult Content Knowledge	**IA:** *Science for All Americans* ▸ Chapter 2, *Mathematical Inquiry,* page 19 ▸ Chapter 9, *Shapes,* page 134 **IB:** *Beyond Numeracy* ▸ *Sorting and Retrieving,* pages 225–226
II. Consider Instructional Implications	**IIA:** *Benchmarks for Science Literacy* ▸ 2B, *Mathematics, Science, and Technology,* grade span essay, page 31 ▸ 9C, *Shapes,* general essay, page 222; grade span essays, pages 223–224 **IIB:** *NCTM Principles and Standards for School Mathematics* ▸ Grades PreK–12 Overview Algebra, *Understand Patterns,* page 38; Geometry general essay, page 41, *Analyze Characteristics,* pages 41–42 ▸ Grades PreK–2 Algebra, *Understand Patterns,* page 91; Geometry general essay, page 97, *Analyze Characteristics,* pages 97–98 ▸ Grades 3–5 Algebra, *Understand Patterns,* pages 159–160; Geometry general essay, page 165, *Analyze Characteristics,* pages 165–166 ▸ Grades 6–8 Geometry general essay, page 233, *Analyze Characteristics,* pages 233–235 ▸ Grades 9–12 Geometry general essay, page 309, *Analyze Characteristics,* pages 310–311
III. Identify Concepts and Specific Ideas	**IIIA:** *Benchmarks for Science Literacy* ▸ 9C, *Shapes,* pages 223–224 ▸ 11B, *Models,* page 268 **IIIB:** *NCTM Principles and Standards for School Mathematics* ▸ Grades PreK–2 Algebra, page 90 or 394; Geometry, page 96 or 396 ▸ Grades 3–5 Algebra, page 158 or 394; Geometry, page 164 or 396 ▸ Grades 6–8 Geometry, page 232 or 397 ▸ Grades 9–12 Geometry, page 308 or 397
IV. Examine Research on Student Learning	**IVA:** *Benchmarks for Science Literacy*: ▸ 9C, *Shapes,* page 352 **IVB:** *Research Companion* ▸ Chapter 11, *Theories of Geometric Thinking,* pages 152–155, *Instructional Tools,* page 155, *Shape, Congruence, and Similarity,* pages 160–162
V. Examine Coherency and Articulation	**V:** *Atlas of Science Literacy:* There are no maps for this topic in Volume 1.
VI. Clarify State Standards and District Curriculum	**VIA:** *State Standards:* Link Sections I–V to learning goals and information from your state standards or frameworks that are informed by the results of the topic study. **VIB:** *District Curriculum Guide:* Link Sections I–V to learning goals and information from your district curriculum guide that are informed by the results of the topic study.
Visit www.curriculumtopicstudy.org for updates or supplementary readings, Web sites, and videos.	

Standards- and Research-Based Study of a Curricular Topic

SPATIAL VISUALIZATION

Section and Outcome	Selected Sources and Readings for Study and Reflection Read and examine *related parts* of:
I. Identify Adult Content Knowledge	**IA:** ***Science for All Americans*** ▸ Chapter 9, *Shapes,* pages 134–135
II. Consider Instructional Implications	**IIA:** ***Benchmarks for Science Literacy*** ▸ 9C, *Shapes* general essay, page 222; grade span essays, pages 223–225 **IIB:** ***NCTM Principles and Standards for School Mathematics*** ▸ Grades PreK–12 Overview Geometry general essay, page 41, *Use Visualization*, page 43 ▸ Grades PreK–2 Geometry general essay, page 97, *Use Visualization,* pages 100–101 ▸ Grades 3–5 Geometry general essay, page 165, *Use Visualization,* pages 168–169 ▸ Grades 6–8 Geometry general essay, page 233, *Use Visualization,* pages 237–239 ▸ Grades 9–12 Geometry general essay, pages 309–310, *Use Visualization,* pages 315–318
III. Identify Concepts and Specific Ideas	**IIIA:** ***Benchmarks for Science Literacy*** ▸ 9C, *Shapes,* pages 223–225 **IIIB:** ***NCTM Principles and Standards for School Mathematics*** ▸ Grades PreK–2 *Geometry,* page 96 or 396 ▸ Grades 3–5 *Geometry,* page 164 or 396 ▸ Grades 6–8 *Geometry,* page 232 or 397 ▸ Grades 9–12 *Geometry,* page 308 or 397
IV. Examine Research on Student Learning	**IVA:** ***Benchmarks for Science Literacy*** ▸ 9C, *Shapes,* page 352 **IVB:** ***Research Companion*** ▸ Chapter 11, *Selected Geometric Topics,* pages 160–167
V. Examine Coherency and Articulation	**V:** ***Atlas of Science Literacy:*** There are no maps for this topic in Volume 1.
VI. Clarify State Standards and District Curriculum	**VIA:** ***State Standards:*** Link Sections I–V to learning goals and information from your state standards or frameworks that are informed by the results of the topic study. **VIB:** ***District Curriculum Guide:*** Link Sections I–V to learning goals and information from your district curriculum guide that are informed by the results of the topic study.
Visit www.curriculumtopicstudy.org for updates or supplementary readings, Web sites, and videos.	

Standards- and Research-Based Study of a Curricular Topic

TRANSFORMATIONS AND SYMMETRY

Section and Outcome	Selected Sources and Readings for Study and Reflection Read and examine *related parts* of:
I. Identify Adult Content Knowledge	**IA:** *Science for All Americans* ▶ Chapter 9, *Shapes,* page 134 ▶ Chapter 11, *Constancy and Change,* page 174 **IB:** *Beyond Numeracy* ▶ *Symmetry and Invariance,* pages 234–236
II. Consider Instructional Implications	**IIA:** *Benchmarks for Science Literacy* ▶ 9C, *Shapes,* general essay page 222; grade span essays, pages 223–224 **IIB:** *NCTM Principles and Standards for School Mathematics* ▶ Grades PreK–12 Overview Geometry general essay, page 41, *Apply Transformations,* page 43 ▶ Grades PreK–2 Geometry general essay, page 97, *Apply Transformations,* pages 99–100 ▶ Grades 3–5 Geometry general essay, page 165, *Apply Transformations,* pages 167–168 ▶ Grades 6–8 Geometry general essay, page 233, *Apply Transformations,* pages 235–237 ▶ Grades 9–12 Geometry general essay, pages 309–310, *Apply Transformations,* pages 314–315
III. Identify Concepts and Specific Ideas	**IIIA:** *Benchmarks for Science Literacy* ▶ 9C, *Shapes,* pages 223–224 **IIIB:** *NCTM Principles and Standards for School Mathematics* ▶ Grades PreK–2 Geometry, page 96 or 396 ▶ Grades 3–5 Geometry, page 164 or 396 ▶ Grades 6–8 Geometry, page 232 or 397 ▶ Grades 9–12 Geometry, page 308 or 397
IV. Examine Research on Student Learning	**IVA:** *Benchmarks for Science Literacy* ▶ 9C, *Shapes,* pages 352–353 **IVB:** *Research Companion* ▶ Chapter 11, *Symmetry and Geometric Motion,* page 162, *Angle, Parallelism,* pages 162–164, *Navigations Coordinates,* pages 164–167
V. Examine Coherency and Articulation	**V:** *Atlas of Science Literacy:* There are no maps for this topic in Volume 1.
VI. Clarify State Standards and District Curriculum	**VIA:** *State Standards:* Link Sections I–V to learning goals and information from your state standards or frameworks that are informed by the results of the topic study. **VIB:** *District Curriculum Guide:* Link Sections I–V to learning goals and information from your district curriculum guide that are informed by the results of the topic study.
Visit www.curriculumtopicstudy.org for updates or supplementary readings, Web sites, and videos.	

Standards- and Research-Based Study of a Curricular Topic

TRIANGLES

Section and Outcome	Selected Sources and Readings for Study and Reflection Read and examine *related parts* of:
I. Identify Adult Content Knowledge	**IA:** *Science for All Americans* ▸ Chapter 9, *Shapes,* pages 134–135 ▸ Chapter 12, *Calculator Skills,* page 189 **IB:** *Beyond Numeracy* ▸ *Areas and Volumes,* pages 18–23 ▸ *The Pythagorean Theorem,* pages 192–194
II. Consider Instructional Implications	**IIA:** *Benchmarks for Science Literacy* ▸ 9C, *Shapes* general essay, page 222; grade span essays, pages 223–225 **IIB:** *NCTM Principles and Standards for School Mathematics* ▸ Grades PreK–12 Overview Geometry general essay, page 41, *Analyze Characteristics,* pages 41–42; Measurement general essay, page 44, *Understand Measurable,* page 44–45, *Apply Appropriate Techniques,* pages 46–47 ▸ Grades PreK–2 Geometry general essay, page 97, *Analyze Characteristics,* pages 97–98 ▸ Grades 3–5 Geometry general essay, page 165, *Analyze Characteristics,* pages 165–166, *Use Visualization,* page 168 ▸ Grades 6–8 Geometry general essay, page 233, *Analyze Characteristics,* pages 233–235, *Use Visualization,* pages 237–239; Measurement general essay, page 241, *Understand Measurable,* page 242, *Apply Appropriate Techniques,* pages 243–245 ▸ Grades 9–12 Geometry general essay, page 309, *Analyze Characteristics,* pages 310–311, page 313, Vignette, pages 311–312, *Specify Locations,* pages 313–314
III. Identify Concepts and Specific Ideas	**IIIA:** *Benchmarks for Science Literacy* ▸ 9C, *Shapes,* pages 223–225 ▸ 12B, *Computation and Estimation,* page 291 **IIIB:** *NCTM Principles and Standards for School Mathematics* ▸ Grades PreK–2 Geometry, page 96 or 396 ▸ Grades 3–5 Geometry, page 164 or 396 ▸ Grades 6–8 Geometry, page 232 or 397; Measurement page 240 or 399 ▸ Grades 9–12 Geometry, page 308 or 397
IV. Examine Research on Student Learning	**IVA:** *Benchmarks for Science Literacy* ▸ 9C, *Shapes,* pages 352–353 **IVB:** *Research Companion* ▸ Chapter 11, *Theories of Geometric Thinking,* pages 152–155, *Shape, Congruence, and Similarity,* page 160 ▸ Chapter 12, *Area Measure,* pages 184–185, *Angle Measure,* page 187
V. Examine Coherency and Articulation	**V:** *Atlas of Science Literacy:* There are no maps for this topic in Volume 1.
VI. Clarify State Standards and District Curriculum	**VIA:** *State Standards:* Link Sections I–V to learning goals and information from your state standards or frameworks that are informed by the results of the topic study. **VIB:** *District Curriculum Guide:* Link Sections I–V to learning goals and information from your district curriculum guide that are informed by the results of the topic study.
Visit www.curriculumtopicstudy.org for updates or supplementary readings, Web sites, and videos.	

Standards- and Research-Based Study of a Curricular Topic

TRIGONOMETRY

Section and Outcome	Selected Sources and Readings for Study and Reflection Read and examine *related parts* of:
I. Identify Adult Content Knowledge	**IA:** *Science for All Americans* ▸ Chapter 9, *Shapes*, pages 134–135 ▸ Chapter 11, *Patterns of Change: Cycles*, pages 175–176 **IB:** *Beyond Numeracy* ▸ *Music, Art, and Digitalization*, pages 154–157 ▸ *Trigonometry*, pages 251–256
II. Consider Instructional Implications	**IIA:** *Benchmarks for Science Literacy* ▸ 9B, *Symbolic Relationships* general essay, page 215–216; grade span essay, pages 218–220 ▸ 9C, *Shapes* general essay, page 222; grade span essays, pages 223–225 **IIB:** *NCTM Principles and Standards for School Mathematics* ▸ Grades PreK–12 Overview Geometry, *Analyze Characteristics*, pages 41–42 ▸ Grades 3–5 Geometry, *Analyze Characteristics*, pages 165–166 ▸ Grades 6–8 Geometry, *Analyze Characteristics*, pages 233–235; Measurement general essay, page 241, *Apply Appropriate Techniques*, page 245 ▸ Grades 9–12 Algebra general essay, page 297, *Understand Patterns*, pages 298–299; Geometry general essay, pages 309–310, *Analyze Characteristics*, pages 310–311, page 313
III. Identify Concepts and Specific Ideas	**IIIA:** *Benchmarks for Science Literacy* ▸ 9B, *Symbolic Relationships*, pages 219–221 ▸ 9C, *Shapes*, pages 223–225 **IIIB:** *NCTM Principles and Standards for School Mathematics* ▸ Grades 3–5 Geometry, page 164 or 396 ▸ Grades 6–8 Geometry, page 232 or 397; Measurement, page 240 or 399 ▸ Grades 9–12 Algebra, page 296 or 395; Geometry, page 308 or 397
IV. Examine Research on Student Learning	**IVA:** *Benchmarks for Science Literacy* ▸ 9B, *Symbolic Relationships*, page 351 ▸ 9C, *Shapes*, pages 352–353 ▸ 12B, *Computation and Estimation*, page 360
V. Examine Coherency and Articulation	**V:** *Atlas of Science Literacy:* There are no maps for this topic in Volume 1.
VI. Clarify State Standards and District Curriculum	**VIA:** *State Standards:* Link Sections I–V to learning goals and information from your state standards or frameworks that are informed by the results of the topic study. **VIB:** *District Curriculum Guide:* Link Sections I–V to learning goals and information from your district curriculum guide that are informed by the results of the topic study.
Visit www.curriculumtopicstudy.org for updates or supplementary readings, Web sites, and videos.	

Measurement

Number of CTS Guides: 10

Overview: The primary focus of this section is on understanding measurable attributes, proficiency with measurement tools and techniques, and understanding systems of measurement. Ideas such as understanding units, systems and processes of measurement and measuring using a variety of techniques, tools and formulas are developed through a study of the topics in this section.

- Angle Measurement
- Area
- Customary Measurement
- Length
- Measurement Systems
- Measurement Tools
- Metric System
- Perimeter, Area, and Volume
- Time, Temperature, Weight, and Capacity
- Volume

Standards- and Research-Based Study of a Curricular Topic

ANGLE MEASUREMENT

Section and Outcome	Selected Sources and Readings for Study and Reflection Read and examine *related parts* of:
I. Identify Adult Content Knowledge	**IA:** *Science for All Americans*: No research available in *Science for All Americans*. **IB:** *Beyond Numeracy* ▸ *Trigonometry,* pages 251–256
II. Consider Instructional Implications	**IIA:** *Benchmarks for Science Literacy* ▸ 9C, *Shapes,* grade span essays, pages 224–225 ▸ 12B, *Computation and Estimation,* general essay, pages 288–289 **IIB:** *NCTM Principles and Standards for School Mathematics* ▸ Grades PreK–12 Overview Geometry, *Analyze Characteristics,* page 42; Measurement, *Understand Measurable,* page 44, *Apply Appropriate Techniques,* page 47 ▸ Grades PreK–2 Geometry, *Analyze Characteristics,* page 98 ▸ Grades 3–5 Geometry, *Analyze Characteristics,* pages 165–166; Measurement, page 171, *Understand Measurable Attributes,* page 172 ▸ Grades 6–8 Geometry, *Analyze Characteristics,* pages 233–234; Measurement, page 241, *Apply Appropriate Techniques,* pages 243–244 ▸ Grades 9–12 Geometry, *Analyze Characteristics,* pages 310–313
III. Identify Concepts and Specific Ideas	**IIIA:** *Benchmarks for Science Literacy* ▸ 9C, *Shapes,* page 225 ▸ 12B, *Computation and Estimation,* page 291 **IIIB:** *NCTM Principles and Standards for School Mathematics* ▸ Grades 3–5 Measurement page 240 or 398 ▸ Grades 6–8 Geometry, page 232 or 397; Measurement page 170 or 399 ▸ Grades 9–12 Geometry page 308 or 397
IV. Examine Research on Student Learning	**IVA:** *Benchmarks for Science Literacy* ▸ 12C, *Manipulation and Observation,* page 360 **IVB:** *Research Companion* ▸ Chapter 12, *Angle Measure,* page 187
V. Examine Coherency and Articulation	**V:** *Atlas of Science Literacy:* There are no maps for this topic in Volume 1.
VI. Clarify State Standards and District Curriculum	**VIA:** *State Standards:* Link Sections I–V to learning goals and information from your state standards or frameworks that are informed by the results of the topic study. **VIB:** *District Curriculum Guide:* Link Sections I–V to learning goals and information from your district curriculum guide that are informed by the results of the topic study.
Visit www.curriculumtopicstudy.org for updates or supplementary readings, Web sites, and videos.	

Standards- and Research-Based Study of a Curricular Topic

AREA

Section and Outcome	Selected Sources and Readings for Study and Reflection Read and examine *related parts* of:
I. Identify Adult Content Knowledge	**IA:** ***Science for All Americans*** ▸ Chapter 2, *Manipulating Mathematical Statements,* page 20 ▸ Chapter 9, *Shapes,* pages 134–135 ▸ Chapter 11, *Scale,* page 180 ▸ Chapter 12, *Habits of Mind,* page 189, *Manipulation and Observation,* page 191 **IB:** ***Beyond Numeracy*** ▸ *Area and Volumes,* pages 18–23 ▸ *The Pythagorean Theorem,* pages 192–194
II. Consider Instructional Implications	**IIA:** ***Benchmarks for Science Literacy*** ▸ 9C, *Shapes,* general essay, page 222, grade span essays, pages 223–225 ▸ 11D, *Scale,* general essay, page 276, grade span essay, page 277 **IIB:** ***NCTM Principles and Standards for School Mathematics*** ▸ Grades K–12 Overview Measurement, pages 44–47 ▸ Grades PreK–2 Geometry, *Analyze Characteristics,* pages 97–98; Measurement, pages 103–106 ▸ Grades 3–5 Geometry, *Analyze Characteristics,* page 166; Measurement, pages 171–174 ▸ Grades 6–8 Geometry, *Analyze Characteristics,* pages 234–235; Measurement, pages 241–244 ▸ Grades 9–12 Measurement, *Apply Appropriate Techniques,* page 323
III. Identify Concepts and Specific Ideas	**IIIA:** ***Benchmarks for Science Literacy*** ▸ 9C, *Shapes,* pages 223–225 ▸ 11D, *Scale,* page 278 ▸ 12B, *Computation and Estimation,* pages 290–291 ▸ 12C, *Manipulation and Observation,* pages 293–294 **IIIB:** ***NCTM Principles and Standards for School Mathematics*** ▸ Grades PreK–2 Geometry, page 96 or 396; Measurement, page 102 or 398 ▸ Grades 3–5 Geometry, page 164 or 396; Measurement, page 170 or 398 ▸ Grades 6–8 Geometry, page 232 or 397; Measurement, page 240 or 399 ▸ Grades 9–12 Measurement, page 320 or 399
IV. Examine Research on Student Learning	**IVA:** ***Benchmarks for Science Literacy*** ▸ 11C, *Constancy and Change,* page 357 ▸ 12C, *Manipulation and Observation,* page 360 **IVB:** ***Research Companion*** ▸ Chapter 12, *Tiling,* page 181, *Area and Volume Measure,* pages 184–187
V. Examine Coherency and Articulation	**V:** ***Atlas of Science Literacy*** ▸ *Ratios and Proportionality,* page 119 noting the conceptual strand "parts and wholes"
VI. Clarify State Standards and District Curriculum	**VIA:** ***State Standards:*** Link Sections I–V to learning goals and information from your state standards or frameworks that are informed by the results of the topic study. **VIB:** ***District Curriculum Guide:*** Link Sections I–V to learning goals and information from your district curriculum guide that are informed by the results of the topic study.
	Visit www.curriculumtopicstudy.org for updates or supplementary readings, Web sites, and videos.

Standards- and Research-Based Study of a Curricular Topic

CUSTOMARY MEASUREMENT

Section and Outcome	Selected Sources and Readings for Study and Reflection Read and examine *related parts* of:
I. Identify Adult Content Knowledge	**IA:** ***Science for All Americans*** ▸ Chapter 11, *Systems,* page 166 ▸ Chapter 12, *Manipulation and Observation,* page 191 **IIA:** ***Benchmarks for Science Literacy*** ▸ 9A, *Numbers,* grade span essays, pages 211–213
II. Consider Instructional Implications	**IIB:** ***NCTM Principles and Standards for School Mathematics*** ▸ Grades PreK–12 Overview Measurement, *Understand Measurable Attributes,* pages 45–46, *Apply Appropriate Techniques,* pages 46–47 ▸ Grades PreK–2 Measurement, *Understand Measurable Attributes,* pages 103–105, *Apply Appropriate Techniques,* pages 105–106 ▸ Grades 3–5 Measurement, page 171, *Understand Measurable Attributes,* page 172, *Apply Appropriate Techniques,* pages 173–174 ▸ Grades 6–8 Measurement, page 241, *Understand Measurable Attributes,* pages 241–242, *Apply Appropriate Techniques,* page 243 ▸ Grades 9–12 Measurement, *Understand Measurable Attributes,* pages 321–322, *Apply Appropriate Techniques,* page 323
III. Identify Concepts and Specific Ideas	**IIIA:** ***Benchmarks for Science Literacy*** ▸ 9A, *Numbers,* pages 211–213 ▸ 12C, *Manipulation and Observation,* page 293 **IIIB:** ***Principles and Standards for School Mathematics*** ▸ Grades PreK–2 Measurement, page 102 or 398 ▸ Grades 3–5 Measurement, page 170 or 398 ▸ Grades 6–8 Measurement, page 240 or 399
IV. Examine Research on Student Learning	**IVA:** ***Benchmarks for Science Literacy*** ▸ 12C, *Manipulation and Observation,* page 360 **IVB:** ***NCTM Research Companion*** ▸ Chapter 12, *Understanding Measure,* page 180–181, *Concluding Comments,* pages 189–190
V. Examine Coherency and Articulation	**V.** ***Atlas of Science Literacy:*** There are no maps for this topic in Volume 1.
VI. Clarify State Standards and District Curriculum	**VIA:** ***State Standards:*** Link Sections I–V to learning goals and information from your state standards or frameworks that are informed by the results of the topic study. **VIB:** ***District Curriculum Guide:*** Link Sections I–V to learning goals and information from your district curriculum guide that are informed by the results of the topic study.
Visit www.curriculumtopicstudy.org for updates or supplementary readings, Web sites, and videos.	

Standards- and Research-Based Study of a Curricular Topic

LENGTH

Section and Outcome	Selected Sources and Readings for Study and Reflection Read and examine *related parts* of:
I. Identify Adult Content Knowledge	**IA:** ***Science for All Americans*** ▸ Chapter 9, *Numbers,* pages 130–131 ▸ Chapter 12, *Estimation,* page 190, *Manipulation and Observation,* page 191 **IB:** ***Beyond Numeracy*** ▸ *The Pythagorean Theorem,* pages 192–194
II. Consider Instructional Implications	**IIA:** ***Benchmarks for Science Literacy*** ▸ 9A, *Numbers,* general essay, page 210, grade span essays, pages 211–212 ▸ 9C, general essay, page 222, grade span essays, pages 223–225 ▸ 12C, *Manipulation and Observation,* general essay, page 292 **IIB:** ***NCTM Principles and Standards for School Mathematics*** ▸ Grades PreK–12 Overview Geometry, *Specify Locations,* page 42; Measurement, pages 44–47 ▸ Grades PreK–2 Geometry, *Specify Locations,* pages 98–99; Measurement, pages 103–106 ▸ Grades 3–5 Geometry, *Analyze Characteristics,* page 166, *Specify Locations,* page 167; Measurement, pages 171–174 ▸ Grades 6–8 Geometry, *Analyze Characteristics,* pages 233–235; Measurement, pages 241–246 ▸ Grades 9–12 Geometry, *Analyze Characteristics,* pages 310–312; Measurement, page 321, *Apply Appropriate Techniques,* pages 322–323
III. Identify Concepts and Specific Ideas	**IIIA:** ***Benchmarks for Science Literacy*** ▸ 9A, *Numbers,* pages 211–212 ▸ 9C, *Shapes,* pages 223–225 ▸ 12B, *Computation and Estimation,* pages 290–291 ▸ 12C, *Manipulation and Observation,* pages 293–294 **IIIB:** ***NCTM Principles and Standards for School Mathematics*** ▸ Grades PreK–2 Geometry, page 96 or 396; Measurement, page 102 or 398 ▸ Grades 3–5 Geometry, page 164 or 396; Measurement, page 170 or 398 ▸ Grades 6–8 Geometry, page 232 or 397; Measurement, page 240 or 399 ▸ Grades 9–12 Geometry, page 308 or 397; Measurement, page 320 or 399
IV. Examine Research on Student Learning	**IVA:** ***Benchmarks for Science Literacy*** ▸ 12C, *Manipulation and Observation,* page 360 **IVB:** ***Research Companion*** ▸ Chapter 12, *Understanding Measure,* page 180–182, *Length Measure,* page 182–184
V. Examine Coherency and Articulation	**V:** ***Atlas of Science Literacy*** ▸ *Ratios and Proportionality,* page 119
VI. Clarify State Standards and District Curriculum	**VIA:** ***State Standards:*** Link Sections I–V to learning goals and information from your state standards or frameworks that are informed by the results of the topic study. **VIB:** ***District Curriculum Guide:*** Link Sections I–V to learning goals and information from your district curriculum guide that are informed by the results of the topic study.
Visit www.curriculumtopicstudy.org for updates or supplementary readings, Web sites, and videos.	

Standards- and Research-Based Study of a Curricular Topic

MEASUREMENT SYSTEMS

Section and Outcome	Selected Sources and Readings for Study and Reflection Read and examine *related parts* of:
I. Identify Adult Content Knowledge	**IA:** *Science for All Americans* ▸ Chapter 9, *Shapes,* pages 134–135 ▸ Chapter 12, *Manipulation and Observation,* pages 191–192 **IB:** *Beyond Numeracy* N/A
II. Consider Instructional Implications	**IIA:** *Benchmarks for Science Literacy* ▸ 9C, *Shapes,* general essay, page 222, grade span essays, pages 223–225 ▸ 12B, *Computation and Estimation,* general essay, pages 288–289 **IIB:** *NCTM Principles and Standards for School Mathematics* ▸ Grades PreK–12 Overview Measurement, page 44, *Understand Measurable Attributes,* pages 44–46 ▸ Grades PreK–2 Measurement, page 103, *Understand Measurable Attributes,* pages 103–105 ▸ Grades 3–5 Measurement, page 171, *Understand Measurable Attributes,* pages 171–173 ▸ Grades 6–8 Measurement, *Understand Measurable Attributes,* pages 241–243 ▸ Grades 9–12 Measurement, page 321, *Understand Measurable Attributes,* pages 321–322
III. Identify Concepts and Specific Ideas	**IIIA:** *Benchmarks for Science Literacy* ▸ 9C, *Shapes,* pages 223–225 ▸ 12B, *Computation and Estimation,* pages 290–291 ▸ 12C, *Manipulation and Observation,* pages 293–294 **IIIB:** *NCTM Principles and Standards for School Mathematics* ▸ Grades PreK–2 Measurement, page 102 or 398 ▸ Grades 3–5 Measurement, page 170 or 398 ▸ Grades 6–8 Measurement, page 240 or 399 ▸ Grades 9–12 Measurement, page 320 or 399
IV. Examine Research on Student Learning	**IVA:** *Benchmarks for Science Literacy* ▸ 12C, *Manipulation and Observation,* page 360 **IVB:** *NCTM Research Companion* ▸ Chapter 7, *Fractions and Multiplicative Reasoning,* pages 100–2 ▸ Chapter 12, *Developing an Understanding of Measurement,* pages 179–192
V. Examine Coherency and Articulation	**V.** *Atlas of Science Literacy* No corresponding maps in Atlas Version 1
VI. Clarify State Standards and District Curriculum	**VIA:** *State Standards:* Link Sections I–V to learning goals and information from your state standards or frameworks that are informed by the results of the topic study. **VIB:** *District Curriculum Guide:* Link Sections I–V to learning goals and information from your district curriculum guide that are informed by the results of the topic study.
Visit www.curriculumtopicstudy.org for updates or supplementary readings, Web sites, and videos.	

Standards- and Research-Based Study of a Curricular Topic

MEASUREMENT TOOLS

Section and Outcome	Selected Sources and Readings for Study and Reflection Read and examine *related parts* of:
I. Identify Adult Content Knowledge	**IA:** ***Science for All Americans*** ▸ Chapter 12, *Manipulation and Observation*, pages 191–192 **IB:** **Beyond Numeracy:** No research available in *Beyond Numeracy.*
II. Consider Instructional Implications	**IIA:** ***Benchmarks for Science Literacy*** ▸ 12C, *Manipulation and Observation*, general essay page 292 **IIB:** ***NCTM Principles and Standards for School Mathematics*** ▸ Grades PreK–12 Overview Measurement, *Apply Appropriate Techniques*, pages 46–47 ▸ Grades PreK–2 Measurement, *Apply Appropriate Techniques*, pages 105–106 ▸ Grades 3–5 Measurement, *Apply Appropriate Techniques*, pages 173–175 ▸ Grades 6–8 Measurement, *Apply Appropriate Techniques*, pages 243–244, 247
III. Identify Concepts and Specific Ideas	**IIIA:** ***Benchmarks for Science Literacy*** ▸ 12C, *Manipulation and Observation*, pages 293–294 **IIIB:** ***Principles and Standards for School Mathematics*** ▸ Grades PreK–2 Measurement, page 102 or 398 ▸ Grades 3–5 Measurement, page 170 or 398 ▸ Grades 6–8 Measurement, page 240 or 399
IV. Examine Research on Student Learning	**IVA:** ***Benchmarks for Science Literacy*** ▸ 12C, *Manipulation and Observation*, page 360 **IVB:** ***Research Companion*** ▸ Chapter 12, pages 179–180, *Understanding Measureable*, pages 180–181, *Length Measure*, pages 182–183, *Angle Measure*, page 187
V. Examine Coherency and Articulation	**V.** ***Atlas of Science Literacy:*** There are no maps for this topic in Volume 1.
VI. Clarify State Standards and District Curriculum	**VIA:** ***State Standards:*** Link Sections I–V to learning goals and information from your state standards or frameworks that are informed by the results of the topic study. **VIB:** ***District Curriculum Guide:*** Link Sections I–V to learning goals and information from your district curriculum guide that are informed by the results of the topic study.
Visit www.curriculumtopicstudy.org for updates or supplementary readings, Web sites, and videos.	

Standards- and Research-Based Study of a Curricular Topic

METRIC SYSTEM

Section and Outcome	Selected Sources and Readings for Study and Reflection Read and examine *related parts* of:	
I. Identify Adult Content Knowledge	**IA:**	***Science for All Americans*** ▶ Chapter 11, *Systems*, page 166 ▶ Chapter 12, *Manipulation and Observation*, page 192
	IB:	***Beyond Numeracy***: No available research in *Beyond Numeracy*.
II. Consider Instructional Implications	**IIA:**	***Benchmarks for Science Literacy*** ▶ 9A, *Numbers,* grade span essays, pages 211–212
	IIB:	***NCTM Principles and Standards for School Mathematics*** ▶ Grades PreK–12 Overview Measurement, *Understand Measurable Attributes*, pages 45–46, *Apply Appropriate Techniques*, pages 46–47 ▶ Grades PreK–2 Measurement, *Understand Measurable Attributes*, pages 103–105, *Apply Appropriate Techniques*, pages 105–106 ▶ Grades 3–5 Measurement, *Understand Measurable Attributes*, pages 172–173, *Apply Appropriate Techniques*, pages 173–174 ▶ Grades 6–8 Measurement, page 241; *Understand Measurable Attributes*, pages 241–242, *Apply Appropriate Techniques*, page 243 ▶ Grades 9–12 Measurement, pages 321–323
III. Identify Concepts and Specific Ideas	**IIIA:**	***Benchmarks for Science Literacy*** ▶ 9A, *Numbers*, pages 211–212 ▶ 12C, *Manipulation and Observation*, page 293
	IIIB:	***NCTM Principles and Standards for School Mathematics*** ▶ Grades PreK–2 Measurement, page 102 or 398 ▶ Grades 3–5 Measurement, page 240 or 398 ▶ Grades 6–8 Measurement, page 170 or 399
IV. Examine Research on Student Learning	**IVA:**	***Benchmarks for Science Literacy*** ▶ 12C, *Manipulation and Observation*, page 360
	IVB:	***NCTM Research Companion*** ▶ Chapter 12, *Understanding Measure*, pages 180–181, *Concluding Comments*, pages 189–190
V. Examine Coherency and Articulation	**V.**	***Atlas of Science Literacy:*** There are no maps for this topic in Volume 1.
VI. Clarify State Standards and District Curriculum	**VIA:**	***State Standards:*** Link Sections I–V to learning goals and information from your state standards or frameworks that are informed by the results of the topic study.
	VIB:	***District Curriculum Guide:*** Link Sections I–V to learning goals and information from your district curriculum guide that are informed by the results of the topic study.
Visit www.curriculumtopicstudy.org for updates or supplementary readings, Web sites, and videos.		

Standards- and Research-Based Study of a Curricular Topic

PERIMETER, AREA, AND VOLUME

Section and Outcome	Selected Sources and Readings for Study and Reflection Read and examine *related parts* of:
I. Identify Adult Content Knowledge	**IA:** ***Science for All Americans*** ▶ Chapter 2, *Manipulating Mathematical Statements,* page 20 ▶ Chapter 9, *Shapes,* pages 134–135 ▶ Chapter 11, *Scale,* page 180 ▶ Chapter 12, *Habits of Mind,* page 189; *Manipulation and Observation,* page 191 **IB:** ***Beyond Numeracy*** ▶ *Area and Volumes,* pages 18–23 ▶ *The Pythagorean Theorem,* pages 192–194
II. Consider Instructional Implications	**IIA:** ***Benchmarks for Science Literacy*** ▶ 9C, *Shapes,* general essay, page 222, grade span essays, pages 223–225 ▶ 11D, *Scale,* general essay page 276, grade span essay, page 277 ▶ 12B, *Computation and Estimation,* general essay, pages 288–289 **IIB:** ***NCTM Principles and Standards for School Mathematics*** ▶ Grades PreK–12 Overview Geometry, pages 41–42; Measurement, pages 44–47 ▶ Grades PreK–2 Geometry, pages 97–98; Measurement, pages 103–106 ▶ Grades 3–5 Geometry, pages 165–166; Measurement, pages 171–175 ▶ Grades 6–8 Geometry, pages 233–235; Measurement, pages 241–247 ▶ Grades 9–12 Measurement, pages 321–323
III. Identify Concepts and Specific Ideas	**IIIA:** ***Benchmarks for Science Literacy*** ▶ 9C, *Shapes,* pages 223–225 ▶ 11D, *Scale,* page 278 ▶ 12B, *Computation and Estimation,* pages 290–291 ▶ 12C, *Manipulation and Observation,* pages 293–294 **IIIB:** ***NCTM Principles and Standards for School Mathematics*** ▶ Grades PreK–2 Geometry, page 96 or 396; Measurement, page 102 or 398 ▶ Grades 3–5 Geometry, page 164 or 396; Measurement, page 170 or 398 ▶ Grades 6–8 Geometry, page 232 or 397; Measurement, page 240 or 399 ▶ Grades 9–12 Measurement, page 320 or 399
IV. Examine Research on Student Learning	**IVA:** ***Benchmarks for Science Literacy*** ▶ 11C, *Constancy and Change,* page 357 ▶ 12C, *Manipulation and Observation,* page 360 **IVB:** ***Research Companion*** ▶ Chapter 12, *Tiling,* page 181, *Area and Volume Measure,* pages 184–187
V. Examine Coherency and Articulation	**V:** ***Atlas of Science Literacy*** ▶ *Ratios and Proportionality,* page 119 noting the conceptual strand "parts and wholes"
VI. Clarify State Standards and District Curriculum	**VIA:** ***State Standards:*** Link Sections I–V to learning goals and information from your state standards or frameworks that are informed by the results of the topic study. **VIB:** ***District Curriculum Guide:*** Link Sections I–V to learning goals and information from your district curriculum guide that are informed by the results of the topic study.
Visit www.curriculumtopicstudy.org for updates or supplementary readings, Web sites, and videos.	

Standards- and Research-Based Study of a Curricular Topic

TIME, TEMPERATURE, WEIGHT, AND CAPACITY

Section and Outcome	Selected Sources and Readings for Study and Reflection Read and examine *related parts* of:
I. Identify Adult Content Knowledge	**IA:** *Science for All Americans* ▸ Chapter 9, *Numbers,* pages 130–131, *Symbolic Relationships,* pages 131–132 ▸ Chapter 11, *Estimation,* page 190, *Manipulation and Observation,* pages 191–192 **IB:** *Beyond Numeracy* ▸ *Area and Volume,* pages 18–23 ▸ *Time, Space, and Immensity,* pages 241–245
II. Consider Instructional Implications	**IIA:** *Benchmarks for Science Literacy* ▸ 9A, *Numbers,* general essay, page 210, grade span essay, page 211 ▸ 9C, *Shapes,* grade span essays, pages 223–224 ▸ 11D, *Scale,* grade span essay, page 277 ▸ 12B, *Computation and Estimation,* general essay, pages 288–289 **IIB:** *NCTM Principles and Standards for School Mathematics* ▸ Grades PreK–12 Overview Measurement, page 44, *Understand Measurable Attributes,* pages 44–46 ▸ Grades PreK–2 Measurement, *Understand Measurable Attributes,* page 103–105 ▸ Grades 3–5 Measurement, page 171, *Understand Measurable Attributes,* page 172 ▸ Grades 6–8 Measurement, page 241, *Understand Measurable Attributes,* page 241, *Apply Appropriate Techniques,* page 243 ▸ Grades 9–12 Measurement, page 321
III. Identify Concepts and Specific Ideas	**IIIA:** *Benchmarks for Science Literacy* ▸ 9A, *Numbers,* pages 212–213 ▸ 9C, *Shapes,* page 225 ▸ 11D, *Scale,* pages 277–278 ▸ 12B, *Computation and Estimation,* pages 290–291 ▸ 12C, *Manipulation and Observation,* pages 293–294 **IIIB:** *NCTM Principles and Standards for School Mathematics* ▸ Grades PreK–2 Measurement, page 102 or 398 ▸ Grades 3–5 Measurement, page 170 or 398 ▸ Grades 6–8 Measurement, page 240 or 399 ▸ Grades 9–12 Measurement, page 320 or 399
IV. Examine Research on Student Learning	**IVA:** *Benchmarks for Science Literacy* ▸ 11C, *Constancy and Change,* page 357 **IVB:** *NCTM Research Companion*: No research available in *Research Companion.*
V. Examine Coherency and Articulation	**V:** *Atlas of Science Literacy* ▸ *Ratio and Proportionality,* page 119 noting the conceptual strand "Parts and Wholes"
VI. Clarify State Standards and District Curriculum	**VIA:** *State Standards:* Link Sections I–V to learning goals and information from your state standards or frameworks that are informed by the results of the topic study. **VIB:** *District Curriculum Guide:* Link Sections I–V to learning goals and information from your district curriculum guide that are informed by the results of the topic study.
Visit www.curriculumtopicstudy.org for updates or supplementary readings, Web sites, and videos.	

Standards- and Research-Based Study of a Curricular Topic

VOLUME

Section and Outcome	Selected Sources and Readings for Study and Reflection Read and examine *related parts* of:
I. Identify Adult Content Knowledge	**IA:** *Science for All Americans* ‣ Chapter 9, *Shapes,* page 134 ‣ Chapter 11, *Scale,* page 180 ‣ Chapter 12, *Calculator Skills,* page 189, *Manipulation and Observation,* page 191 **IB:** *Beyond Numeracy* ‣ *Area and Volumes,* pages 18–23
II. Consider Instructional Implications	**IIA:** *Benchmarks for Science Literacy* ‣ 9C, *Shapes,* general essay, page 222, grade span essays, pages 223–225 ‣ 11D, *Scale,* general essay, page 276, grade span essay, page 277 **IIB:** *NCTM Principles and Standards for School Mathematics* ‣ Grades PreK–12 Overview Measurement, pages 44–47 ‣ Grades PreK–2 Geometry, *Analyze Characteristics,* pages 97–98; Measurement, pages 103–106 ‣ Grades 3–5 Geometry, *Analyze Characteristics,* page 166; Measurement, pages 171–174 ‣ Grades 6–8 Geometry, *Analyze Characteristics,* pages 234–235; Measurement, pages 241–244 ‣ Grades 9–12 Measurement, *Apply Appropriate Techniques,* page 323
III. Identify Concepts and Specific Ideas	**IIIA:** *Benchmarks for Science Literacy* ‣ 9C, *Shapes,* pages 223–225 ‣ 11D, *Scale,* page 278 ‣ 12B, *Computation and Estimation,* pages 290–291 ‣ 12C, *Manipulation and Observation,* pages 293–294 **IIIB:** *NCTM Principles and Standards for School Mathematics* ‣ Grades PreK–2 Geometry, page 96 or 396; Measurement, page 102 or 398 ‣ Grades 3–5 Geometry, page 164 or 396; Measurement, page 170 or 398 ‣ Grades 6–8 Geometry, page 232 or 397; Measurement, page 240 or 399 ‣ Grades 9–12 Measurement, page 320 or 399
IV. Examine Research on Student Learning	**IVA:** *Benchmarks for Science Literacy* ‣ 11C, *Constancy and Change,* page 357 ‣ 12C, *Manipulation and Observation,* page 360 **IVB:** *Research Companion* ‣ Chapter 12, *Tiling,* page 181, *Volume Measure,* pages 186–187
V. Examine Coherency and Articulation	**V:** *Atlas of Science Literacy* ‣ *Ratios and Proportionality,* page 119 noting the conceptual strand "Parts and Wholes"
VI. Clarify State Standards and District Curriculum	**VIA:** *State Standards:* Link Sections I–V to learning goals and information from your state standards or frameworks that are informed by the results of the topic study. **VIB:** *District Curriculum Guide:* Link Sections I–V to learning goals and information from your district curriculum guide that are informed by the results of the topic study.
Visit www.curriculumtopicstudy.org for updates or supplementary readings, Web sites, and videos.	

Data Analysis

Number of CTS Guides: 9

Overview: The primary focus of this section is on gathering and using data to answer questions that arise from a variety of situations. Ideas such as collecting, organizing and displaying data, selecting and using various statistical methods, and predicting and inferring from data and concepts of probability are developed through a study of the topics in this section.

- Line Graphs, Bar Graphs, and Histograms
- Line Plots, Stem and Leaf Plots, Box Plots, and Histograms
- Measures of Center and Spread
- Probability
- Sampling
- Scatterplots and Correlation
- Simulation
- Statistical Reasoning
- Summarizing Data

Standards- and Research-Based Study of a Curricular Topic

LINE GRAPHS, BAR GRAPHS, AND HISTOGRAMS

Section and Outcome	Selected Sources and Readings for Study and Reflection Read and examine *related parts* of:
I. Identify Adult Content Knowledge	**IA:** ***Science for All Americans*** ▸ Chapter 9, *Shapes,* page 135 ▸ Chapter 12, *Communication,* page 193, *Critical Response Skills,* page 194 **IB:** ***Beyond Numeracy***: No research available in *Beyond Numeracy.*
II. Consider Instructional Implications	**IIA:** ***Benchmarks for Science Literacy*** ▸ 9B, *Symbolic Relationship,* general essay, page 216, grade span essays, pages 217–220 ▸ 9C, *Shapes,* grade span essays, pages 223–224 **IIB:** ***NCTM Principles and Standards for School Mathematics*** ▸ Grades K–12 Overview Data Analysis and Probability, pages 48–50 ▸ Grades PreK–2 Data Analysis and Probability, page 109, *Formulate Questions,* pages 109–112 ▸ Grades 3–5 Data Analysis and Probability, page 177, *Formulate Questions,* pages 177–178, *Develop and Evaluate,* pages 180–181 ▸ Grades 6–8 Data Analysis and Probability, page 249, *Formulate Questions,* pages 249–250, *Select and Use,* page 251, *Develop and Evaluate,* pages 251–252 ▸ Grades 9–12 Data Analysis and Probability, *Select and Use,* pages 327–328
III. Identify Concepts and Specific Ideas	**IIIA:** ***Benchmarks for Science Literacy*** ▸ 9B, *Symbolic Relationship,* pages 218–221 ▸ 9C, *Shapes,* pages 223–224 ▸ 12D, *Communication,* pages 296–297 **IIIB:** ***NCTM Principles and Standards for School Mathematics*** ▸ Grades PreK–2 Data Analysis and Probability, page 108 or 400 ▸ Grades 3–5 Data Analysis and Probability, page 176 or 400 ▸ Grades 6–8 Data Analysis and Probability, page 248 or 401 ▸ Grades 9–12 Data Analysis and Probability, page 324 or 401
IV. Examine Research on Student Learning	**IVA:** ***Benchmarks for Science Literacy*** ▸ 9B, *Graphs,* page 351 **IVB:** ***Research Companion*** ▸ Chapter 13, *Organizing and Displaying Data,* pages 199–202, *Describing and Interpreting Data,* pages 202–203 ▸ Chapter 17, *Two Uses of Graphs,* pages 250–256
V. Examine Coherency and Articulation	**V:** ***Atlas of Science Literacy*** ▸ *Graphic Representation,* page 115 ▸ *Describing Change,* page 121
VI. Clarify State Standards and District Curriculum	**VIA:** ***State Standards:*** Link Sections I–V to learning goals and information from your state standards or frameworks that are informed by the results of the topic study. **VIB:** ***District Curriculum Guide:*** Link Sections I–V to learning goals and information from your district curriculum guide that are informed by the results of the topic study.
Visit www.curriculumtopicstudy.org for updates or supplementary readings, Web sites, and videos.	

Study of a Mathematical Topic or Theme

LINE PLOTS, STEM AND LEAF PLOTS, BOX PLOTS, AND HISTOGRAMS

Section and Outcome	Selected Sources and Readings for Study and Reflection Read and examine *related parts* of:
I. Identify Adult Content Knowledge	**IA:** ***Science for All Americans*** ▸ Chapter 9, *Shapes,* page 135, *Summarizing Data,* page 137 ▸ Chapter 12, *Communication,* page 193 **IB:** ***Beyond Numeracy*** ▸ *Mean, Median, and Mode,* pages 141–143
II. Consider Instructional Implications	**IIA:** ***Benchmarks for Science Literacy*** ▸ 9C, *Shapes,* grade span essays, page 223 ▸ 9D, *Uncertainty,* grade span essays, pages 227–230 **IIB:** ***NCTM Principles and Standards for School Mathematics*** ▸ Grades K–12 Overview Data Analysis and Probability, page 48, *Formulate Questions,* page 49, *Select and Use,* pages 49–50 ▸ Grades PreK–2 Data Analysis and Probability, page 109, *Formulate Questions,* pages 109–112, *Select and Use,* page 113 ▸ Grades 3–5 Data Analysis and Probability, page 177, *Formulate Questions,* page 178, *Select and Use,* pages 179–180 ▸ Grades 6–8 Data Analysis and Probability, page 249, *Formulate Questions,* pages 249–250, *Select and Use,* pages 250–251, *Develop and Evaluate,* page 252 ▸ Grades 9–12 Data Analysis and Probability, *Select and Use,* pages 327–328
III. Identify Concepts and Specific Ideas	**IIIA:** ***Benchmarks for Science Literacy*** ▸ 9C, *Shapes,* pages 223–224 ▸ 9D, *Uncertainty,* pages 228–230 ▸ 12D, *Communication Skills,* page 297 **IIIB:** ***NCTM Principles and Standards for School Mathematics*** ▸ Grades K–2 Data Analysis and Probability, page 108 or 400 ▸ Grades 3–5 Data Analysis and Probability, page 176 or 400 ▸ Grades 6–8 Data Analysis and Probability, page 248 or 401 ▸ Grades 9–12 Data Analysis and Probability, page 324 or 401
IV. Examine Research on Student Learning	**IVA:** ***Benchmarks for Science Literacy*** ▸ 9D, *Summarizing Data,* pages 353–354 **IVB:** ***Research Companion*** ▸ Chapter 13, *Deciding About Scale,* page 201, *Describing and Interpreting Data,* pages 202–207 ▸ Chapter 17, *Ways of Making Meaning,* pages 252–256
V. Examine Coherency and Articulation	**V:** ***Atlas of Science Literacy*** ▸ *Averages and Comparisons,* page 123, noting the conceptual strands "Comparing Groups" and "Averages and Spreads" ▸ *Graphic Representation,* page 115
VI. Clarify State Standards and District Curriculum	**VIA:** ***State Standards:*** Link Sections I–V to learning goals and information from your state standards or frameworks that are informed by the results of the topic study. **VIB:** ***District Curriculum Guide:*** Link Sections I–V to learning goals and information from your district curriculum guide that are informed by the results of the topic study.
	Visit www.curriculumtopicstudy.org for updates or supplementary readings, Web sites, and videos.

Study of a Mathematical Topic or Theme

MEASURES OF CENTER AND SPREAD

Section and Outcome	Selected Sources and Readings for Study and Reflection Read and examine *related parts* of:
I. Identify Adult Content Knowledge	**IA:** *Science for All Americans* ▸ Chapter 9, *Summarizing Data,* pages 137–138 ▸ Chapter 12, *Critical Response Skills,* page 194 **IB:** *Beyond Numeracy* ▸ *Mean, Median, and Mode,* pages 141–143
II. Consider Instructional Implications	**IIA:** *Benchmarks for Science Literacy* ▸ 9D, *Uncertainty,* general essay, page 226; grade span essays, pages 227–230 **IIB:** *NCTM Principles and Standards for School Mathematics* ▸ Grades PreK–12 Overview Data Analysis and Probability, pages 48–50 ▸ Grades PreK–2 Data Analysis and Probability, page 109, *Select and Use,* pages 113–114, *Develop and Evaluate,* page 114 ▸ Grades 3–5 Data Analysis and Probability, page 117, *Select and Use,* pages 179–181, *Develop and Evaluate,* pages 180–181 ▸ Grades 6–8 Data Analysis and Probability, page 249, *Select and Use,* pages 250–251, *Develop and Evaluate,* pages 251–252 ▸ Grades 9–12 Data Analysis and Probability, page 325, *Select and Use,* pages 327–329
III. Identify Concepts and Specific Ideas	**IIIA:** *Benchmarks for Science Literacy* ▸ 9D, *Uncertainty,* pages 227–230 ▸ 12D, *Communication Skills,* page 297 ▸ 12E, *Critical Response Skills,* page 300 **IIIB:** *NCTM Principles and Standards for School Mathematics* ▸ Grades PreK–2 Data Analysis and Probability, page 108 or 400 ▸ Grades 3–5 Data Analysis and Probability, page 176 or 400 ▸ Grades 6–8 Data Analysis and Probability, page 248 or 401 ▸ Grades 9–12 Data Analysis and Probability, page 324 or 401
IV. Examine Research on Student Learning	**IVA:** *Benchmarks for Science Literacy* ▸ 9D, *Summarizing Data,* pages 353–354 **IVB:** *Research Companion.* ▸ Chapter 13, *Overview,* page 194, *Describing and Interpreting Data,* pages 202–209
V. Examine Coherency and Articulation	**V:** *Atlas of Science Literacy* ▸ *Averages and Comparisons,* page 123, noting the conceptual strands "Comparing Groups" and "Averages and Spreads"
VI. Clarify State Standards and District Curriculum	**VIA:** *State Standards:* Link Sections I–V to learning goals and information from your state standards or frameworks that are informed by the results of the topic study. **VIB:** *District Curriculum Guide:* Link Sections I–V to learning goals and information from your district curriculum guide that are informed by the results of the topic study.
Visit www.curriculumtopicstudy.org for updates or supplementary readings, Web sites, and videos.	

Standards- and Research-Based Study of a Curricular Topic

PROBABILITY

Section and Outcome	Selected Sources and Readings for Study and Reflection Read and examine *related parts* of:
I. Identify Adult Content Knowledge	**IA:** **Science for All Americans** ▶ Chapter 9, *Probability,* pages 135–137 **IB:** **Beyond Numeracy** ▶ *Coincidences,* pages 38–41 ▶ *Probabilities,* pages 187–191 ▶ *Statistics: Two Theorems,* pages 227–230
II. Consider Instructional Implications	**IIA:** **Benchmarks for Science Literacy** ▶ 9D, *Uncertainty,* general essay, page 226, grade span essays, pages 227–230 **IIB:** **NCTM Principles and Standards for School Mathematics** ▶ Grades PreK–12 Overview Data Analysis and Probability, page 48, *Understand and Apply,* page 51 ▶ Grades PreK–2 Data Analysis and Probability, page 109, *Understand and Apply,* page 114 ▶ Grades 3–5 Data Analysis and Probability, *Understand and Apply,* page 181 ▶ Grades 6–8 Data Analysis and Probability, *Understand and Apply,* pages 253–255 ▶ Grades 9–12 Data Analysis and Probability, page 325, *Understand and Apply,* pages 331–333
III. Identify Concepts and Specific Ideas	**IIIA:** **Benchmarks for Science Literacy** ▶ 9D, *Uncertainty,* pages 227–230 **IIIB:** **NCTM Principles and Standards for School Mathematics** ▶ Grades PreK–2 Data Analysis and Probability, page 108 or 400 ▶ Grades 3–5 Data Analysis and Probability, page 176 or 400 ▶ Grades 6–8 Data Analysis and Probability, page 248 or 401 ▶ Grades 9–12 Data Analysis and Probability, page 324 or 401
IV. Examine Research on Student Learning	**IVA:** **Benchmarks for Science Literacy** ▶ 9D, *Probability,* page 353 **IVB:** **Research Companion** ▶ Chapter 14, *Research on Students' Understanding of Probability,* pages 216–224
V. Examine Coherency and Articulation	**V:** **Atlas of Science Literacy** ▶ *Statistical Reasoning,* page 127 noting the conceptual strand "Probability"
VI. Clarify State Standards and District Curriculum	**VIA:** **State Standards:** Link Sections I–V to learning goals and information from your state standards or frameworks that are informed by the results of the topic study. **VIB:** **District Curriculum Guide:** Link Sections I–V to learning goals and information from your district curriculum guide that are informed by the results of the topic study.
	Visit www.curriculumtopicstudy.org for updates or supplementary readings, Web sites, and videos.

Standards- and Research-Based Study of a Curricular Topic

SAMPLING

Section and Outcome	Selected Sources and Readings for Study and Reflection Read and examine *related parts* of:
I. Identify Adult Content Knowledge	**IA:** *Science for All Americans* ▸ Chapter 9, *Sampling,* pages 139–140 **IB:** *Beyond Numeracy* ▸ *Correlation, Intervals, Testing,* pages 56–58 ▸ *Statistics: Two Theorems,* pages 227–230
II. Consider Instructional Implications	**IIA:** *Benchmarks for Science Literacy* ▸ 9D, *Uncertainty,* general essay, page 226, grade span essays, pages 227–230 **IIB:** *NCTM Principles and Standards for School Mathematics* ▸ Grades PreK–12 Overview Data Analysis, *Develop and Evaluate,* page 50 ▸ Grades PreK–2 Data Analysis, *Select and Use,* pages 113–114 ▸ Grades 3–5 Data Analysis, page 177, *Formulate Questions,* pages 177–178, *Develop and Evaluate,* pages 180–181 ▸ Grades 6–8 Data Analysis, page 249, *Formulate Questions,* page 249 ▸ Grades 9–12 Data Analysis, *Formulate Questions,* pages 325–327, *Select and Use,* page 327, *Develop and Evaluate,* pages 329–331
III. Identify Concepts and Specific Ideas	**IIIA:** *Benchmarks for Science Literacy* ▸ 9D, *Uncertainty,* pages 227–230 **IIIB:** *NCTM Principles and Standards for School Mathematics* ▸ Grades PreK–2 Data Analysis, page 108 or 400 ▸ Grades 3–5 Data Analysis, page 176 or 400 ▸ Grades 6–8 Data Analysis, page 248 or 401 ▸ Grades 9–12 Data Analysis, page 324 or 401
IV. Examine Research on Student Learning	**IVA:** *Benchmarks for Science Literacy* ▸ 9D, *Uncertainty,* pages 353–354 **IVB:** *Research Companion* ▸ Chapter 13, *Sampling,* pages 196–97
V. Examine Coherency and Articulation	**V:** *Atlas of Science Literacy* ▸ *Statistical Reasoning,* page 127 noting the conceptual strand "Sampling"
VI. Clarify State Standards and District Curriculum	**VIA:** *State Standards:* Link Sections I–V to learning goals and information from your state standards or frameworks that are informed by the results of the topic study. **VIB:** *District Curriculum Guide:* Link Sections I–V to learning goals and information from your district curriculum guide that are informed by the results of the topic study.
	Visit www.curriculumtopicstudy.org for updates or supplementary readings, Web sites, and videos.

Standards- and Research-Based Study of a Curricular Topic

SCATTERPLOTS AND CORRELATION

Section and Outcome	Selected Sources and Readings for Study and Reflection Read and examine *related parts* of:
I. Identify Adult Content Knowledge	**IA:** ***Science for All Americans*** ▸ Chapter 9, *Symbolic Relationships,* pages 132–133, *Shapes,* page 135, *Summarizing Data,* pages 138–139, *Reasoning,* pages 140–143 ▸ Chapter 12, *Communication,* page 193 **IB:** ***Beyond Numeracy*** ▸ *Correlation, Intervals, and Testing,* pages 56–58
II. Consider Instructional Implications	**IIA:** ***Benchmarks for Science Literacy*** ▸ 9B, *Symbolic Relationships,* general essay, pages 215–216, grade span essays, pages 218–220 ▸ 9D, *Uncertainty,* general essay, page 226, grade span essay, page 230 **IIB:** ***NCTM Principles and Standards for School Mathematics*** ▸ Grades PreK–12 Overview Data Analysis and Probability, *Select and Use,* page 50 ▸ Grades 6–8 Data Analysis and Probability, page 249, *Formulate Questions,* page 249, *Develop and Evaluate,* pages 251–253 ▸ Grades 9–12 Data Analysis and Probability, page 325, *Formulate Questions,* pages 326–327, *Select and Use,* pages 328–329, *Develop and Evaluate Predictions,* page 329
III. Identify Concepts and Specific Ideas	**IIIA:** ***Benchmarks for Science Literacy*** ▸ 9B, *Symbolic Relationships,* pages 218–221 ▸ 9D, *Uncertainty,* page 230 ▸ 12D, *Communication Skills,* page 297 ▸ 12E, *Critical Response Skills,* pages 299–300 **IIIB:** ***NCTM Principles and Standards for School Mathematics*** ▸ Grades 6–8 Data Analysis and Probability, page 248 or 401 ▸ Grades 9–12 Data Analysis and Probability, page 324 or 401
IV. Examine Research on Student Learning	**IVA:** ***Benchmarks for Science Literacy*** ▸ 12E, *Interpretation of Data,* page 361 **IVB:** ***Research Companion*** ▸ Chapter 13, *Judgments About Covariation,* page 208, *Comparing two numeric variables,* pages 209–211
V. Examine Coherency and Articulation	**V:** ***Atlas of Science Literacy*** ▸ *Correlation,* page 125
VI. Clarify State Standards and District Curriculum	**VIA:** ***State Standards:*** Link Sections I–V to learning goals and information from your state standards or frameworks that are informed by the results of the topic study. **VIB:** ***District Curriculum Guide:*** Link Sections I–V to learning goals and information from your district curriculum guide that are informed by the results of the topic study.
	Visit www.curriculumtopicstudy.org for updates or supplementary readings, Web sites, and videos.

Standards- and Research-Based Study of a Curricular Topic

SIMULATION

Section and Outcome	Selected Sources and Readings for Study and Reflection Read and examine *related parts* of:
I. Identify Adult Content Knowledge	**IA:** ***Science for All Americans*** ▸ Chapter 9, *Probability*, pages 135–137 **IB:** ***Beyond Numeracy*** ▸ *Monte Carlo Method of Simulation*, pages 147–149 ▸ *Statistics: Two Theorems*, pages 227–230
II. Consider Instructional Implications	**IIA:** ***Benchmarks for Science Literacy*** ▸ 9D, *Uncertainty*, grade span essay, page 229 **IIB:** ***NCTM Principles and Standards for School Mathematics*** ▸ Grades K–12 Overview Data Analysis and Probability, *Develop and Evaluate Inferences*, page 50, *Understand and Apply*, page 51 ▸ Grades 6–8 Data Analysis and Probability, *Understand and Apply*, page 254 ▸ Grades 9–12 Data Analysis and Probability, page 325, *Develop and Evaluate*, pages 329–330, *Understand and Apply*, pages 332–333
III. Identify Concepts and Specific Ideas	**IIIA:** ***Benchmarks for Science Literacy*** ▸ 9D, *Uncertainty*, pages 229–230 **IIIB:** ***NCTM Principles and Standards for School Mathematics*** ▸ 6–8 Data Analysis and Probability, page 248 or 401 ▸ 9–12 Data Analysis and Probability, page 324 or 401
IV. Examine Research on Student Learning	**IVA:** ***Benchmarks for Science Literacy*** ▸ 9D, *Probability*, page 353 **IVB:** ***Research Companion*** ▸ Chapter 14, *The Outcome Approach*, page 218, *Some Thoughts on Teaching*, pages 224–225
V. Examine Coherency and Articulation	**V:** ***Atlas of Science Literacy*** ▸ *Statistical Reasoning*, page 127 noting the conceptual strand "Probability"
VI. Clarify State Standards and District Curriculum	**VIA:** ***State Standards:*** Link Sections I–V to learning goals and information from your state standards or frameworks that are informed by the results of the topic study. **VIB:** ***District Curriculum Guide:*** Link Sections I–V to learning goals and information from your district curriculum guide that are informed by the results of the topic study.
Visit www.curriculumtopicstudy.org for updates or supplementary readings, Web sites, and videos.	

Standards- and Research-Based Study of a Curricular Topic

STATISTICAL REASONING

Section and Outcome	Selected Sources and Readings for Study and Reflection Read and examine *related parts* of:		
I. Identify Adult Content Knowledge	**IA:**	***Science for All Americans***	
		▸ Chapter 9, *Summarizing Data,* pages 137–140, *Reasoning,* pages 140–143 ▸ Chapter 12, *Critical Response Skills,* pages 193–194	
	IB:	***Beyond Numeracy***	
		▸ *Correlation, Intervals, and Testing,* pages 56–58 ▸ *Mean, Median, and Mode,* pages 141–143 ▸ *Statistics: Two Theorems,* pages 227–230	
II. Consider Instructional Implications	**IIA:**	***Benchmarks for Science Literacy***	
		▸ 9D, *Uncertainty,* general essay, page 226, grade span essays, pages 227–230 ▸ 9E, *Reasoning,* general essay, page 231, grade span essays, pages 232–234 ▸ 12E, *Critical Response Skills,* general essay, page 298	
	IIB:	***NCTM Principles and Standards for School Mathematics***	
		▸ Grades PreK–12 Overview Data Analysis and Probability, pages 48–50 ▸ Grades PreK–2 Data Analysis and Probability, pages 109–114 ▸ Grades 3–5 Data Analysis and Probability, pages 177–181 ▸ Grades 6–8 Data Analysis and Probability, pages 249–253 ▸ Grades 9–12 Data Analysis and Probability, pages 325–331	
III. Identify Concepts and Specific Ideas	**IIIA:**	***Benchmarks for Science Literacy***	
		▸ 9D, *Uncertainty,* pages 227–230 ▸ 9E, *Reasoning,* pages 232–234 ▸ 12E, *Critical Response Skills,* pages 298–300	
	IIIB:	***NCTM Principles and Standards for School Mathematics***	
		▸ Grades PreK–2 Data Analysis and Probability, page 108 or 400 ▸ Grades 3–5 Data Analysis and Probability, page 176 or 400 ▸ Grades 6–8 Data Analysis and Probability, page 248 or 401 ▸ Grades 9–12 Data Analysis and Probability, page 324 or 401	
IV. Examine Research on Student Learning	**IVA:**	***Benchmarks for Science Literacy***	
		▸ 9D, *Uncertainty,* pages 353–354 ▸ 12E, *Interpretation of Data,* page 361	
	IVB:	***Research Companion***	
		▸ Chapter 13, *Reasoning About Data,* pages 193–213	
V. Examine Coherency and Articulation	**V:**	***Atlas of Science Literacy***	
		▸ *Averages and Comparisons,* page 123 ▸ *Statistical Reasoning,* page 127	
VI. Clarify State Standards and District Curriculum	**VIA:**	***State Standards:*** Link Sections I–V to learning goals and information from your state standards or frameworks that are informed by the results of the topic study.	
	VIB:	***District Curriculum Guide:*** Link Sections I–V to learning goals and information from your district curriculum guide that are informed by the results of the topic study.	
Visit www.curriculumtopicstudy.org for updates or supplementary readings, Web sites, and videos.			

Standards- and Research-Based Study of a Curricular Topic

SUMMARIZING DATA

Section and Outcome	Selected Sources and Readings for Study and Reflection Read and examine *related parts* of:
I. Identify Adult Content Knowledge	**IA:** *Science for All Americans* ▸ Chapter 9, *Summarizing Data*, pages 137–139 **IB:** *Beyond Numeracy* ▸ *Correlation, Intervals, and Testing*, pages 56–58 ▸ *Mean, Median, and Mode*, pages 141–143 ▸ *Statistics: Two Theorems*, pages 227–230
II. Consider Instructional Implications	**IIA:** *Benchmarks for Science Literacy* ▸ 9D, *Uncertainty*, general essay, page 226; grade span essays, pages 227–230 ▸ 12D, *Communication*, general essay, page 295 **IIB:** *NCTM Principles and Standards for School Mathematics* ▸ Grades PreK–12 Overview Data Analysis and Probability, pages 48–50 ▸ Grades PreK–2 Data Analysis and Probability, pages 109–114 ▸ Grades 3–5 Data Analysis and Probability, pages 177–181 ▸ Grades 6–8 Data Analysis and Probability, pages 249–253 ▸ Grades 9–12 Data Analysis and Probability, pages 325–331
III. Identify Concepts and Specific Ideas	**IIIA:** *Benchmarks for Science Literacy* ▸ 9D, *Uncertainty*, pages 227–230 ▸ 12D, *Communication*, pages 296–297 **IIIB:** *NCTM Principles and Standards for School Mathematics* ▸ Grades PreK–2 Data Analysis and Probability, page 108 or 400 ▸ Grades 3–5 Data Analysis and Probability, page 176 or 400 ▸ Grades 6–8 Data Analysis and Probability, page 248 or 401 ▸ Grades 9–12 Data Analysis and Probability, page 324 or 401
IV. Examine Research on Student Learning	**IVA:** *Benchmarks for Science Literacy* ▸ 9D, *Uncertainty*, pages 353–354 **IVB:** *Research Companion* ▸ Chapter 13, *Reasoning About Data*, pages 202–215
V. Examine Coherency and Articulation	**V:** *Atlas of Science Literacy* ▸ *Averages and Comparisons*, page 123, *Correlation*, page 125
VI. Clarify State Standards and District Curriculum	**VIA:** *State Standards:* Link Sections I–V to learning goals and information from your state standards or frameworks that are informed by the results of the topic study. **VIB:** *District Curriculum Guide:* Link Sections I–V to learning goals and information from your district curriculum guide that are informed by the results of the topic study.
Visit www.curriculumtopicstudy.org for updates or supplementary readings, Web sites, and videos.	

Integrated Topics

Number of CTS Guides: 10

Overview: The primary focus of this section is developing an understanding of the connection among mathematical ideas, how connected ideas build on one another, and connections of topics to context outside of mathematics. These topics help provide coherence to the mathematics curriculum and are threaded through multiple content areas.

- Connections
- Connections Outside
- Connections Within
- Constancy and Change
- Discrete Mathematics
- Equivalence
- Estimation
- Graphic Representation
- Matrices and Vectors
- Proportionality

Standards- and Research-Based Study of a Curricular Topic

CONNECTIONS

Section and Outcome	Selected Sources and Readings for Study and Reflection Read and examine *related parts* of:	
I. Identify Adult Content Knowledge	**IA:**	**Science for All Americans** ▸ Chapter 2, *Patterns and Relationships,* pages 16–17, *Mathematics, Science, and Technology,* pages 17–18 ▸ Chapter 13, *Effective Learning and Teaching,* pages 198–199
	IB:	**Beyond Numeracy** ▸ *Mathematics in Ethics,* pages 66–70 ▸ *Music, Art, and Digitalization,* pages 154–157
II. Consider Instructional Implications	**IIA:**	**Benchmarks for Science Literacy** ▸ 2A, *Patterns and Relationships,* general essay, pages 25–26, grade span essays, pages 28–29 ▸ 2B, *Mathematics, Science, and Technology,* general essay, page 30, grade span essays, pages 31–33 ▸ 14, *Issues and Language,* pages 315, 320
	IIB:	**NCTM Principles and Standards for School Mathematics** ▸ Grade PreK–12 Overview Number and Operations, page 32; Algebra, page 37; Geometry, page 41; Measurement, page 44; Data Analysis and Probability, page 48; Connections, pages 64–66 ▸ Grade PreK–2 Connections, pages 132–135 ▸ Grade 3–5 Connections, pages 200–205 ▸ Grade 6–8 Connections, pages 274–279 ▸ Grade 9–12 Connections, pages 354–359
III. Identify Concepts and Specific Ideas	**IIIA:**	**Benchmarks for Science Literacy** ▸ 2A, *Patterns and Relationships,* pages 26–29 ▸ 2B, *Mathematics, Science, and Technology,* pages 32–33
	IIIB:	**NCTM Principles and Standards for School Mathematics** ▸ Grade PreK–12 Connections, page 64 or 402
IV. Examine Research on Student Learning	**IVA:**	**Benchmarks for Science Literacy** ▸ 2A, *Patterns and Relationships,* page 334 ▸ 2B, *Mathematics, Science, and Technology,* page 334
	IVB:	**Research Companion** ▸ Chapter 23, *The Need for Meaning,* pages 358–360, *The Need for Significance and Relevance,* pages 367–370
V. Examine Coherency and Articulation	**V.**	**Atlas of Science Literacy** ▸ *Graphic Representation,* page 115, noting the conceptual strand "Alternative Representations"
VI. Clarify State Standards and District Curriculum	**VIA:**	**State Standards:** Link Sections I–V to learning goals and information from your state standards or frameworks that are informed by the results of the topic study.
	VIB:	**District Curriculum Guide:** Link Sections I–V to learning goals and information from your district curriculum guide that are informed by the results of the topic study.
Visit www.curriculumtopicstudy.org for updates or supplementary readings, Web sites, and videos.		

Standards- and Research-Based Study of a Curricular Topic

CONNECTIONS OUTSIDE

Section and Outcome	Selected Sources and Readings for Study and Reflection Read and examine *related parts* of:
I. Identify Adult Content Knowledge	**IA:** *Science for All Americans* ▸ Chapter 2, *Mathematics, Science, and Technology,* pages 17–18 **IB:** *Beyond Numeracy* ▸ *Mathematics in Ethics,* pages 66–70 ▸ *Music, Art, and Digitalization,* pages 154–157 ▸ *Voting Systems,* pages 262–265
II. Consider Instructional Implications	**IIA:** *Benchmarks for Science Literacy* ▸ 2B, *Mathematics, Science, and Technology,* general essay, page 30, grade span essays, pages 31–33 ▸ 14, *Issues and Language,* pages 315, 320 **IIB:** *NCTM Principles and Standards for School Mathematics* ▸ Grade PreK–12 Overview Measurement, page 44; Connections, page 64, *Recognize and Apply Mathematics,* pages 65–66 ▸ Grade PreK–2 Geometry, page 97; Connections, pages 132–135 ▸ Grade 3–5 Measurement, page 171; Connections, *What Should Connections,* pages 200–202, *What Should Be,* page 203–205 ▸ Grade 6–8 Measurement, page 241; Connections, *What Should Be,* pages 277–279 ▸ Grade 9–12 Geometry, page 309; Measurement, page 321; Connections, page 354, *What Should Be,* page 359
III. Identify Concepts and Specific Ideas	**IIIA:** *Benchmarks for Science Literacy* ▸ 2B, *Mathematics, Science, and Technology,* pages 32–33 **IIIB:** *NCTM Principles and Standards for School Mathematics* ▸ Grade PreK–12 Connections, page 64 or 402
IV. Examine Research on Student Learning	**IVA:** *Benchmarks for Science Literacy* ▸ 2B, *Mathematics, Science, and Technology,* page 334 **IVB:** *NCTM Research Companion* ▸ Chapter 23, *The Need for Meaning,* pages 358–360
V. Examine Coherency and Articulation	**V.** *Atlas of Science Literacy:* There are no maps for this topic in Volume 1.
VI. Clarify State Standards and District Curriculum	**VIA:** *State Standards:* Link Sections I–V to learning goals and information from your state standards or frameworks that are informed by the results of the topic study. **VIB:** *District Curriculum Guide:* Link Sections I–V to learning goals and information from your district curriculum guide that are informed by the results of the topic study.
Visit www.curriculumtopicstudy.org for updates or supplementary readings, Web sites, and videos.	

Standards- and Research-Based Study of a Curricular Topic

CONNECTIONS WITHIN

Section and Outcome	Selected Sources and Readings for Study and Reflection Read and examine *related parts* of:
I. Identify Adult Content Knowledge	**IA:** *Science for All Americans* ▸ Chapter 2, *Patterns and Relationships,* pages 16–17 ▸ Chapter 13, *Effective Learning and Teaching,* pages 198–199 **IB:** *Beyond Numeracy* ▸ *Analytic Geometry,* pages 10–14
II. Consider Instructional Implications	**IIA:** *Benchmarks for Science Literacy* ▸ 2A, *Patterns and Relationships,* general essay, pages 25–26, grade span essays, pages 28–29 ▸ 14, *Issues and Language,* page 315 **IIB:** *NCTM Principles and Standards for School Mathematics* ▸ Grade PreK–12 Overview Number and Operations, page 32; Algebra, page 37; Geometry, page 41; Measurement, page 44; Data Analysis and Probability, page 48; Connections, page 64, *Recognize and Use,* pages 64–65, *Understand How,* page 65 ▸ Grade PreK–2 Number and Operations, page 79; Geometry, page 97; Measurement, page 103; Connections, pages 132–135 ▸ Grade 3–5 Measurement, page 171; Connections, pages 200–203 ▸ Grade 6–8 Algebra, page 223; Measurement, page 241; Connections, pages 274–278 ▸ Grades 9–12 Number and Operations, page 291; Geometry, page 309; Measurement, page 321; Data Analysis and Probability, page 325; Connections, pages 354–359
III. Identify Concepts and Specific Ideas	**IIIA:** *Benchmarks for Science Literacy* ▸ 2A, *Patterns and Relationships,* pages 26–29 **IIIB:** *NCTM Principles and Standards for School Mathematics* ▸ Grades PreK–12 Connections, page 64 or 402
IV. Examine Research on Student Learning	**IVA:** *Benchmarks for Science Literacy* ▸ 2A, *Patterns and Relationships,* page 334 **IVB:** *Research Companion* ▸ Chapter 23, *The Need for Meaning,* pages 358–360, *The Need for Significance and Relevance,* pages 367–370
V. Examine Coherency and Articulation	**V.** *Atlas of Science Literacy* ▸ *Graphic Representation,* page 115, noting the conceptual strand "Alternative Representations"
VI. Clarify State Standards and District Curriculum	**VIA:** *State Standards:* Link Sections I–V to learning goals and information from your state standards or frameworks that are informed by the results of the topic study. **VIB:** *District Curriculum Guide:* Link Sections I–V to learning goals and information from your district curriculum guide that are informed by the results of the topic study.
	Visit www.curriculumtopicstudy.org for updates or supplementary readings, Web sites, and videos.

Standards- and Research-Based Study of a Curricular Topic

CONSTANCY AND CHANGE

Section and Outcome	Selected Sources and Readings for Study and Reflection Read and examine *related parts* of:
I. Identify Adult Content Knowledge	**IA:** ***Science for All Americans*** ▸ Chapter 9, *Symbolic Relationships*, pages 133–134, *Shapes*, page 135 ▸ Chapter 11, *Conservation*, pages 173–174, *Patterns of Change*, pages 174–176 **IB:** ***Beyond Numeracy*** ▸ *Calculus*, pages 27–31, *Symmetry and Invariance*, pages 234–236
II. Consider Instructional Implications	**IIA:** ***Benchmarks for Science Literacy*** ▸ 9B, *Symbolic Relationships*, general essay, page 216, grade span essays, pages 217–220 ▸ 9C, *Shapes*, grade span essays, page 223–224 ▸ 11C, *Constancy and Change*, general essay, pages 271–272, grade span essays, pages 272–275 **IIB:** ***NCTM Principles and Standards for School Mathematics*** ▸ Grades PreK–2 Numbers and Operations, *Understand Numbers*, page 79–80, *Understand Meanings*, pages 83–84; Algebra, *Analyze Change*, page 95; Geometry, *Use Visualization*, page 100; Measurement, *Understand Measurable*, page 104 ▸ Grades 3–5 Numbers, *Understand Numbers*, pages 149–150; Algebra, *Analyze Change*, page 163; Geometry, *Analyze Characteristics*, page 166; Measurement, *Understand Measurable*, pages 172–173 ▸ Grades 6–8 Numbers, *Understand Numbers*, page 217; Algebra, *Analyze Change*, pages 229–231; Geometry, *Analyze Characteristics*, pages 234–235, *Use Transformations*, pages 235–237; Measurement, *Understand Measurable*, pages 242–243, *Apply Techniques*, pages 243–245; Data Analysis and Probability, *Select and Use*, page 251, *Develop and Evaluate*, pages 252–253 ▸ Grades 9–12 Algebra, *Analyze Change*, pages 305–306; Measurement, *Apply Techniques*, page 323; Data Analysis and Probability, *Select and Use*, pages 327–328
III. Identify Concepts and Specific Ideas	**IIIA:** ***Benchmarks for Science Literacy*** ▸ 9B, *Symbolic Relationships*, pages 217–220 ▸ 9C, *Shapes*, pages 223–224 ▸ 11C, *Constancy and Change*, pages 272–275 **IIIB:** ***NCTM Principles and Standards for School Mathematics*** ▸ Grades PreK–2 Numbers and Operations, page 78 or 392; Algebra, page 90 or 394; Geometry, page 96 or 396; Measurement, page 102 or 398 ▸ Grades 3–5 Numbers and Operations, page 148 or 392; Algebra, page 158 or 394; Geometry, page 164 or 396; Measurement, page 170 or 398 ▸ Grades 6–8 Numbers and Operations, page 214 or 393; Algebra, page 222 or 395; Geometry, page 232 or 397; Measurement, page 240 or 399; Data Analysis, page 248 or 401 ▸ Grades 9–12 Algebra, page 296 or 395; Measurement, page 320 or 399; Data Analysis, page 324 or 401
IV. Examine Research on Student Learning	**IVA:** ***Benchmarks for Science Literacy*** ▸ 9B, *Graphs*, page 351 ▸ 11C, *Constancy and Change*, pages 357–358 **IVB:** ***Research Companion*** ▸ Chapter 10, *Stasis and Change*, pages 136–148 ▸ Chapter 17, *Representation in School Mathematics*, pages 252–260
V. Examine Coherency and Articulation	**V:** ***Atlas of Science Literacy*** ▸ *Graphic Representation*, page 115; *Symbolic Representation*, page 117; *Describing Change*, pages 121; *Correlation*, page 125
VI. Clarify State Standards and District Curriculum	**VIA:** ***State Standards:*** Link Sections I–V to learning goals and information from your state standards or frameworks that are informed by the results of the topic study. **VIB:** ***District Curriculum Guide:*** Link Sections I–V to learning goals and information from your district curriculum guide that are informed by the results of the topic study.
	Visit www.curriculumtopicstudy.org for updates or supplementary readings, Web sites, and videos.

Standards- and Research-Based Study of a Curricular Topic

DISCRETE MATHEMATICS

Section and Outcome	Selected Sources and Readings for Study and Reflection Read and examine *related parts* of:
I. Identify Adult Content Knowledge	**IA:** ***Science for All Americans:*** ▸ Chapter 9, *Shapes,* page 135 **IB:** ***Beyond Numeracy*** ▸ *Combinatorics, Graphs, and Maps,* pages 42–46 ▸ *Fractals,* pages 82–86 ▸ *The Multiplication Principle,* pages 151–153 ▸ *Pascal's Triangle,* pages 171–174 ▸ *Recursion—From Definitions to Life,* pages 209–213
II. Consider Instructional Implications	**IIA:** ***Benchmarks for Science Literacy*** ▸ 2A, *Patterns and Relationships,* general essay, page 25, grade span essays, pages 26–29 **IIB:** ***NCTM Principles and Standards for School Mathematics*** ▸ Grades PreK–12 Overview *Where Is Discrete,* page 31; Algebra, *Understand Patterns,* page 38; Geometry, page 41, *Specify Locations,* page 42 ▸ Grades PreK–2 Algebra, *Understand Patterns,* pages 91–92; Geometry, *Specify Locations,* pages 98–99 ▸ Grades 3–5 Algebra, page 159, *Understand Patterns,* pages 159–160; Geometry, *Specify Locations,* page 167 ▸ Grades 6–8 Geometry, *Use Visualization,* pages 237–239; Data Analysis and Probability, *Understand and Apply,* pages 254–255 ▸ Grades 9–12 Number and Operations, page 291, *Understand Meanings,* pages 292–294, *Compute Fluently,* page 294; Algebra, page 297, *Understand Patterns,* pages 297–300; Geometry, *Use Visualization,* pages 315–318; Data Analysis and Probability, *Understand and Apply,* page 331
III. Identify Concepts and Specific Ideas	**IIIB:** ***NCTM Principles and Standards for School Mathematics*** ▸ Grades PreK–2 Algebra, page 90 or 394; Geometry, page 96 or 396 ▸ Grades 3–5 Algebra, page 158 or 394; Geometry, page 164 or 396 ▸ Grades 6–8 Geometry, page 232 or 397; Data Analysis and Probability, page 248 or 401 ▸ Grades 9–12 Number and Operations, page 290 or 393; Algebra, page 296 or 395; Geometry, page 308 or 397
IV. Examine Research on Student Learning	**IVA:** ***Benchmarks for Science Literacy***: No research available in *Benchmarks.* **IVB:** ***Research Companion*** No research available in *Research Companion.*
V. Examine Coherency and Articulation	**V:** ***Atlas of Science Literacy***: There are no maps for this topic in Volume 1.
VI. Clarify State Standards and District Curriculum	**VIA:** ***State Standards:*** Link Sections I–V to learning goals and information from your state standards or frameworks that are informed by the results of the topic study. **VIB:** ***District Curriculum Guide:*** Link Sections I–V to learning goals and information from your district curriculum guide that are informed by the results of the topic study.
Visit www.curriculumtopicstudy.org for updates or supplementary readings, Web sites, and videos. (after publication in 2005)	

Standards- and Research-Based Study of a Curricular Topic

EQUIVALENCE

Section and Outcome	Selected Sources and Readings for Study and Reflection Read and examine *related parts* of:
I. Identify Adult Content Knowledge	**IA:** *Science for All Americans* ▸ Chapter 9, *Numbers*, pages 130–131, *Symbolic Relationships*, pages 132–133 ▸ Chapter 11, *Conservation*, pages 173–174, *Symmetry*, page 174 ▸ Chapter 12, *Computation*, page 188, *Calculator Skills*, page 189 **IB:** *Beyond Numeracy* ▸ *Algebra–Some Basic Principles*, pages 7–9 ▸ *Symmetry and Invariance*, pages 234–236
II. Consider Instructional Implications	**IIA:** *Benchmarks for Science Literacy* ▸ 9A, *Numbers,* grade level essay, page 211 ▸ 9B, *Symbolic Relationships*, general essay, page 215, grade span essays, page 217 ▸ 11C, *Constancy and Change*, general essay, page 271, grade span essays, page 273 **IIB:** *NCTM Principles and Standards for School Mathematics* ▸ Grades PreK–12 Overview Number and Operations, *Understand Numbers,* page 33; Algebra, *Represent and Analyze,* pages 38–39; Measurement, *Understand Measurable,* pages 44–45 ▸ Grades PreK–2 Number and Operations, *Understand Numbers,* pages 79–80, *Understand Meanings,* pages 83–84; Algebra, *Represent and Analyze,* pages 93–94; Geometry, *Use Visualization,* page 100; Measurement, *Understand Measurable,* page 104 ▸ Grades 3–5 Number and Operations, *Understand Numbers,* pages 149–150; Algebra, *Represent and Analyze,* pages 160–162; Geometry, *Analyze Characteristics,* page 166, *Apply Transformations* pages 167–168; Measurement, *Understand Measurable,* pages 172–173; Connections, page 200 ▸ Grades 6–8 Number and Operations, *Understand Numbers,* page 215; Algebra, page 223; *Represent and Analyze,* pages 225–227; Geometry, *Analyze Characteristics,* page 234, *Apply Transformations,* pages 235–236; Measurement, *Understand Measurable,* page 241 ▸ Grades 9–12 Connections, *What Should,* page 354
III. Identify Concepts and Specific Ideas	**IIIA:** *Benchmarks for Science Literacy* ▸ 9B, *Symbolic Relationships,* pages 218–219 ▸ 11C, *Constancy and Change,* page 274 **IIIB:** *NCTM Principles and Standards for School Mathematics* ▸ Grades PreK–2 Number and Operations, page 78 or 392; Algebra, page 90 or 394; Geometry, page 96 or 396 ▸ Grades 3–5 Number and Operations, page 148 or 392; Algebra, page 158 or 394; Geometry, page 164 or 396 ▸ Grades 6–8 Algebra, page 222 or 395; Geometry, page 232 or 397; Data Analysis, page 248 or 401
IV. Examine Research on Student Learning	**IVA:** *Benchmarks for Science Literacy* ▸ 9A, *Rational Numbers,* page 350 ▸ 9B, *Algebraic Equations,* pages 351–352 ▸ 11C, *Constancy and Change,* pages 357–358 **IVB:** *Research Companion* ▸ Chapter 10, *Introduction,* pages 138–139 ▸ Chapter 12, *Additivity,* page 181
V. Examine Coherency and Articulation	**V:** *Atlas of Science Literacy* ▸ *Mathematical Processes,* page 27 noting the conceptual strand "Computation and Operations" ▸ *Symbolic Representation,* page 117
VI. Clarify State Standards and District Curriculum	**VIA:** *State Standards:* Link Sections I–V to learning goals and information from your state standards or frameworks that are informed by the results of the topic study. **VIB:** *District Curriculum Guide:* Link Sections I–V to learning goals and information from your district curriculum guide that are informed by the results of the topic study.

Visit www.curriculumtopicstudy.org for updates or supplementary readings, Web sites, and videos.

Standards- and Research-Based Study of a Curricular Topic

ESTIMATION

Section and Outcome	Selected Sources and Readings for Study and Reflection Read and examine *related parts* of:
I. Identify Adult Content Knowledge	**IA:** *Science for All Americans* ▸ Chapter 12, *Habits of Mind,* pages 190–191
II. Consider Instructional Implications	**IIA:** *Benchmarks for Science Literacy* ▸ 9A, *Numbers* general essay, page 210; grade span essays, pages 211–214 ▸ 12B, *Computation and Estimation* general essay, pages 288–289 **IIB:** *NCTM Principles and Standards for School Mathematics* ▸ Grades PreK–12 Overview Number and Operations general essay, page 32, *Compute Fluently,* pages 35–36 ▸ Grades PreK–2 Number and Operations general essay, page 79, *Understand Numbers,* page 80; Measurement, *Apply Appropriate Techniques,* page 106 ▸ Grades 3–5 Number and Operations general essay, page 149, *Compute Fluently,* pages 155–156; Measurement, *Apply Appropriate Techniques,* page 174 ▸ Grades 6–8 Number and Operations, *Compute Fluently,* pages 220–221; Measurement, *Apply Appropriate Techniques,* page 243 ▸ Grades 9–12 Number and Operations, *Compute Fluently,* page 294; Measurement, *Apply Appropriate Techniques,* pages 322–323
III. Identify Concepts and Specific Ideas	**IIIA:** *Benchmarks for Science Literacy* ▸ 9A, *Number,* page 211, page 214 ▸ 12B, *Computation and Estimation,* pages 290–291 **IIIB:** *NCTM Principles and Standards for School Mathematics* ▸ Grades PreK–2 Number and Operations, page 78 or 392; Measurement, page 102 or 398 ▸ Grades 3–5 Number and Operations, page 148 or 392; Measurement, page 170 or 398 ▸ Grades 6–8 Number and Operations, page 214 or 393; Measurement, page 240 or 399 ▸ Grades 9–12 Number and Operations, page 290 or 393; Measurement, page 320 or 399
IV. Examine Research on Student Learning	**IVA:** *Benchmarks for Science Literacy* ▸ 9A, *Estimation,* page 350 ▸ 12B, *Estimation Skills,* page 360 **IVB:** *Research Companion* ▸ Chapter 12, *Precision and Error,* page 188
V. Examine Coherency and Articulation	**V.** *Atlas of Science Literacy* ▸ *Mathematical Processes,* page 27 ▸ *Mathematical Models,* page 29
VI. Clarify State Standards and District Curriculum	**VIA:** *State Standards:* Link Sections I–V to learning goals and information from your state standards or frameworks that are informed by the results of the topic study. **VIB:** *District Curriculum Guide:* Link Sections I–V to learning goals and information from your district curriculum guide that are informed by the results of the topic study.
Visit www.curriculumtopicstudy.org for updates or supplementary readings, Web sites, and videos.	

Standards- and Research-Based Study of a Curricular Topic

GRAPHIC REPRESENTATION

Section and Outcome	Selected Sources and Readings for Study and Reflection Read and examine *related parts* of:	
I. Identify Adult Content Knowledge	**IA:**	*Science for All Americans* ▸ Chapter 9, *Shapes,* pages 134–134, *Summarizing Data,* pages 137–138 ▸ Chapter 12, *Communication,* page 193
	IB:	*Beyond Numeracy* ▸ *Analytic Geometry,* pages 10–14 ▸ *Linear Programming,* pages 133–135 ▸ *The Quadratic and Other Formulas,* pages 198–201 ▸ *Trigonometry,* pages 251–256
II. Consider Instructional Implications	**IIA:**	*Benchmarks for Science Literacy* ▸ 9B, *Symbolic Relationships,* general essay, pages 215–216, grade span essays, pages 217–221 ▸ 9C, *Shapes,* grade span essays, pages 223–225
	IIB:	*NCTM Principles and Standards for School Mathematics* ▸ K–12 Overview Algebra, *Understand Patterns,* page 38; Geometry, page 41, *Specify Locations,* pages 42–43; Data Analysis and Probability, page 48, *Select and Use,* pages 49–50; Representation, pages 67–71 ▸ Grades PreK–2 Data Analysis and Probability, page 109, *Formulate Questions,* pages 109–112; Representation, pages 136–141 ▸ Grades 3–5 Algebra, page 159, *Understand patterns,* page 160, *Analyze change,* page 163; Geometry, page 165, *Specify Locations,* page 167; Data Analysis and Probability, page 177, *Formulate Questions,* page 178, *Select and Use,* page 179; Representation, pages 206–209 ▸ Grades 6–8 Algebra, pages 223–231; Geometry, *Specify Locations,* page 235; Data Analysis and Probability, page 249, *Formulate Questions,* pages 249–250, *Select and Use,* page 251, *Develop and Evaluate,* pages 251–252; Representation, pages 280–285 ▸ Grades 9–12 Algebra, pages 297–306; Geometry, page 309, *Specify Locations,* pages 313–315; Data Analysis and Probability, *Select and Use,* pages 327–329, *Develop and Evaluate,* pages 329–330; Representation, pages 360–364
III. Identify Concepts and Specific Ideas	**IIIA:**	*Benchmarks for Science Literacy* ▸ 9B, *Symbolic Relationships,* pages 217–221 ▸ 9C, *Shapes,* pages 223–225 ▸ 12D, *Communication Skills,* pages 296–297
	IIIB:	*NCTM Principles and Standards for School Mathematics* ▸ Grades Pre–K–2 Algebra, page 90 or 394; Data Analysis and Probability, page 108 or 400; Representation, page 136 ▸ Grades 3–5 Algebra, page 158 or 394; Geometry, page 164 or 396; Data Analysis and Probability, page 176 or 400; Representation, page 206 ▸ Grades 6–8 Algebra, page 222 or 395; Geometry, page 232 or 397; Data Analysis and Probability, page 248 or 401; Representation, page 280 ▸ Grades 9–12 Algebra, page 296 or 395; Geometry, page 308 or 397; Data Analysis and Probability, page 248 or 401; Representation, page 360
IV. Examine Research on Student Learning	**IVA:**	*Benchmarks for Science Literacy* ▸ 9B, *Graphs,* page 351
	IVB:	*Research Companion* ▸ Chapter 13, *Organizing and Displaying,* pages 199–202 ▸ Chapter 17, *Representation in School: Learning to Graph and Graphing to Learn,* pages 250–260
V. Examine Coherency and Articulation	**V:**	*Atlas of Science Literacy* ▸ *Graphic Representation,* page 115 ▸ *Describing Change,* page 121 noting the conceptual strand "Related Changes"
VI. Clarify State Standards and District Curriculum	**VIA:**	*State Standards:* Link Sections I–V to learning goals and information from your state standards or frameworks that are informed by the results of the topic study.
	VIB:	*District Curriculum Guide:* Link Sections I–V to learning goals and information from your district curriculum guide that are informed by the results of the topic study.
Visit www.curriculumtopicstudy.org for updates or supplementary readings, Web sites, and videos. (after publication in 2005)		

Standards- and Research-Based Study of a Curricular Topic

MATRICES AND VECTORS

Section and Outcome	Selected Sources and Readings for Study and Reflection Read and examine *related parts* of:
I. Identify Adult Content Knowledge	**IA:** *Science for All Americans*: No research available in *Science for All Americans*. **IB:** *Beyond Numeracy* ▸ *Matrices and Vectors*, pages 136–140
II. Consider Instructional Implications	**IIB:** *NCTM Principles and Standards for School Mathematics* ▸ Grades PreK–12 Overview Number and Operation, *Understand Meanings* page 34, *Compute Fluently* page 36; Geometry, *Apply Transformations,* page 43 ▸ Grades 9–12 Number and Operations, *Understand Numbers,* page 292, *Understand Meanings of Operations,* page 293, *Compute Fluently,* page 294; Geometry, page 309, *Apply Transformations,* pages 314–315
III. Identify Concepts and Specific Ideas	**IIIA:** *Benchmarks for Science Literacy:* No research available in *Benchmarks*. **IIIB:** *NCTM Principles and Standards for School Mathematics* ▸ 9–12 Number and Operations, page 290 or 393; Geometry, page 308 or 397
IV. Examine Research on Student Learning	**IVA:** *Benchmarks for Science Literacy:* No research available in *Benchmarks*. **IVB:** *Research Companion*: No research available in *Research Companion*.
V. Examine Coherency and Articulation	**V:** *Atlas of Science Literacy:* There are no maps for this topic in Volume 1.
VI. Clarify State Standards and District Curriculum	**VIA:** *State Standards:* Link Sections I–V to learning goals and information from your state standards or frameworks that are informed by the results of the topic study. **VIB:** *District Curriculum Guide:* Link Sections I–V to learning goals and information from your district curriculum guide that are informed by the results of the topic study.
Visit www.curriculumtopicstudy.org for updates or supplementary readings, Web sites, and videos.	

Standards- and Research-Based Study of a Curricular Topic

PROPORTIONALITY

Section and Outcome	Selected Sources and Readings for Study and Reflection Read and examine *related parts* of:
I. Identify Adult Content Knowledge	**IA:** *Science for All Americans* ▸ Chapter 9, *Symbolic Relationships,* pages 132–134, *Shapes,* page 135, *Probability,* page 137 ▸ Chapter 11, *Mathematical Models,* page, 171, *Patterns of Change,* page 174–175, *Scale,* pages 180–181 **IB:** *Beyond Numeracy* ▸ *Areas and Volume,* pages 21–22, *Exponential Growth,* page 71, *Trigonometry,* pages 251–253
II. Consider Instructional Implications	**IIA:** *Benchmarks for Science Literacy* ▸ 9B, *Mathematical Inquiry,* general essay, page 216, grade span essays, pages 217–221 ▸ 9C, *Shapes,* grade span essays, page 223–225 ▸ 11C, *Constancy and Change,* general essay, page 271, grade span essays, pages 273–275 ▸ 11D, *Scale,* general essay, page 276, grade span essays, pages 277–279 **IIB:** *NCTM Principles and Standards for School Mathematics* ▸ Grades PreK–12 Overview Number and Operations, *Understand Numbers,* page 33, *Understand Meanings,* page 34; Measurement, *Apply Appropriate,* page 47; Connections, *Recognize and Use,* pages 64–65, *Understand How Mathematical,* page 65 ▸ Grades 3–5 Number and Operations, page 144, *Understand Numbers,* page 150; Connections, page 200 ▸ Grades 6–8 Number and Operations, pages 212–213, 215, *Understand Numbers,* page 217, *Compute Fluently,* pages 220–221; Algebra, page 223; Geometry, *Analyze Characteristics,* pages 234–235, *Apply Transformations,* pages 236–237; Measurement, page 241, *Apply Appropriate,* pages 245–247; Data Analysis and Probability, *Understand and Apply,* page 254; Connections, page 274–279 ▸ Grades 9–12 Geometry, *Analyze Characteristics,* pages 310–312; Measurement, *Apply Appropriate,* pages 322–323
III. Identify Concepts and Specific Ideas	**IIIA:** *Benchmarks for Science Literacy* ▸ 9B, *Mathematical Inquiry,* pages 217–221 ▸ 9C, *Shapes,* pages 223–225 ▸ 11C, *Constancy and Change,* pages 273–275 ▸ 11D, *Scale,* pages 278–279 ▸ 12B, *Computation and Estimation,* pages 290–291 **IIIB:** *NCTM Principles and Standards for School Mathematics* ▸ Grades 3–5 Numbers and Operations, page 148 or 392 ▸ Grades 6–8 Numbers and Operations, page 214 or 393; Geometry, page 232 or 397; Measurement, page 240 or 399; Data Analysis and Probability, page 248 or 401 ▸ Grades 9–12 Geometry, page 308 or 397
IV. Examine Research on Student Learning	**IVA:** *Benchmarks for Science Literacy* ▸ 12B, *Proportional Reasoning,* page 360 **IVB:** *Research Companion* ▸ Chapter 7, *Understand Fractions,* pages 100–105 ▸ Chapter 11, *Shape, Congruence, and Similarity,* pages 160–161 ▸ Chapter 12, *Developing Understanding of Measurement,* page 181 ▸ Chapter 14, *The Ratio Concept,* page 217
V. Examine Coherency and Articulation	**V:** *Atlas of Science Literacy* ▸ *Ratios and Proportionality,* page 119; *Describing Change,* page 121
VI. Clarify State Standards and District Curriculum	**VIA:** *State Standards:* Link Sections I–V to learning goals and information from your state standards or frameworks that are informed by the results of the topic study. **VIB:** *District Curriculum Guide:* Link Sections I–V to learning goals and information from your district curriculum guide that are informed by the results of the topic study.
Visit www.curriculumtopicstudy.org for updates or supplementary readings, Web sites, and videos. (coming in 2006)	

Problem Solving and Processes

Number of CTS Guides: 9

Overview: The primary focus of this section is on solving problems, communicating understanding, representing and justifying ideas, and use of mathematical vocabulary. Ideas such as building new knowledge through problem solving, organizing and consolidating thinking through the communication of ideas, using the language of mathematics to express ideas and using various representations and tools to organize ideas are developed through a study of the topics in this section.

- Communication in Mathematics
- Conjecture, Proof, and Justification
- Creating Representations
- Modeling
- Problem Solving
- Reasoning
- Representations
- Technology
- Vocabulary

Standards- and Research-Based Study of a Curricular Topic

COMMUNICATION IN MATHEMATICS

Section and Outcome	Selected Sources and Readings for Study and Reflection Read and examine *related parts* of:
I. Identify Adult Content Knowledge	**IA:** **Science for All Americans** ▶ Chapter 12, *Communication,* pages 192–193
II. Consider Instructional Implications	**IIA:** **Benchmarks for Science Literacy** ▶ 12D, *Communication Skills* general essay, page 295 **IIB:** **NCTM Principles and Standards for School Mathematics** ▶ Grades K–12 Overview Communication, pages 60–63 ▶ Grades PreK–2 Communication, pages 128–131 ▶ Grades 3–5 Communication, pages 194–199 ▶ Grades 6–8 Communication, pages 268–273 ▶ Grades 9–12 Communication, pages 348–352
III. Identify Concepts and Specific Ideas	**IIIA:** **Benchmarks for Science Literacy** ▶ 12D, *Communication Skills,* pages 296–297 **IIIB:** **NCTM Principles and Standards for School Mathematics** ▶ Grades PreK–2 Communication, page 128 or 402 ▶ Grades 3–5 Communication, page 194 or 402 ▶ Grades 6–8 Communication, page 268 or 402 ▶ Grades 9–12 Communication, page 348 or 402
IV. Examine Research on Student Learning	**IVB:** **Research Companion** ▶ Chapter 16, Communication and Language, pages 237–247
V. Examine Coherency and Articulation	**V:** **Atlas of Science Literacy:** There are no maps for this topic in Volume 1.
VI. Clarify State Standards and District Curriculum	**VIA:** **State Standards:** Link Sections I–V to learning goals and information from your state standards or frameworks that are informed by the results of the topic study. **VIB:** **District Curriculum Guide:** Link Sections I–V to learning goals and information from your district curriculum guide that are informed by the results of the topic study.
Visit www.curriculumtopicstudy.org for updates or supplementary readings, Web sites, and videos.	

Standards- and Research-Based Study of a Curricular Topic

CONJECTURE, PROOF, AND JUSTIFICATION

Section and Outcome	Selected Sources and Readings for Study and Reflection Read and examine *related parts* of:
I. Identify Adult Content Knowledge	**IA:** **Science for All Americans** ▸ Chapter 9, *Reasoning,* pages 140–143 ▸ Chapter 12, *Critical Response Skills,* pages 193–194 **IB:** **Beyond Numeracy** ▸ *Mathematical Induction,* pages 121–123 ▸ *The Philosophy of Mathematics,* pages 175–177 ▸ *QED, Proofs, and Theorems,* pages 195–197
II. Consider Instructional Implications	**IIA:** **Benchmarks for Science Literacy** ▸ 9C, *Shapes,* grade span essays, page 224–225 ▸ 9E, *Reasoning,* general essay, page 231, grade span essays, pages 232–234 ▸ 12E, *Critical Response Skills,* general essay, page 298 **IIB:** **NCTM Principles and Standards for School Mathematics** ▸ Grades PreK–12 Overview Geometry, page 41, *Analyze Characteristics,* pages 41–42; Reasoning and Proof, pages 56–59 ▸ Grades PreK–2 Geometry, *Analyze Characteristics,* pages 97–98; Reasoning and Proof, pages 122–126 ▸ Grades 3–5 Geometry, page 165, *Analyze Characteristics,* pages 165–166; Reasoning and Proof, pages 188–192 ▸ Grades 6–8 Geometry, page 233, *Analyze Characteristics,* pages 234–235; Reasoning and Proof, pages 262–267 ▸ Grades 9–12 Geometry, pages 309–310, *Analyze Characteristics,* pages 310–313; Reasoning and Proof, pages 342–346
III. Identify Concepts and Specific Ideas	**IIIA:** **Benchmarks for Science Literacy** ▸ 9E, *Reasoning,* pages 232–234 ▸ 12E, *Critical Response Skills,* pages 298–300 **IIIB:** **NCTM Principles and Standards for School Mathematics** ▸ Grades PreK–2 Geometry, page 96 or 396; Reasoning and Proof, page 122 or 402 ▸ Grades 3–5 Geometry, page 164 or 396; Reasoning and Proof, page 188 or 402 ▸ Grades 6–8 Geometry, page 232 or 397; Reasoning and Proof, page 262 or 402 ▸ Grades 9–12 Geometry, page 308 or 397; Reasoning and Proof, page 342 or 402
IV. Examine Research on Student Learning	**IVA:** **Benchmarks for Science Literacy** ▸ 9C, *Shapes; Proof,* pages 352–353 ▸ 12E, *Critical Response Skills,* page 361 **IVB:** **Research Companion** ▸ Chapter 11, *The van Hieles Levels,* pages 152–154, *Proof,* pages 167–169 ▸ Chapter 15, *Reasoning and Proof,* pages 227–234
V. Examine Coherency and Articulation	**V:** **Atlas of Science Literacy** ▸ *Evidence and Reasoning in Inquiry,* page 17
VI. Clarify State Standards and District Curriculum	**VIA:** *State Standards:* Link Sections I–V to learning goals and information from your state standards or frameworks that are informed by the results of the topic study. **VIB:** *District Curriculum Guide:* Link Sections I–V to learning goals and information from your district curriculum guide that are informed by the results of the topic study.
Visit www.curriculumtopicstudy.org for updates or supplementary readings, Web sites, and videos. (after publication in 2005)	

Standards- and Research-Based Study of a Curricular Topic

CREATING REPRESENTATIONS

Section and Outcome	Selected Sources and Readings for Study and Reflection Read and examine *related parts* of:
I. Identify Adult Content Knowledge	**IA:** ***Science for All Americans*** ▸ Chapter 2, *Mathematical Inquiry,* page 19, *Manipulating Mathematical Statements,* page 20 **IB:** ***Beyond Numeracy*** ▸ *Arabic Numerals,* pages 15–17 ▸ *Notation,* pages 163–165
II. Consider Instructional Implications	**IIA:** ***Benchmarks for Science Literacy*** ▸ 2B, *Mathematical Inquiry* general essay, pages 34–35, grade span essays, pages 36–37 **IIB:** ***NCTM Principles and Standards for School Mathematics*** ▸ Grades PreK–12 Overview Representation, pages 67–69 ▸ Grades PreK–2 Representation general essay, page 136, *What Should Representation Look Like,* pages 136–139, *What Should Be the Teacher's Role,* pages 139–141 ▸ Grades 3–5 Representation, pages 206–209 ▸ Grades 6–8 Representation, *What Should Representation Look Like,* pages 280–282, *What Should Be the Teacher's Role,* pages 284–285 ▸ Grades 9–12 Representation, pages 360–364
III. Identify Concepts and Specific Ideas	**IIIA:** ***Benchmarks for Science Literacy*** ▸ 2B, *Mathematical Inquiry,* pages 36–37 **IIIB:** ***NCTM Principles and Standards for School Mathematics*** ▸ Grades PreK–2 Representation, page 136 or 402 ▸ Grades 3–5 Representation, page 206 or 402 ▸ Grades 6–8 Representation, page 280 or 402 ▸ Grades 9–12 Representation, page 360 or 402
IV. Examine Research on Student Learning	**IVB:** ***Research Companion*** ▸ Chapter 17, *Graphs and Related Representational Forms,* pages 258–260 ▸ Chapter 18, Representation School Mathematics: Children's Representation of Problems, pages 263–273 ▸ Chapter 19, *Some Types and Characteristics of Representational Systems,* pages 278–279
V. Examine Coherency and Articulation	**V.** ***Atlas of Science Literacy*** ▸ *Mathematical Processes,* page 27 ▸ *Mathematical Models,* page 29
VI. Clarify State Standards and District Curriculum	**VIA:** ***State Standards:*** Link Sections I–V to learning goals and information from your state standards or frameworks that are informed by the results of the topic study. **VIB:** ***District Curriculum Guide:*** Link Sections I–V to learning goals and information from your district curriculum guide that are informed by the results of the topic study.
Visit www.curriculumtopicstudy.org for updates or supplementary readings, Web sites, and videos.	

Standards- and Research-Based Study of a Curricular Topic

MODELING

Section and Outcome	Selected Sources and Readings for Study and Reflection Read and examine *related parts* of:
I. Identify Adult Content Knowledge	**IA:** ***Science for All Americans*** ▶ Chapter 2, *Application*, pages 20–22 ▶ Chapter 11, *Models*, page 168, *Mathematical Models*, pages 171–172 **IB:** ***Beyond Numeracy*** ▶ *Functions*, pages 87–90 ▶ *Non–Euclidean Geometry*, pages 158–162
II. Consider Instructional Implications	**IIA:** ***Benchmarks for Science Literacy*** ▶ 2C, *Mathematical Inquiry*, general essay, pages 34–35, grade span essays, pages 36–38 ▶ 9B, *Symbolic Relationships*, general essay, pages 215–216, grade span essays, pages 217–220 ▶ 11B, *Models*, general essay, page 267, grade span essays, pages 268–270 **IIB:** ***NCTM Principles and Standards for School Mathematics*** ▶ Grades PreK–12 Overview Algebra, *Use Mathematical*, pages 39–40; Geometry, *Use Visualization*, page 43; Representations, pages 67–71 ▶ Grades PreK–2 Algebra, *Use Mathematical*, page 95; Geometry, *Use Visualization*, pages 100–101; Representations, pages 136–141 ▶ Grades 3–5 Algebra, *Use Mathematical*, pages 162–163; Geometry, *Use Visualization*, pages 168–169; Representations, pages 206–209 ▶ Grades 6–8 Algebra, *Use Mathematical*, pages 227–228; Geometry, *Use Visualization*, pages 237–239; Representations, pages 280–285 ▶ Grades 9–12 Algebra, *Use Mathematical*, pages 303–305; Geometry, *Use Visualization*, pages 315–318; Representations, pages 360–364
III. Identify Concepts and Specific Ideas	**IIIA:** ***Benchmarks for Science Literacy*** ▶ 2C, *Mathematical Inquiry*, pages 36–38 ▶ 9B, *Symbolic Relationships*, pages 217–220 ▶ 11B, *Models*, pages 268–270 **IIIB:** ***NCTM Principles and Standards for School Mathematics*** ▶ Grades PreK–2 Algebra, page 90 or394; Geometry, page 96 or 396 ▶ Grades 3–5 Algebra, page 158 or 394; Geometry, page 164 or 396 ▶ Grades 6–8 Algebra, page 222 or 395; Geometry, page 232 or 397 ▶ Grades 9–12 Algebra, page 296 or 395; Geometry, page 308 or 397
IV. Examine Research on Student Learning	**IVA:** ***Benchmarks for Science Literacy*** ▶ 2C, *Mathematical Inquiry*, page 334 ▶ 11B, *Models*, page 357 **IVB:** ***Research Companion*** ▶ Chapter 10, *Algebra*, pages 138–141, *Discussion*, pages 148–149 ▶ Chapter 11, *Diagrams, Manipulatives*, pages 155–156, *Navigation, Coordinates*, pages 165–166 ▶ Chapter 18, *Definitions of Representations*, pages 264–265
V. Examine Coherency and Articulation	**V:** ***Atlas of Science Literacy*** ▶ *Mathematical Processes*, page 27 ▶ *Mathematical Models*, page 29
VI. Clarify State Standards and District Curriculum	**VIA:** ***State Standards:*** Link Sections I–V to learning goals and information from your state standards or frameworks that are informed by the results of the topic study. **VIB:** ***District Curriculum Guide:*** Link Sections I–V to learning goals and information from your district curriculum guide that are informed by the results of the topic study.

Visit www.curriculumtopicstudy.org for updates or supplementary readings, Web sites, and videos.
(coming in 2005)

Standards- and Research-Based Study of a Curricular Topic

PROBLEM SOLVING

Section and Outcome	Selected Sources and Readings for Study and Reflection Read and examine *related parts* of:
I. Identify Adult Content Knowledge	**IA:** **Science for All Americans** ▸ Chapter 2, *Mathematical Inquiry*, page 19
II. Consider Instructional Implications	**IIA:** **Benchmarks for Science Literacy** ▸ 2A, *Patterns and Relationships* general essay, page 25, grade span essays, pages 28–29 ▸ 2B, *Mathematics, Science, and Technology* general essay, page 30, grade span essays, pages 31–32 ▸ 2C, *Mathematical Inquiry* general essay, pages 34–35, grade span essays, pages 37–38 ▸ 9, *The Mathematical World* chapter overview, page 209 **IIB:** **NCTM Principles and Standards for School Mathematics** ▸ Grades PreK–12 Overview Problem Solving, pages 52–55 ▸ Grades PreK–2 Problem Solving, pages 116–121 ▸ Grades 3–5 Problem Solving, pages 182–187 ▸ Grades 6–8 Problem Solving, pages 256–261 ▸ Grades 9–12 Problem Solving, pages 334–341
III. Identify Concepts and Specific Ideas	**IIIA:** **Benchmarks for Science Literacy** ▸ 2A, *Patterns and Relationships*, pages 27–29 ▸ 2C, *Mathematical Inquiry*, pages 37–38 **IIIB:** **NCTM Principles and Standards for School Mathematics** ▸ Grades PreK–2 Problem Solving, page 116 or 402 ▸ Grades 3–5 Problem Solving, page 182 or 402 ▸ Grades 6–8 Problem Solving, page 256 or 402 ▸ Grades 9–12 Problem Solving, page 334 or 402
IV. Examine Research on Student Learning	**IVA:** **Benchmarks for Science Literacy** ▸ 2, *The Nature of Mathematics*, page 333 ▸ 2C, *Mathematical Inquiry*, page 334 **IVB:** **Research Companion** ▸ Chapter 18, *Impact of Reform on Representations*, pages 263–264
V. Examine Coherency and Articulation	**V:** **Atlas of Science Literacy:** There are no maps currently available for this topic in Volume 1.
VI. Clarify State Standards and District Curriculum	**VIA:** **State Standards:** Link Sections I–V to learning goals and information from your state standards or frameworks that are informed by the results of the topic study. **VIB:** **District Curriculum Guide:** Link Sections I–V to learning goals and information from your district curriculum guide that are informed by the results of the topic study.
Visit www.curriculumtopicstudy.org for updates or supplementary readings, Web sites, and videos.	

Standards- and Research-Based Study of a Curricular Topic

REASONING

Section and Outcome	Selected Sources and Readings for Study and Reflection Read and examine *related parts* of:
I. Identify Adult Content Knowledge	**IA:** ***Science for All Americans*** ▸ Chapter 9, *Reasoning,* pages 140–143 ▸ Chapter 12, *Critical Response Skills,* pages 193–194 **IB:** ***Beyond Numeracy*** ▸ *Mathematical Induction,* pages 121–123 ▸ *The Philosophy of Mathematics,* pages 175–177
II. Consider Instructional Implications	**IIA:** ***Benchmarks for Science Literacy*** ▸ 9E, *Reasoning,* general essay, page 231, grade span essays, pages 232–234 ▸ 12E, *Critical Response Skills,* general essay, page 298 **IIB:** ***NCTM Principles and Standards for School Mathematics*** ▸ Grades PreK–12 Overview Reasoning and Proof, pages 56–59 ▸ Grades PreK–2 Reasoning and Proof, pages 122–126 ▸ Grades 3–5 Reasoning and Proof, pages 188–192 ▸ Grades 6–8 Reasoning and Proof, pages 262–267 ▸ Grades 9–12 Reasoning and Proof, pages 342–346
III. Identify Concepts and Specific Ideas	**IIIA:** ***Benchmarks for Science Literacy*** ▸ 9E, *Reasoning,* pages 232–234 ▸ 12E, *Critical Response Skills,* pages 298–300 **IIIB:** ***NCTM Principles and Standards for School Mathematics*** ▸ Grades PreK–2 Reasoning and Proof, page 122 or 402 ▸ Grades 3–5 Reasoning and Proof, page 188 or 402 ▸ Grades 6–8 Reasoning and Proof, page 262 or 402 ▸ Grades 9–12 Reasoning and Proof, page 342 or 402
IV. Examine Research on Student Learning	**IVA:** ***Benchmarks for Science Literacy*** ▸ 9C, *Proof,* pages 352–353 ▸ 12E, *Critical Response Skills,* page 361 **IVB:** ***Research Companion*** ▸ Chapter 15, *Reasoning and Proof,* pages 227–234
V. Examine Coherency and Articulation	**V:** ***Atlas of Science Literacy*** ▸ *Evidence and Reasoning in Inquiry,* page 17
VI. Clarify State Standards and District Curriculum	**VIA:** ***State Standards:*** Link Sections I–V to learning goals and information from your state standards or frameworks that are informed by the results of the topic study. **VIB:** ***District Curriculum Guide:*** Link Sections I–V to learning goals and information from your district curriculum guide that are informed by the results of the topic study.
Visit www.curriculumtopicstudy.org for updates or supplementary readings, Web sites, and videos. (after publication in 2005)	

Standards- and Research-Based Study of a Curricular Topic

REPRESENTATIONS

Section and Outcome	Selected Sources and Readings for Study and Reflection Read and examine *related parts* of:
I. Identify Adult Content Knowledge	**IA:** *Science for All Americans* ▸ Chapter 2, *Mathematical Inquiry*, page 19; *Manipulating Mathematical Statements*, page 20 **IB:** *Beyond Numeracy* ▸ *Arabic Numerals*, pages 15–17 ▸ *Notation*, pages 163–165
II. Consider Instructional Implications	**IIA:** *Benchmarks for Science Literacy* ▸ 2B, *Mathematical Inquiry* general essay, pages 34–35; grade span essays, pages 36–37 **IIB:** *NCTM Principles and Standards for School Mathematics* ▸ Grades PreK–12 Overview Representation, pages 67–71 ▸ Grades PreK–2 Representation, pages 136–141 ▸ Grades 3–5 Representation, pages 206–209 ▸ Grades 6–8 Representation, pages 280–285 ▸ Grades 9–12 Representation, pages 360–364
III. Identify Concepts and Specific Ideas	**IIIA:** *Benchmarks for Science Literacy* ▸ 2B, *Mathematical Inquiry,* pages 36–38 **IIIB:** *NCTM Principles and Standards for School Mathematics* ▸ Grades PreK–2 Representation, page 136 or 402 ▸ Grades 3–5 Representation, page 206 or 402 ▸ Grades 6–8 Representation, page 280 or 402 ▸ Grades 9–12 Representation, page 360 or 402
IV. Examine Research on Student Learning	**IVB:** *NCTM Research Companion* ▸ Chapter 17, Representation in School Mathematic: Learning to Graph and Graphing to Learn, pages 250–260 ▸ Chapter 18, Representation in School Mathematics: Children's Representation of Problems, pages 263–273 ▸ Chapter 19, Representation in School Mathematics: A Unifying Research Perspective, pages 275–283
V. Examine Coherency and Articulation	**V:** *Atlas of Science Literacy* ▸ *Mathematical Processes*, page 27 ▸ *Mathematical Models*, page 29
VI. Clarify State Standards and District Curriculum	**VIA:** *State Standards:* Link Sections I–V to learning goals and information from your state standards or frameworks that are informed by the results of the topic study. **VIB:** *District Curriculum Guide:* Link Sections I–V to learning goals and information from your district curriculum guide that are informed by the results of the topic study.
Visit www.curriculumtopicstudy.org for updates or supplementary readings, Web sites, and videos.	

Standards- and Research-Based Study of a Curricular Topic

TECHNOLOGY

Section and Outcome	Selected Sources and Readings for Study and Reflection Read and examine *related parts* of:
I. Identify Adult Content Knowledge	**IA:** *Science for All Americans* ▸ Chapter 2, *Mathematics, Science, and Technology,* page 18 ▸ Chapter 12, *Calculator Skills,* pages 188–190, *Manipulation and Observation,* page 191
II. Consider Instructional Implications	**IIA:** *Benchmarks for Science Literacy* ▸ 2B, *Mathematics, Science, and Technology* general essay, page 30; grade span essays, pages 31–33 ▸ 9B, *Symbolic Relationships,* general essay, page 216; grade span essay, page 220 ▸ 12B, *Computation and Estimation* general essay, page 289 ▸ 12C, *Manipulation and Observation* general essay, page 292 **IIB:** *NCTM Principles and Standards for School Mathematics* ▸ Chapter 2, *The Technology Principle,* pages 24–27 ▸ Grades PreK–12 Overview Number, pages 32–33, *Compute Fluently,* pages 35–36; Algebra overview, page 37, *Use Mathematical Models,* page 40; Geometry overview, page 41; Data Analysis, *Formulate Questions,* page 49 ▸ Grades PreK–2 Number, *Understand Number,* pages 81–82, *Compute Fluently,* pages 87–88 ▸ Grades 3–5 Number, *Compute Fluently,* page 156; Geometry general essay, page 165, *Use Visualization,* page 169 ▸ Grades 6–8 Number, *Compute Fluently,* page 220; Algebra, *Use Mathematical Models,* pages 227–229, *Analyze Change,* page 230; Geometry, *Analyze Characteristics,* pages 233–235; Measurement, *Apply Appropriate Techniques,* page 247; Data Analysis, *Understand and Apply,* page 254; Problem Solving, *What Should Problem Solving,* page 258 ▸ Grades 9–12 Number, *Understand Meaning,* page 293, *Compute Fluently,* page 294; Algebra general essay, page 297, *Understand Patterns,* pages 299–300; Geometry, *Analyze Characteristics,* page 311; Problem Solving, vignette, pages 338–340
III. Identify Concepts and Specific Ideas	**IIIA:** *Benchmarks for Science Literacy* ▸ 2B, *Mathematics, Science, and Technology,* pages 32–33 ▸ 12B, *Computation and Estimation,* pages 290–291 ▸ 12C, *Manipulation and Observation,* pages 293–294 **IIIB:** *NCTM Principles and Standards for School Mathematics* ▸ Grades PreK–2 Number, page 78 or 392 ▸ Grades 3–5 Number, page 148 or 392 ▸ Grades 6–8 Number, page 214 or 393 ▸ Grades 9–12 Number, page 290 or 393; Algebra, page 296 or 395
IV. Examine Research on Student Learning	**IVA:** *Benchmarks for Science Literacy* ▸ Chapter 12, *Calculators,* page 359 ▸ Chapter 9, *Graphs,* page 351 **IVB:** *Research Companion* ▸ Chapter 9, *Adding Representations,* pages 130–132 ▸ Chapter 11, *Instructional Tools,* pages 156–160, *Angle, Parallelism,* page 164
V. Examine Coherency and Articulation	**V:** *Atlas of Science Literacy:* There are no maps for this topic in Volume 1.
VI. Clarify State Standards and District Curriculum	**VIA:** *State Standards:* Link Sections I–V to learning goals and information from your state standards or frameworks that are informed by the results of the topic study. **VIB:** *District Curriculum Guide:* Link Sections I–V to learning goals and information from your district curriculum guide that are informed by the results of the topic study.
	Visit www.curriculumtopicstudy.org for updates or supplementary readings, Web sites, and videos.

Standards- and Research-Based Study of a Curricular Topic

VOCABULARY

Section and Outcome	Selected Sources and Readings for Study and Reflection Read and examine *related parts* of:
I. Identify Adult Content Knowledge	**IA:** **Science for All Americans** ▸ Chapter 12, *Communication,* pages 192–193
II. Consider Instructional Implications	**IIA:** **Benchmarks for Science Literacy** ▸ 12D, *Communication Skills* general essay, page 295 **IIB:** **NCTM Principles and Standards for School Mathematics** ▸ Grades K–12 Overview Communication, *Communicate Their Mathematical Thinking,* page 62; *Use of Language of Mathematics,* page 63 ▸ Grades PreK–2 Communication general essay, page 128, *What Should Communication Look Like* page 128, page 130, *What Should Be the Teacher's Role,* page 130, page 131 ▸ Grades 3–5 Communication general essay, page 194, *What Should Be the Teacher's Role,* page 198 ▸ Grades 6–8 Communication, *What Should Be the Teacher's Role,* page 272 ▸ Grades 9–12 Communication, *What Does Communication Look Like,* page 349
III. Identify Concepts and Specific Ideas	**IIIA:** **Benchmarks for Science Literacy** ▸ 12D, *Communication Skills,* pages 296–297 **IIIB:** **NCTM Principles and Standards for School Mathematics** ▸ Grades PreK–2 Communication, page 128 or page 402 ▸ Grades 3–5 Communication, page 194 or page 402 ▸ Grades 6–8 Communication, page 268 or page 402 ▸ Grades 9–12 Communication, page 348 or page 402
IV. Examine Research on Student Learning	**IVB:** **Research Companion** ▸ Chapter 16, *Negotiated Defining and Genre Instruction,* pages 242–243
V. Examine Coherency and Articulation	**V:** ***Atlas of Science Literacy:*** There are no maps available for this topic in Volume 1.
VI. Clarify State Standards and District Curriculum	**VIA:** ***State Standards:*** Link Sections I–V to learning goals and information from your state standards or frameworks that are informed by the results of the topic study. **VIB:** ***District Curriculum Guide:*** Link Sections I–V to learning goals and information from your district curriculum guide that are informed by the results of the topic study.
Visit www.curriculumtopicstudy.org for updates or supplementary readings, Web sites, and videos.	

Resource A: Additional Resources to Support Curriculum Topic Study

CURRICULUM TOPIC STUDY WEB SITE

The Curriculum Topic Study (CTS) project maintains a project Web site at www.curriculumtopicstudy.org. New information about CTS, updated guides, and new tools will be available here. A searchable database allows CTS users to search by CTS Guide for additional articles, videos, Web sites, and so on to supplement readings from the CTS Guides. The Web site also provides information about participating in CTS national workshops or arranging for CTS professional development at your site.

SCIENCE CURRICULUM TOPIC STUDY

Science Curriculum Topic Study: Bridging the Gap Between Standards and Practice (Keeley, 2005) contains 147 topics in science. The science and mathematics CTS books have parallel chapters, resources, and tools. The science CTS book includes several topics that overlap with mathematics such as correlation, data collection and analysis, graphs and graphing, mathematical modeling, mathematics in science and technology, scientific sampling, and summarizing and representing data. Both books can be used for integrating mathematics and science.

FACILITATOR'S GUIDE TO CURRICULUM TOPIC STUDY

The third book in the National Science Foundation-funded Curriculum Topic Project will be geared toward professional developers, higher education faculty, teacher leaders, and others who facilitate group learning using CTS. The book will be developed in partnership with WestEd and will use a national professional development and higher education design team to produce tools, processes, and professional development materials to use with CTS. The book will also describe how CTS is used with study groups, action research, examination of student work and thinking, lesson study, inquiry immersion, content immersion, curriculum and assessment development, online learning, mentoring and coaching, curriculum and assessment implementation, workshops and courses, case discussions, demonstration lessons, and other strategies. Information on the facilitator's guide is available on the CTS Web site.

OTHER PROJECT 2061 MATERIALS

Project 2061 produces several supporting resources to use with *Benchmarks for Science Literacy* (AAAS, 1993), *Science for All Americans* (AAAS, 1990), and *Atlas of Science Literacy* (AAAS, 2001). Recommended resources to extend CTS include *Designs for Science Literacy* (AAAS, 2000), the Project 2061 Curriculum Materials Analysis Procedure, Project 2061's evaluation of middle grades textbooks and algebra textbooks, and Project 2061's assessment resources. Information about these tools, including ordering information for the Project 2061 materials used in CTS, and other Project 2061 initiatives are available at http://www.project2061.org.

NATIONAL COUNCIL OF TEACHERS OF MATHEMATICS (NCTM)

The National Council of Teachers of Mathematics (NCTM) is the leading professional association in the United States for mathematics educators. NCTM offers a variety of different resources used as supplemental resources for CTS including *Research Ideas for the Classroom* and the *Navigations* Series. NCTM has an online bookstore that carries the materials used in CTS. You can visit the NCTM Web site at http://www.nctm.org.

MAINE MATHEMATICS AND SCIENCE ALLIANCE (MMSA)

The Maine Mathematics and Science Alliance (MMSA) is a not-for-profit organization based in Maine that provides professional development in mathematics and science, including CTS. The MMSA mathematics and science staff also coordinates various projects and initiatives in the areas of teacher leadership, technology, formative assessment, mentoring and new teacher support, and data usage, all of which include a CTS component. To learn more about the work of the MMSA, please visit the Web site at www.mmsa.org.

CORWIN PRESS SPEAKERS BUREAU

Corwin Press maintains a Speakers Bureau that arranges presentations by Corwin authors, including CTS co-authors Page Keeley and Cheryl Rose. For information on arranging a CTS presentation or workshop session at your school, please visit the Corwin Press Web site at www.corwinpress.com.

Resource B:
Worksheets
for Curriculum
Topic Study

Resource B.1   Topic Study Reflection: Capturing Your Thoughts

Capture Your Thoughts

★ Important Ideas	◉ Specific Insights
? Questions Raised	⇨ Implications for Action

SOURCE: Adapted from *Reflective Practice to Improve Schools: An Action Guide for Educators,* by York-Barr, Sommers, Ghere, & Montie (2001).

Resource B.2   CTS Content Summary Guide for Instructional Materials Review

CTS Topic: **Grade Level:**

Concepts for Teacher Background Information (Sec. I, II)	Students' Content Knowledge (Sec. III, V, VI)
Instructional Implications (Sec. II, IV)	**Student Difficulties and Misconceptions (Sec. II, IV)**
Prerequisite Knowledge (Sec. III, V)	**Connections to Other Topics (Sec. II, V)**

Resource B.3   Four-Square Elicitation Organizer

Prior Knowledge Related to the Topic

Adult Content Knowledge	Student Knowledge
Misconceptions or Difficulties	Connections

Resource B.4 CTS Content Summary Review Match for Instructional Materials

Unit: _____ Grade Level: _____ Developer: _____

Please rate the CTS summary categories, on a scale of 1–5, to the extent that the material showed evidence of matching the findings and recommendations in the CTS Summary Guide: **1**—No evidence; **2**—Minimal evidence; **3**—Sufficient evidence; **4**—Strong evidence; **5**—Strong evidence that includes additional useful and relevant material that exceeds the CTS findings and recommendations.

Concepts for Teacher Background Information

Evidence: 1   2   3   4   5

Comments:

Students' Content Knowledge

Evidence: 1   2   3   4   5

Comments:

Instructional Implications

Evidence: 1   2   3   4   5

Comments:

Student Difficulties and Misconceptions

Evidence: 1   2   3   4   5

Comments:

Prerequisite Knowledge

Evidence: 1   2   3   4   5

Comments:

Connections to Other Topics

Evidence: 1   2   3   4   5

Comments:

References

Abbott, A. A. (1964). *Flatland: A romance of many dimensions.* Mineola, NY: Dover.

American Association for the Advancement of Science. (2001). *Atlas of science literacy.* Washington, DC: Author; Arlington, VA: National Science Teachers Association.

American Association for the Advancement of Science. (2000). *Designs for Science Literacy.* New York: Oxford University Press.

American Association for the Advancement of Science. (1993). *Benchmarks for science literacy.* New York: Oxford University Press.

American Association for the Advancement of Science. (1990). *Science for all Americans.* New York: Oxford University Press.

Audet, R., & Jordan, L. (2003). *Standards in the classroom: An implementation guide for teachers of science and mathematics.* Thousand Oaks, CA: Corwin.

Barnett, C., Goldenstein, D., & Jackson, B. (1994). Mathematics teaching cases: *Fractions, decimals, ratios, and percents hard to teach and hard to learn?* Portsmouth, NH: Heinemann.

Beane, J. A. (1995). *Toward a coherent curriculum* (1995 Yearbook of the Association for Supervision and Curriculum Development. Alexandria, VA: Association for Supervision and Curriculum Development.

Bransford, J., Brown, A., & Cocking, R. (2000). *How people learn.* Washington, DC: National Academy Press.

Bright, G., & Joyner, J. (2004). *Dynamic classroom assessment: Linking mathematical understanding to instruction.* Vernon Hills, IL: ETA/Cuisenaire.

Chen, I.-E., & Lin, F.-L. (2004). *The investigative teaching of mathematical conjecturing and refuting.* Retrieved December 1, 2005, from http://www.math.ntnu.edu.tw/~cyc/_private/mathedu/me1/me1_2002_2/cheninger.doc

Clermont, C. P., Krajcik, J. S., & Borko, H. (1993). The influence of an intensive inservice workshop on pedagogical content knowledge growth among novice teachers. *Journal of Research in Science Teaching, 30,* 21–43.

Cochran, K. F., DeRuiter, J. A., & King, R. A. (1993). Pedagogical content knowing: An integrative model for teacher preparation. *Journal of Teacher Education, 44,* 263–272.

Danielson, C. (1996). *Enhancing professional practice: A framework for teaching.* Alexandria, VA: Association for Supervision and Curriculum Development.

Darling-Hammond, L. (2000). Teacher quality and student achievement: A review of state policy and evidence. *Education Policy Archives, 8.* Retrieved from Web site: http://epaa.asu.edu

De Lange, J. (1999). *Framework for assessment in mathematics.* Madison, WI: National Center for Improving Student Learning and Achievement.

Donovan, S., & Bransford, J. (2005). *How students learn mathematics in the classroom.* Washington, DC: National Academy Press.

Driver, R., Squires, A., Rushworth, P., & Wood-Robinson, V. (1994). *Making sense of secondary science.* New York: Routledge.

Erickson, L. (1998). *Concept-based curriculum and instruction.* Thousand Oaks, CA: Corwin.

Fendel, F., Resek, D., Alper, L., & Fraser, S. (1997). *Interactive mathematics program: Year 1.* Emeryville, CA: Key Curriculum Press.

Fernández-Balboa, J. M., & Stiehl, J. (1995). The generic nature of pedagogical content knowledge among college professors. *Teaching & Teacher Education, 11,* 293–306.

Gregory, G., & Chapman, C. (2002). *Differentiated instructional strategies: One size doesn't fit all.* Thousand Oaks, CA: Corwin.

Gregory, G., & Kuzmich, L. (2004). *Data-driven differentiations in the standards-based classroom.* Thousand Oaks, CA: Corwin.

Hazen, R., & Trefil, J. (1991). *Science matters: Achieving scientific literacy.* New York: Anchor Books.

Hiebert, J. (1997). Making sense: Teaching and learning mathematics with understanding. Portsmouth, NH: Heinemann.

Horizon Research. (2001). The status of high school mathematics teaching. Chapel Hill, NC: Author.

Jacobs, H. (1997). *Mapping the big picture: Integrating curriculum and assessment K–12.* Alexandria, VA: Association for Supervision and Curriculum Development.

Jonassen, D. H. (1994). Thinking technology: Toward a constructivist design model. *Educational Technology, 34*(4), 34–37.

Keeley, P. (2005). *Science curriculum topic study: Bridging the gap between standards and practice.* Thousand Oaks, CA: Corwin.

Kahle, J. B. (June 1999). Testimony, U.S. House of Representatives, Washington, DC.

Lappan, G., Fey, J., Fitzgerald, W., Friel, S., & Phillips, E. (1996). *Getting to know connected mathematics.* White Plains, NY: Dale Seymour.

Lewis, C. C. (2002). *Lesson study: A handbook of teacher-led instructional change.* Philadelphia: Research for Better Schools.

Loucks-Horsley, S., Love, N., Stiles, K., Mundry, S., & Hewson, P. (2003). *Designing professional development for teachers of science and mathematics.* Thousand Oaks, CA: Corwin.

Ma, L. (1999). *Knowing and teaching elementary mathematics.* Mahwah, NJ: Lawrence Erlbaum.

Maine Department of Education. (1997). *Maine's learning results.* Augusta: State of Maine Printing Office.

Marzano, R., Pickering, D., & Pollock, J. (2001). *Classroom instruction that works: Research-based strategies for increasing student achievement.* Alexandria, VA: Association for Supervision and Curriculum Development.

Mezirow, J. (1997). Transformative learning: Theory to practice. In *Transformative learning in action: Insights from practice.* San Franscisco: Jossey-Bass.

Monk, D. H. (1994). Subject area preparation of secondary mathematics and science teachers and student achievement. *Economics of Education Review, 13,* 125–145.

Murphy, C., & Lick, D. (2001). *Whole-faculty study groups: Creating student-based professional development* (2nd ed.). Thousands Oaks, CA: Corwin.

National Council of Teachers of Mathematics. (2003). *Research companion to principles and standards for school mathematics.* Reston, VA: Author.

National Council of Teachers of Mathematics. (2000). *Principles and standards for school mathematics.* Reston, VA: Author.

National Council of Teachers of Mathematics. (1989). *Curriculum and evaluation standards for school mathematics.* Reston, VA: Author.

National Research Council. (2001). *Educating teachers of science, mathematics, and technology: New practices for the new millennium.* Washington, DC: National Academy Press.

National Research Council. (2005). *How students learn: Mathematics in the Classroom.* Washington, DC: National Academy Press.

National Research Council. (2002). *Investigating the influence of standards.* Washington, DC: National Academy Press.

National Research Council. (2001). *Adding it up: Helping children learn mathematics.* Washington, DC: National Academy Press.

National Research Council. (1996). *National science education standards.* Washington, DC: National Academy Press.

National Science Foundation. (2002). *Professional development that supports school mathematics reform* (Foundations Monograph, Vol. 3). Washington, DC: Author.

Paulos, J. (1992). *Beyond numeracy.* New York: Vintage.

Schmidt, W., McKnight, C., & Raizen, S. (1997). *A splintered vision: An investigation of U.S. science and mathematics education.* Norwell, MA: Kluwer Academic.

Shulman, L. S. (1986). Those who understand: Knowledge growth in teaching. *Educational Researcher, 15*(2), 4–14.

Shulman, L., & Grossman, p. (1988). *Knowledge growth in teaching: A final report to the Spencer Foundation.* Stanford, CA: Stanford University.

Stigler, J., & Hiebert, J. (1999). *The teaching gap: Best ideas from the world's teachers for improving education in the classroom.* New York: Free Press.

Thompson, A. (1992). Teachers' beliefs and conceptions: A synthesis of research. In D. A. Grouws (Ed.), *Handbook of research on mathematics teaching and learning.* New York: MacMillan.

TIMS Curriculum: University of Illinois at Chicago. (2003). *Math Trailblazers Grade 2* (2nd ed.). Dubuque, IA: Kendall Hunt.

Van Driel, J. H., Verloop, N., & DeVos, W. (1998). Developing science teachers' pedagogical knowledge. *Journal of Teacher Education, 41,* 3–11.

Whittington, D. (2002). *The status of high school mathematics teaching.* Chapel Hill, NC: Horizon Research.

York-Barr, J., Sommers, W., Ghere, G., Montie, J. (2001). *Reflective practice to improve schools.* Thousand Oaks, CA: Corwin Press.

Weiss, I. R., Pasley, J. D., Smith, P. S., Banilower, E. R., & Heck, D. J. (2003). *Looking inside the classroom: A study of K–12 mathematics and science education in the United States.* Chapel Hill, NC: Horizon Research.

Wiggins, G., & McTighe, J. (1998). *Understanding by design.* Alexandria, VA: Association for Supervision and Curriculum Development.

Index

CORWIN
PRESS

The Corwin Press logo—a raven striding across an open book—represents the union of courage and learning. Corwin Press is committed to improving education for all learners by publishing books and other professional development resources for those serving the field of K–12 education. By providing practical, hands-on materials, Corwin Press continues to carry out the promise of its motto: **"Helping Educators Do Their Work Better."**